ONE SWEET GUY
And What He Is Doing To You

Arthur E. Rowse

Consumer News Inc.
Washington, D.C. 20045

To one sweet gal

How doth the little crocodile
　　Improve his shining tail,
And pour the waters of the Nile
　　On every golden scale

How cheerfully he seems to grin
　　How neatly spreads his claws,
And welcomes little fishes in
　　With gently smiling jaws

Lewis Carroll, Alice's Adventures in Wonderland

ACKNOWLEDGEMENTS

Special mention should be made of my wife, Ruth, without whose inspiration and dogged assistance this book could never have been written. Her contributions ranged from helping plan the book to editing and typing.

Also assisting in important ways but not responsible for any of the content were many people. They included: Leonard Appel, Jeanne Atkinson, Richard Bradee, Richard Corrigan, Theodore Jacobs, Mary Gardiner Jones, Barbara Kraft, Joe Luppino, Ed Murray, Tama Reasonover, Vic Reinemer, Betty Ann Rowse, David Swankin, Richard Thomas, Rick Weinberg and Karen Washington.

The front cover photograph is from United Press International.

All references to months in the book are for 1981 unless otherwise specified.

Arthur E. Rowse
Washington, D.C.
October, 1981

Table of Contents

Members, Individual Tax Cuts, Commercials for Congress, Tilt Toward Upper Brackets, Summary of Major Tax Changes, Busting the Budget.

Action Belies Promises, Change of Tune, Hit List Strikes the Heart, Safety Net Comes Apart, Promise of Prosperity, Shipping Problems to the States, Attacking Legal Aid for the Poor, Aid to Families With Dependent Children, Food Stamps, Health Care Programs, Job Programs, Social Security, Education, Housing, Transportation, Child Nutrition, Veterans Programs, Arts and Communications, Community Development, Supplemental Security Income, Consumer Cooperative Bank, Dire Predictions, Saving Business Programs, Working Poor Hit Hardest, Crunch at the Local Level, Other Victims.

A 1950 View of the World, Boosting the Pentagon, Gaps in Weapon Data, Reviving Old Ideas, Overlooking Waste, Recruiting Problems, The Haig Problem, Seeing Red in the Mideast, El Salvador, Helping the Juntas, Corporate Considerations, Tilt Towards South Africa, Aid for Multinational Firms, Expanding Arms Sales, Nuclear Proliferation, Increasing Tensions With Allies, Dangers of Nuclear War.

Introduction

"Where's the rest of me?"

That is the title of Ronald Reagan's autobiography. He chose the words from a movie in which he portrayed a man who wakes up in bed after an accident with both legs missing.

That also could be the theme of his first year since being elected President of the United States. For the first six months, nearly everything came up roses. By claiming to have a mandate for his sweeping plans for reducing federal spending and taxes, he obtained virtually all his requests from Congress despite some painful political decisions by many legislators. In response to other alleged mandates, he relegated hundreds of regulations to the deep freezer for review, revision or elimination. And to fulfill campaign promises to shore up the Nation's prestige around the world, he launched the biggest military buildup in history.

Initial reactions were generally positive. Many people obviously liked Reagan's pledge to "restore faith" in the American ideals of individual initiative and his plan to reduce dependence on government for so many things in life. It was clear that the Great Society and War on Poverty had not solved the big social problems. So why not try a new approach, many people asked.

Early polls showed substantial approval of Reagan's program and policies. Prices on Wall Street zoomed over the magic 1,000-mark, and the dollar gained value on international exchanges. After Congress put the finishing touches on the huge budget and tax cuts, Reagan and his supporters left Washington for a long vacation to savor their impressive political victories.

But when they came back at the end of summer, they suddenly discovered some important things missing. One was a loss of business confidence in the Reagan programs. Prices of stocks and bonds were skidding precipitously, and continued high interest rates not only were causing unprecedented havoc in the housing industry but were disrupting overseas economics, too. In addition, normally friendly governments abroad were voicing misgivings about the massive buildup of the Pentagon and the penchant of Reagan officials to bait the Russians around the world. A new wave of terrorist attacks struck American military bases in Germany to dramatize opposition to Reagan arms policies. Relations with Israel and Arab nations were becoming frayed over the AWAC plane deal and bombing raids by the Israelis. And policies affecting Africa were being roundly criticized. It was beginning to look as if Ronald Reagan, instead of restoring American prestige in international affairs, had pushed it below where it allegedly was when he took office.

In this country, public polls indicated that Reagan's popularity was also falling. More than a quarter-million people gathered in Washington to protest the Administration's budget cuts and efforts to reduce worker-safety rules as well as other policies. And major environmental groups were unanimous in demanding the resignation of Interior Secretary James Watt. News reports began reporting personal hardship stories as the first budget cuts of the 1982 fiscal year ran into the human factor.

These were all signs that the Reagan program was approaching a critical stage before it had scarcely started. To salvage the situation, President Reagan pleaded for patience. He urged critics to wait until the tax and budget cuts had time to take effect. Meanwhile, he vowed to continue a "firm, steady course," seemingly unperturbed by the change of events. In response to persistent worries, he promised once again that the "truly needy" would not be hurt by his program.

But he could not stand by and ignore complaints from the truly rich and others who were being hurt on Wall Street. It came as a shock to him — and many other people — that those who stood to gain the most from the Reagan program were making it clear that they were not buying it.

First reactions of Administration leaders were to turn against their friends in the investment community. Treasury Secretary Donald T. Regan, former head of a leading brokerage house, lashed out at "worry-warts in the bond market" and others with "too simplistic" views of the situation. Republican leaders who had pushed the drastic cuts through Congress became threatening. "It's time," said Senate Majority Leader Howard Baker, "that the financial

markets realize that they're playing a dangerous game."
Unless trends change within "days," he warned, he would seek
new restrictions, including credit controls and an excess profits tax on interest. President Reagan, deploring "Chicken Lit-
tles" in the business world, called some leaders of that world to
the White House for pep talks.

It was a bizarre turn of events, with Republicans scolding
Republicans, and a business-minded Administration chastis-
ing a marketplace where prices are determined by economic
forces rather than political policies. Strangely, an administration devoted to improving business was unable to gain the confidence of the business community.

But there was nothing mysterious behind the reactions of
Wall Street. Investors were simply saying that the Reagan
program did not add up. They feared that instead of a projected deficit of $42.5 billion in fiscal 1982, the shortage would
be nearly twice that figure, as the bipartisan Congressional
Budget Office (CBO) had estimated. And they were worried
about estimates by Federal Reserve Board Chairman Paul
Volcker that another $100 billion would be needed to balance
the budget by 1984, as Reagan had promised. They felt that
the $750 billion loss of tax revenues over five years was too
much for the government to give up. And they had serious
doubts about the advisability of a Pentagon budget of $1.5
trillion over the same period. Business leaders were beginning
to feel that the Reagan program was ill-conceived and would
bring on a serious recession unless big changes were made.
They also felt, along with the Federal Reserve Board and CBO,
that the Administration's economic projections were based on
assumptions that were much too optimistic.

When leading Republicans in Congress joined the chorus of
doubters, President Reagan reluctantly agreed to consider
making some changes while continuing to insist that the program passed by Congress was right on target. But all he could
find for 1982 were $13 billion in new budget cuts and $3 billion
in new tax revenues (which he chose to call "revenue
enhancements" because of his repeated pledge not to raise
taxes). The figures included only $2 billion from the $222
billion Pentagon budget. The new proposed savings for both
1982 and subsequent years fell far short of what Congressional
Republicans were hoping for from the White House. They were
thus put on the spot to come up with enough additional sav-

ings to restore the credibility of the Reagan Administration.

Yet prospects for passage of even the President's own modest proposals were dim. Making the outlook still grimmer was the feeling of many legislators that social programs had already been cut to the bone, particularly those affecting the "truly needy." A number of key Republicans and Democrats who had backed the earlier proposals indicated that they would oppose further cuts in social programs without reductions in military spending far beyond what Reagan said he would accept.

Some legislators accused the President of having reneged on earlier deals for their votes by going back to sensitive social programs for further cuts after agreeing to accept less than his original requests for cuts. Legislators were particularly angry at the President's lack of candor in saying that most of the new cuts would come from 12 per cent across-the-board reductions when the actual reductions would be much greater in many cases. The reason for the differences was that the President based his figures on his original pared-down requests, not the level finally approved by Congress in July. Thus, the "12 per cent cut" would be equivalent to reductions of 32 per cent for energy assistance to low-income families, 29 per cent for education for the handicapped, 43 per cent for guaranteed student loans, 89 per cent for Conrail and local public works projects, 26 per cent for impact aid to public schools and 100 per cent for energy conservation and solar development projects.[1]

State and local officials were also up in arms. A delegation of 18 governors visited President Reagan in September to express misgivings about any further cuts in programs affecting the poor and the near poor. Vermont Governor Richard Snelling, the delegation leader, told Reagan that further budget cuts "could result in a public backfire."[2] The National Governors' Association had voted earlier to ask the Administration to keep responsibility for income support programs such as welfare and Medicaid rather than shift it to the states. The governors were especially concerned about further proposed cuts in revenue sharing and block grants.

Early signs of a "public backfire" forced Administration leaders to "eat" some of their plans to implement the original budget cuts. One was the attempt of the Agriculture Department to cut $1.5 billion from school lunch costs by designating catsup and pickle relish as vegetables and cutting portions of milk to four ounces and meat to one ounce per meal. This proposal generated so much ridicule that President Reagan withdrew it as soon as he learned about it. But Secretary of Agriculture John R. Block continued to call the proposal "sound" and "in step with the Administration's goal of reducing regulation . . ."[3]

Although Administration officials were forced by adverse publicity to hold the catsup and relish, they went ahead with equally sensitive new limits on eligibility for welfare, food stamps and other government services. What began to bother people of both parties was not so much the effort to reduce government benefits to those who did not clearly need them but to cut so deeply into basic benefits while leaving the Pentagon virtually immune to cuts and while giving so many tax breaks to the wealthy.

Many people near the poverty line or below faced cutbacks that could cause severe hardships, and many of the "working poor" were likely to wind up on welfare or charity because of reductions or losses of benefits. Yet there was no provision for handling such imbalances in the Reagan budget. By September, 10 states had set up plans to require welfare recipients to seek work, including mothers in some states with children only 3 years old. The nice old movie cowboy was increasingly being accused of cutting the heart out of American society with changes like these.

Americans of all income levels were bound to be affected by the wholesale elimination of health and safety regulations. Hundreds of rules and standards designed to reduce job hazards, dangerous products and harmful chemicals in the environment were shoved aside at the request of business interests claiming that they cost too much. With nearly all regulatory agencies under the control of people from the regulated industries, assaults on public protections were beginning to pick up speed.

Far more worrisome for many Americans was the Administration's rapidly accelerating plans to wage nuclear war. Despite widely accepted facts indicating that a first strike by either superpower would inevitably lead to devastation of both nations, President Reagan pushed ahead with plans for waging a lengthy nuclear war. Secretary of Defense Caspar Weinberger told a television audience on October 4 about a network of orbiting satellites, some already capable of relaying information about missile attacks to ground stations. It was part of a $180-billion nuclear arsenal announced a few days earlier by the White House.

Part of the grand plan was placement of 100 MX missiles in existing silos containing Titan missiles. Although the plan avoided opposition from Nevada and Utah where a mobile MX system had been planned by the Carter Administration, the revised plan aroused new criticism because its lack of mobility would not close the so-called "window of vulnerability" from Russian missiles.

What bothered an increasing number of people, however, was the underlying assumption that nuclear war was "winnable" and that the Soviets thought so, too, as President Reagan told a press conference on October 1. Most experts on the subject were unable to find any indication that the Soviets considered nuclear war anything but a disaster.

By giving top priority to such a massive arms buildup, the Administration claimed it was increasing the possibility that the Russians would agree to substantial arms controls. But the more likely prospect was what the Soviets promised: to match or surpass every new American weapon. The emphasis on the military also effectively reduced the prospects of obtaining international solutions to other critical world problems such as hunger, disease, pollution and dwindling natural resources.

By October, it was too early to declare the "Reagan Revolution" a total failure, since no bombs had fallen and the tax and budget cuts had just begun. But it was not too early to see the direction in which the "new beginning" was going. It was not just paring down the size of government; it was reversing course. It was not just trying to cut out waste; it was trying to repeal generations of social legislation by wiping out operating funds. And it was not just assaulting those most dependent on public assistance, as offensive as that was to many Americans; it was assaulting the conscience of many people by doing so. Reaganism was leading a massive shift from investing in people to investing in dollars and weapons.

By the same token, its attack on regulations and taxes was not designed so much to save money, as claimed, but to give business and industry more freedom to make money without restraint. Yet the loss of public protections against health and safety hazards alone could cost society many times the cost of regulations to business. By virtually eliminating taxes on business and the well-to-do, Reaganism was shifting the burden of government onto the backs of the poor and middle class and away from those who could afford it better.

While aiming somehow to bring back a purer form of Americanism, the Reagan Administration was undermining the foundations of democracy itself. Often without realizing it, these champions of law and order chipped away at some basic Constitutional rights in their crusades against communism and crime. By making government more secretive, they wound up reducing the flow of information so vital to the functioning of a free society.

Reaganites even worked at cross purpose to their own goals. While basing their whole economic program on faith that business competition will correct the imbalances, they encouraged less competition by relaxing antitrust enforcement and other policing of the marketplace. While turning over more government functions to private business, they condoned public subsidies to those interests with heavy costs to taxpayers.

The ultimate irony may be the attempt to cloak many of these initiatives in a mantle of moralism. By endorsing attempts of the religious right to impose its own brand of Christianity on all of society, the President and his cohorts in Congress displayed a disregard for the feelings of non-Christians and a misunderstanding of the value of dissent to democracy.

A growing number of people were beginning to wonder how the country got into such a situation only a year after the election of 1980. They were also asking how Ronald Reagan and the New Right got elected in the first place? Did they really get a mandate for such drastic changes? And how did they manage to win Congressional approval for them? Why has there been so much adverse reaction in other countries? Finally, how did your representatives in Congress vote on key proposals affecting you, your family and friends?

Here is a timely book with some answers.

1

Cowboy Capitalists Take Over

In this present crisis, government is not the solution to our problems; government is the problem.

Ronald Reagan[1]

"Mr. President, Mr. President," shouted a reporter, who then proceeded to allege that the only woman member of the Federal Trade Commission (FTC) had been passed over for the chairmanship after she had objected to proposed budget cuts for the agency. "Did you mean to give a signal to other Republicans that if they don't conform, off will go their heads?"

President Reagan paused in semi-shock at the accusation by Sarah McClendon, noted for her feisty questions. He fidgeted a moment, then purred: "How can you say that about a sweet fellow like me?" Amid laughter from the reporters at the televised press conference in March, the former movie actor countered with a smile that the FTC job had not been promised to anyone, as claimed, and that all candidates for the job had been treated equally.

Sweet fellow indeed. His easy quip and denial immediately disarmed the questioner and the audience. Yet he undoubtedly knew that Republican Patricia Bailey had been passed over after she had spoken out publicly against his FTC budget cuts and for the Equal Rights Amendment.

It is easy to like Ronald Reagan. He acts like a friendly granddad, quick with a smile and ready with an aw-shucks reaction to unfriendly gibes and complicated questions. He is a natural charmer, especially in a social setting. And he can pour oil over turbulent waters as well as anyone who ever held the office. In televised debates, Jimmy Carter learned how hard it is to pick a fight with Ronald Reagan and win. The fact that

Reagan spewed out a number of inaccuracies and exaggerations in defending his record as governor of California was less important than his coolness and wit under fire. Most of the large audience did not know the answers were fudged; they saw him as a likable man who would not lie or be mean.

In an age when television can make the difference between victory and defeat, appearance counts far more than substance, and Reagan knew it well. He may have been a Grade B movie actor, but he had become a Grade A politician. The ultimate compliment came from Jesse Unruh, a power in his own right in California politics. After trying without success to keep Reagan from becoming re-elected as governor in 1970, he acknowledged that Reagan had been "nearly masterful."

GOP publicist Richard J. Whalen claimed to have spotted Reagan's secret of success: his ability to get people to underestimate his political skills. In a newspaper article, Whalen noted the usual put-downs of the former actor: that he is not sufficiently aware of the issues and tends to oversimplify them. What makes him a winner, said Whalen, is his abillity to charm the voting populace, particularly via television. The article, entitled "Why Ronald Reagan Will Be The Next President," was published seven months before the election.[2]

Some nagging questions still remain, however, about Reagan as President. Is he really as ignorant of the real world as he often seems or is he a sly fox who knows exactly what he is doing when he disarms his opponents into complacency while his aides swing their knives? Does he really believe that his reverse-Robin Hood policies can actually help ordinary people or is he consciously playing front-man for the rich with a cold and villainous heart?

For some revealing clues, one needs only to open his autobiography, *Where's The Rest Of Me?* Here is the story of an idyllic youth filled with apple pies, turkey dinners, adventures on the creek, football games, film-making and corny stories. Like Huck Finn, his life reads like a series of old family movies as he takes the reader on a saunter through several small towns and Hollywood.

The only thing missing is the other side of life. He skims lightly over the fact that his father was an alcoholic shoe salesman who had trouble keeping a job, thus forcing frequent moves. He omits all but a few of his disappointments. All through the book, he tends to block out the unpleasant and concentrate on the lucky breaks and good times. In describing a day when he found his father in a drunken stupor on the front porch, he wrote: "I wanted to let myself in the house and go to bed and pretend he wasn't there."

As Gregg Easterbrook summed it up in *The Washington Monthly*, "Life for Reagan is one uninterrupted march to the top. No setbacks, no despair, and certainly nobody falling by the wayside. The sorrows, like [his father's] alcoholism, fold into the landscape as Reagan pretends they aren't there. Potentially painful stories are introduced but quickly capped by a happy ending, as if to suggest that every story ends happily."[3]

The book helps to explain why as President, Ronald Reagan is so surprised at unfriendly questions from reporters, why he prefers to confront reporters on the run rather than at formal press conferences so he can pick out the questions he wants to answer briefly. His own words, strained through numerous ghost writers, reveal a lot about his views of life and the world around him. And they help explain why he is willing to delegate so many responsibilities and nasty tasks to loyal lieutenants.

FROM POVERTY TO RICHES

It is not quite so easy to explain Reagan's evolution from a Democratic, pro-union, "poverty-stricken" background to right-wing Republicanism with policies designed to make the wealthy wealthier and poor poorer. One explanation is that Ronald Reagan was so preoccupied with the glamor of sports and movies during his adult life that he became isolated from the struggling masses and the injustice they face. Another is that he never had the time or inclination for intellectual pursuits that could have given him a more balanced picture of life.

A further explanation for his transformation is the natural tendency of people to move politically to the right as their possessions pile up. There is also the inclination of those who have "made it" to revel in the aura of wealth and influence simply because they remember so well being without such things. Like their wealthy friends, Ronald and Nancy Reagan surrounded themselves with luxury, including a large, isolated ranch where they kept horses.

None of the various books or articles on Reagan, including his 1965 autobiography, provide much insight as to why he changed so much politically. But it apparently happened after he moved from the movie screen to the TV screen as the host of the GE Theatre as his movie career was fading into the sunset. Having made a name for himself in Hollywood, he was no doubt looked on by business executives as an equal and a hale fellow in the bargain. The more goodwill he produced for General Electric, the more he, too, became a product of the corporate world.

As he began to enjoy the adulation and riches from television, he gradually lost his desire to fight the old actors' guild battles. At one point, he was asked to take another turn as head of the union. "I didn't want to answer the question at all," he wrote in his autobiography, "I just wanted to hide someplace."[4]

THE CATALYST

Although he did return for one more painful fling that involved a long, costly strike, he had already made the transition to being a publicist for big business and critic of big government. Beginning in the mid-1950s, he wrote, "I talked on this theme of big government. . .and was accepted as presenting a non-partisan viewpoint." Then, everything changed when Kennedy became President. "The same speech delivered *after* January 20, 1961, brought down thunders of wrath on my head, the charge that my speech was a partisan political attact, an expression of right-wing extremism." He did a double take when his former union colleagues took the same view. He used the occasion in the book to say that his critics were not liberals at all and that the traditional definitions of liberal and conservative had suddenly become reversed. He began to generalize: "The liberal used to believe in freedom under law. He now takes the ancient feudal position that power is everything. He believes in a stronger and stronger central government and in the philosophy that control is better than freedom . . . . The conservatives believe the collective responsibility of the qualified men in a community should decide its course. . . .The conservatives believe in the unique powers of the individual and his personal opinions."⁵

Note Reagan's Hamiltonian endorsement of "qualified men" deciding the course for everyone else, while praising the "unique powers" of the individual. He appeared to favor autocracy while praising democracy. He did not see the contradiction nor the fact that he was espousing the same elitist control he criticized.

Having found a home in the business world and having discovered belatedly that he was a political conservative, he warmed to the challenge and polished The Speech. In 1962, he switched party allegiances from Democrat to Republican. But it was not until 1964 that he really blossomed as a political spokesman for the conservative cause.

The catalyst was a speech he made at the Republican convention for Barry Goldwater, the right-wing candidate for President that year. Reagan did not get much public notice when he delivered his remarks, but he caught the eye of some influential Republicans. Video tapes of the address were used later that year to raise millions of dollars for party coffers despite fears of some leaders that his views would cause a backlash and hurt Goldwater's chances. In the speech, Reagan had suggested "voluntary features" for Social Security and strongly endorsed Taiwan as the representative of the Chinese people.

IMPRESSING BIG WHEELS

Among those most impressed was Holmes Tuttle, an old friend who owned a large Ford dealership in California. He and Henry Salvatori, who had made a fortune in oil drilling equipment, decided that Ronald Reagan was a viable candidate for governor to run against Democratic Governor Edmund (Pat) Brown, whom they had come to abhor. They sounded out other businessmen of like mind and jointly put the proposition to Reagan. Although flattered by the invitation, he did not want to leave his job of selling "free enterprise" for General Electric, so his fans formed "Friends of Ronald Reagan" and began to raise money to show him they were serious.

In addition to Tuttle and Salvatori, his guiding lights included Theodore E. Cummings, who built a supermarket chain; Justin Dart, chairman of Dart Industries, later Dart & Kraft

Inc.; Jack Wrather, head of an oil, entertainment and real
estate conglomerate; Alfred S. Bloomingdale, former head of
the Diners' Club and other firms; Earle M. Jorgensen, head of
a steel company; and William French Smith, Reagan's personal attorney, senior partner of a large law firm and director of
numerous corporations. All were conservative, self-made
millionaires.

PAVING THE WAY

By the time he finally agreed to run for governor in 1965, his
way was already paved. A campaign organization had been
started and financed with initial donations. His backers hired
political professionals to help him plan a strategy. They hired
publicists to handle the media. They arranged advertising, and
they helped set the tone of the campaign. Reagan had little to
do but show up when scheduled and read the remarks written
for him. For a product of the movies and the business world,
being merchandised in politics was a natural evolution. As a
veteran actor, it was not a big change for him to start taking
cues from enthusiastic admirers on the political stage.

Once he jumped in, Reagan took to the stump like a duck to
water. And he played the part with consummate skill. He deft-
ly depicted himself as a moderate conservative and relegated
his opponent to the far left as a reckless spender who had
brought the state to the brink of financial collapse. The gross
exaggerations never caught up with him. He won by a landslide.

Once in the governor's chair, Reagan naturally turned to his
friends and boosters to help select key people and plan policy.
In Tuttle's words, "He asked us to fill 35 to 40 of the top jobs.
We met for 10 hours a day for weeks, and with the help of other
people, we looked for the best people we could find and made
the recommendations to Ron. He didn't have to accept them,
but I'll say this, in all but one or two cases, he did."[6]

According to Robert Lindsey, co-author of *Reagan, The Man,
The President*, almost all of the people nominated for state
jobs by the search committee were employees of corporations
and conservative Republicans. Many took jobs regulating the
industries they came from, but no major controversies tran-
spired.[7]

Considerable criticism arose, however, over some of

Reagan's decisions. Among them was his effort to close down government legal services for the poor; cut benefits for crippled children, the blind and the elderly; and impose a Workfare scheme to force people off the state dole and into jobs. But he managed to weather these storms by emphasizing his basic themes of cutting taxes and spending, which had tremendous appeal to blue collar workers, the bulk of the swing vote in California (and the nation). He was re-elected for another four years in 1970 over Jesse Unruh, speaker of the state legislature.

EYEING THE WHITE HOUSE

Visions of a Reagan presidency began to dance in the eyes of Tuttle and others of Reagan's "Kitchen Cabinet" shortly after Reagan became governor. Within two years, they had started to lay the groundwork for a White House run. Thomas Reed was hired away from the Governor's staff to work along with Cliff White, a professional political manager. Their efforts did not immediately bear fruit, as Reagan was soundly beaten by Richard Nixon for the Republican nomination in 1968 and edged out by President Gerald Ford in 1976.

But neither Reagan nor his backers gave up, even though he was getting to the point where his age might become a political handicap. Using $1 million in leftover campaign funds, Reagan and his friends set up "Citizens for the Republic," which became one of the richest Political Action Committees (PACs), for the purpose of raising still more money for a repeat run in 1980.

Meanwhile, Michael Deaver and Peter Hannaford, two of Reagan's top gubernatorial aides, set up a public relations firm bearing their names, partly to help sell him to national voters. They gave Reagan an office and served as business coordinators, arranged speaking tours, wrote a regular radio commentary and tended to political fence-building. He kept an office there until November, 1979, when he formally launched his campaign for the Presidency. Deaver and Hannaford continued to assist him on a voluntary basis after that.

They also unwittingly caused him some problems because of various clients who may have seen the firm as a handy means for channeling their view to the candidate. One was the Republic of China, otherwise known as Nationalist China or

Taiwan. According to *Washington Post* reporter Don Ober-
dorfer, the firm, "while receiving large sums from the Taiwan
account, worked on speeches, press releases, newspaper columns and other public statements by Reagan, including a
number backing Taiwan and opposing U.S. ties with its adver-
sary, the People's Republic of China."[8] Deaver and Hannaford
denied any impropriety, pointing out that Reagan had
previously been a strong supporter of Taiwan. But from that
point on, there were stronger and more frequent endorsements
of Taiwan in Reagan's basic speech. The endorsements were to
haunt him throughout the campaign and into the White House
because of the official government policy of recognizing
mainland China, a policy instituted by President Nixon.

SIDING WITH BUSINESS

The firm's corporate clients were less of a problem, because
of the confluence of Reagan's views with theirs. From the
beginning of his political life, Reagan has unabashedly sided
with big business on almost every issue. He has made no
apologies. He has seen the need for none. He has firmly believed that what is good for business is good for the country,
although he has never put it exactly the way Charles Wilson
put it. Whatever ails the economy and society, in his view, has
been the government's fault because of high taxes, "over-
regulation," spending that is "out of control" and loose
monetary policies. From his perspective, government social
programs have also been basically wrong because they have
destroyed individual initiative. In his autobiography, he
quoted Plutarch's warning: "The real destroyer of the liberties
of the people is he who spreads among them bounties, donations and benefits."[9]

The great masses of hapless people do not seem to exist in
his mind. In response to a question from television reporter
Bill Moyers during the campaign on what he would do to help
those who cannot fend for themselves, he launched into a story
of an acquaintance who became rich by inventing a simple device for holding a beer can with a handle. It's just a matter of
old-fashioned gumption that separates the haves from the
havenots, in his opinion. With such an attitude, he could con-
veniently rationalize the sufferings of the masses as a fault of

the liberals and big government and ignore the need for compassionate assistance.

Reagan's basic attitude has been pure and simple *laissez-faire*: Get the government out of human affairs except as policemen and soldier. "Outside of its legitimate function," he said in his stock campaign speech, "government does nothing as well or as economically as the private sector of the economy."[10] He simply skipped over the primary government roles in protecting the environment, assuring economic justice, equal rights, public health and safety, none of which can be handled as well by the private sector.

SIMPLE THEMES

One of his pet peeves has been the network of government regulations set up over a century to protect the citizenry from economic abuses of the marketplace as well as unnecessary health and safety hazards. "Under bureaucratic regulations adopted with no regard for the wish of the people," he said in the same stock speech, "we have lost much of our Constitutional freedom. He then cited an example of a government inspector "invading" a business firm to check on worker safety as a violation of human rights. Again, he looked at the situation from the business point of view, not the workers'.[11]

In an ever more complex world, Reagan saw only simple solutions. Former Governor Pat Brown observed that "his ideas, his philosophy, his perceptions, his comprehension of human affairs and society are neatly confined to a simple framework of thought and action that permits no doubts and acknowledges no sobering complexities.[12]

Reagan's themes in the Presidential campaign were equally uncomplicated: reduce government spending and regulations; encourage economic growth through reduced taxes and tighter control of money, and improve the nation's image in world affairs. To drive home these points, he used a series of catchy slogans repeated over and over again a la Madison Avenue: "Big government is the problem." "Let's turn the economy around." "Get rid of fraud, waste and abuse." "Get the government off our backs." He vowed to make certain that the United States would never be "second best" or be "pushed around."

Reagan honed these well worn cliches with the skill of a

master salesman. He knew the importance of having a few major themes and simple slogans to appeal to the great bulk of voters. His strategy was perfectly designed for television. Here was a "supreme communicator" at work. That was the term given to him by former Nixon press aide Herbert Klein, a veteran communicator in his own right.

One of his underlying themes was the need for renewed faith in America. "We need to make America great again," he told audience after audience. This "call to faith," with its religious overtones and occasional references to God, was his most effective device in getting votes, according to a study by the Connecticut Mutual Life Insurance Company. "Perhaps the election was not decided on 'issues' in the customary sense," said the report, "but rather by the overriding issue of belief in our established American traditions."

PROGRAMMED RESPONSES

Reagan had spouted these lines so often over the years that they had become second nature to him. To almost any question, he reverted to a programmed response. Questioned about inflation, he would say it was the government's fault because of tax and regulatory burdens on business. Questioned about pollution, this man who had spent much of his life in smogbound Los Angeles would say that it was no longer a serious problem. On almost any national problem, he would blame the government, saying that to reduce its size would bring prosperity to all.

The press, by and large, accepted his pat answers and rarely challenged the numerous contradictions between his views and the real world. In a typical interview allowing him freedom to present his stock responses without hard questions, he told *U.S. News & World Report* that he would reduce the "centralized authority of Washington" and eliminate "waste, fraud and abuse" without harming people dependent on social programs. He was not pressed on how he would do that.

He also was not pressed by reporters to explain how the *laissez-faire* theory would work in an economy where many major industries are dominated by a few large firms that control prices and supplies without fear of being undercut. His campaign managers made it difficult for reporters by greatly limiting their access to him except for media outlets known to be friendly to him.

Reagan's view of foreign affairs was just as simple. One of his top aides who left the campaign because of a staff disagreement linked the candidate to outdated concepts. Said John Sears: "His is a kind of 1950 world" when the United States and Russia completely dominated the rest of the globe and the Cold War was under way in earnest.[13] Even though much has changed since then, Reagan still clings to the same outlook. He holds the Soviet Union responsible for virtually every act of terrorism and violence. After an especially bitter denunciation of Russia, Reagan was asked if he was seeking to resume the Cold War. He replied: "When did it ever end?"

With his broad generalities, he found it easy to convice voters that President Carter had weakened the U.S. position, especially with his handling of the Iranian crisis. By comparing the number of this country's missiles, submarines, planes and troops with Russia's, he implied that a bigger stockpile of these items could somehow have solved the hostage matter, the Cuban situation and other sticking points when that was not the case.

Happily for Ronald Reagan and the Republicans, the American people are famous for accepting political candidates at face value. They tend to weigh personality and appearances more than policies and issues. According to a number of polls, the 1980 election hinged more on differences in style of the two main candidates than on differences in views. Most voters apparently felt that Carter had failed to exert proper leadership and, although they did not know as much about Reagan, they were ready to give him an opportunity to run the country.

WINNING BIG

When the votes were tallied, it was clear that the Reagan strategy had worked. The 489-to-49 margin of his electoral victory surprised even his most optmistic supporters. He was also given much of the credit for the astounding capture of the Senate by Republicans and increased dominance of conservatives in the House.

Not since Calvin Coolidge, whom Reagan openly admired, had a victorious Presidential candidate so openly espoused conservative, pro-business points of view. And not since FDR had there been such a sudden shift in government direction.

For people with money, the election was an emancipation.
They began to act as though a great weight had been lifted
from their shoulders. No longer did they feel that they should
hide their wealth or their interest in cutting taxes. For several
days before and after the Inauguration, the Nation's Capital
was virtually taken over by propertied interests. Limousines
and company cars filled the streets while corporate jets jam-
med the airports. Conspicuous consumption and the flaunting
of wealth were suddenly back in style, with mink furs and
gaudy jewelry mixed with the Reagan movie theme of cowboy
boots and 10-gallon hats. The First Lady's wardrobe for the occasion was said to cost more than $25,000. Washington had
never seen such opulence.

The incoming Republicans felt they had a clear mandate for
turning the government upside down. The President-elect
wasted no time in seizing the initiative. On the day he was in-
augurated, he signed an executive order freezing federal hiring,
even making the order retroactive to election day, a move that
was later declared illegal by an appeals court. He quickly
followed with a freeze of pending regulations, another move
challenged on legal grounds. And he proposed sweeping reductions in taxes and spending on social programs offset by record
increases in the military budget.

THE "NEW BEGINNING"

Equally sweeping were some of the terms used. Reagan
himself spoke of a "new beginning," which he repeated often
despite the redundancy, later opting for the equally redundant
"new renaissance." To the Republican National Committee, it
was nothing less than an "economic revolution." The latter
term implied that the voters were behind all the major changes
made by the new Administration. Whether that was indeed
true may not become known until the 1982 or 1984 elections.

In any case, the new crowd lost no time in reversing the
course of government. It planned to "hit the ground running,"
in Reagan's words, and it surely did. Washington was soon
swarming with representatives of conservative causes, single-
issue groups such as anti-abortionists and the far-right fringe
of the Republican Party. They not only came to cash in their
chips for campaign support but to consolidate the Washington
foothold as quickly and surely as possible.

The most influential group was the Heritage Foundation, a right-wing think tank financed largely by Joseph Coors of brewery fame and Richard Mellon Scaife, an heir to the Mellon fortune. Just in time for the new wave came publication of several thick volumes from the Foundation, headed by the 1,093-page *Mandate For Leadership*, providing guidelines for the conservative conquest of Washington. Everything was laid out in detail, including proposed budget cuts for each agency, suggested taxes to slash and regulations to be put into storage. Many Reagan aides had already endorsed the proposals or written them while at the Foundation. Budget Director David Stockman called the book " a blueprint. . . for the 1980s," and Presidential Counsellor Ed Meese III said the "Administration will rely heavily" on it.

The rest looked simple. Simply duplicate the pages, bind them together and forward them to the President and Congress. Although many of the projected savings were altered — usually upward — the basic outlines of the Heritage proposal were swallowed whole by the new crew. Never had a private organization shaped a new administration so completely and so rapidly.

President Reagan outlined his plans publicly in staged television appearances and formal statements. He kept out in front with broad, general themes while his aides who did the work stayed off camera. He limited formal press conferences to only three in the first eight months, far less than almost all previous chief executives back for more than 50 years. He chose to concentrate on formal events which could be more carefully controlled. The strategy was to capitalize on the election euphoria and keep the momentum going as long as possible.

FEEDING THE PRESS

A key element of success was the press. Front-line reporters were generally kept in line with carefully crafted handouts and minor tidbits. The proverbial honeymoon given by the press to all new Presidents was especially long and sweet for Ronald Reagan, since he had so much to propose and the press had so little time to analyze it. He and his aides knew that they could probably get more done if they overwhelmed both Congres and the press. And overwhelm they did. The budget and tax pack-

ages themselves were so monstrous and complicated that there
was no way that their full import could be communicated to
the general public. And on Capitol Hill, the chief complaint of
legislators became the lack of time to look into all the Reagan
proposals.

Adding to the problem of digestibility was Reagan's special
standing with media owners and managers back home. He not
only enjoyed the editorial endorsement of most newspapers
that took a stand, but he wound up on the receiving end of
many favorable features and news reports. Some of the largest
news organizations started a process of cheerleading that
Democratic Presidents had never experienced. (See Chapter 3
for details) Reporters and correspondents in Washington did
not even have to read between the lines of their homes papers
to learn how far they should go in slanting stories for the new
regime. They could merely read the White House guest lists
showing their bosses and other media executives dining with
the President and his wife, Nancy.

Even cartoonists were neutralized. Most are relatively free
spirits who occasionally defy their own paper's political
stance. But with Ronald Reagan, many began to pull their
punches rather than let their feelings out. In a roundup of
leading artists, *The Washington Post* found a surprising
amount of editorial restraint for such normally independent artists. Among those admitting to having problems getting
around Reagan's nice-guy image were Jack Ohman, Dwane
Powell, Mike Peters, Tony Auth, even Herblock. Among the
better known artists, only Doug Marlette and Paul Conrad appeared unwilling "to play the Reagan game," as Conrad put it.
"It's a cop out," he said. Marlette added: "You have to sort of
educate people into what's really going on. These people (the
Reagan Administration) are really mean-spirited... they may
be nice to their families and pay their mortgages on time and
contribute to the United Way, but their problem is a serious
hardness of heart. It comes out in the policies. And Reagan is a
perfect front man for them."[14]

Whether one agrees that Reagan is really an evil person
wrapped up in a smile, the result of all this journalistic adulation was that the American public got only part of the news
from Washington about the "new beginning." Too much happened too fast to fit into the usual radio bulletins, TV news

segments and newspaper reports. Congress also was snowed under. Thus, the two forces that the public depended on most to provide a check on the executive branch were bowled over by the Reagan bulldozer.

SELLING THE PROGRAM

In the absence of full discussion, not to mention a truly national debate, the Reagan Administration had relatively clear sailing for its mammoth program of budget cuts, tax reductions, regulatory changes and shifts in policies. Rather than encouraging full examination of the proposals in the press and in Congress, the Reagan crew resorted to a selling process: applying pressure on Congress and imparting propaganda to the public.

Instead of issuing rationales for the wrenching reversals of past government policies and programs, Reagan officials threw their weight into lobbying and advertising campaigns to win Congressional approval for their budget cuts. They leaned heavily on the corporate community, which had the most to gain from the programs, to spread the word. A nationwide advertising campaign financed by a number of large corporations was arranged secretly by the White House staff working with members of the President's "Kitchen Cabinet." Full-page newspaper ads proclaimed an urgent need to enact Reagan's program—for the public's own good, of course. Some companies urged stockholders and employees to contact legislators and ask them to support the President. Among the firms were Standard Oil of Indiana and Dow Chemical Company. Mail favorable to the Administration flooded Congressional offices, much of it clearly part of organized efforts by business and conservative groups.

White House lobbyists even agreed to hold off on certain potential budget cuts in order not alienate key Senators and Representatives. For example, the Office of Management and Budget wanted to slash federal subsidies to tobacco farmers but was thwarted by other Presidential aides who did not want to incur the wrath of Senator Jesse Helms, the North Carolina Republican who heads the Agriculture Committee.

By proposing so many changes at once, the Administration succeeded in putting potential critics on the defensive. Congressional discussions revolved around questions of how much to cut from the budget rather than around more basic questions of whether to reduce—or raise—the level of spending for particular programs. By pushing the entire program at once while the first favorable responses were pouring in from the public, Reaganites managed to force many reluctant and doubting Democrats into quick approval of the controversial proposals before there was time to review the changes fully or get feedback from their constituents. Reagan aides pursued this type of offensive with full knowledge that parts of the package contained some bitter pills for many Americans. They appeared willing to risk a massive backlash at a later date rather than allow time for full analysis and thus risk losing impetus.

PUTTING CRITICS ON THE DEFENSIVE

Much was made of the expected battle in Congress over the monumental changes requested by the Reagan forces. But the outcome was never really in doubt. In recent years, both the House and Senate have been controlled by conservative coalitions. The capture of the Senate by Republicans and the increase in Republican numbers in the House merely increased their control.

Both friends and critics of the Reagan proposals found themselves besieged by letters and phone calls from local business executives and large contributors urging a positive vote. They were also lobbied by fellow legislators as well as the President himself.

After the final votes were in, and Congress had locked the country into three years of greatly reduced social programs, record military expenditures and five years of generous tax breaks, mostly for the wealthy, Congress and the President left town for summer vacations.

But some haunting questions remained in the empty halls of government. One was whether the final product would fly. Another was whether the American people really knew what happened. It was clear from their comments that members of Congress did not.

2

What Mandate?

The era of self-doubt is over.
President Reagan[1]

What caused the election of Ronald Reagan and the new crop of conservative politicians in Congress and elsewhere? Did the election bring a mandate, as they claim, for the sweeping changes they have begun?

Since the 1980 election, there have been many claims of a "massive" victory of "landslide" proportions for Republicans and conservative policies. According to the *U.S. News & World Report*, the election was a "massive shift to the right," in which voters "left no doubt what they wanted."[2] Whether the news media started such talk, or the victorious candidates did, they fed on each other until the assumptions became accepted by almost everyone.

There was certainly no doubt about who won. Ronald Reagan captured 10 times more electoral votes than Jimmy Carter, becoming the first challenger to defeat an incumbent President since 1932. Republicans also picked up 12 seats in the Senate for a 53-to-46 majority and gained 33 seats in the house, cutting a 2-to-1 Democratic margin to 243 to 192. Republicans also won new strength at the state level, winning four governorships from Democrats and gaining control of both houses of legislatures in two more states.

CLOSE POPULAR VOTE

But a closer look shows a different picture. What *U.S. News & World Report* called a "runaway popular-vote victory" was only a bare majority for Reagan.[3] He got 51 per cent of total ballots, with Carter and other candidates splitting the rest. The 43 million people who voted for the former movie actor represented only 27 per cent of adults of voting age. Some 41 million people voted against Reagan, while 76 million other Americans of voting age chose not to vote for any Presidential candidate. The 52 per cent turnout of voters was the lowest since 1948, a clear sign that many eligible voters were not enchanted by any of the available candidates.

Outside the Presidential race, the results were less conclusive. Democrats actually outpolled Republicans in balloting for both the House and Senate, because their large pluralities in a few races exceeded the total margins in many close races won by Republicans. Although Republicans won four governorships, they wound up holding less than a majority. And although they gained control of both houses of the legislature in two additional states, only 39 per cent of state legislators in the nation were Republicans. Altogether, such results did not indicate a landslide but a relatively close election.

Even conservative writer Kevin P. Phillips cautioned against reading too much into the 1980 election. "There's been very little upheaval," he wrote, "the closer you get to the grassroots... This is one reason why I'm skeptical of the idea of 1980 as a 'fundamental realignment' election. I don't believe it was." Phillips was the author of the seminal book, *The Emerging Republican Majority.*[4]

In another analysis of the results, liberal author Mark Green concluded: "Americans did not explicitly decide to endorse right-wing policies throughout the government—to ditch human rights, clean air and food stamps for the hungry. Instead, a confluence of economic and political events fortuitously broke in favor of an attractive nonincumbent, who happened to be extremely conservative.[5]

NEGATIVE PUBLIC MOOD

More evidence that the election was a negative popularity contest emerged from a poll by Yankelovich, Skelly and White for Time Inc. It showed that 63 per cent felt that Reagan won because voters had rejected Carter. Only 24 per cent felt that the election was a mandate for more conservative policies.[6] A Gallup poll of Reagan voters themselves reported that only 10 per cent chose him because he was more "conservative." Gallup concluded that there was "no strong political movement to the right."

Similar readings came from a survey of Reagan voters leaving the polling booths. According to a CBS News/*New York Times* survey that asked which qualifications best described their choice of Reagan, 38 per cent said it was because they felt it was time for a change. Only 21 per cent said it was because Reagan was a strong leader. A significant 14 per cent said they did not know or gave no answer.[7]

During the campaign, a sour mood among the people was detected by numerous reporters. Haynes Johnson, one of the best, reported after a five-week tour of the country "a clear lack of enthusiasm for any candidate." He said: "Everywhere, people are yearning for a special, if not impossible, brand of national leadership—leadership that answers the unanswerable, solves the insoluble, removes frustration and doubt." He added that this yearning, coupled with the lack of enthusiasm for the candidates for President, "is going to make it all the more difficult for the new leader to unite the country and move it forward."[8]

Obviously, many voters felt that Carter had had a chance to improve the economy and failed; therefore, it was time to try someone else. Continuing double-digit inflation and high interest rates, the lag in productivity and jobs and the frustrating Iranian hostage situation all worked against Carter. To voters, Reagan was a pleasant alternative, the least offensive of the major candidates, certainly not a strong endorsement of him or his views.

But Reagan made the most of what he had in the campaign. His choice of issues to emphasize was masterful. By concentrating on economic matters, he focused public interest on Carter's most prominent failures, at least to the extent that a President can be blamed for such things. Polls of voters leaving the polling booths showed that inflation was indeed the top issue in their minds, followed by budget deficits and military power. Reagan staked out a strong position on these matters, but he avoided getting specific about how he would proceed.

PUBLIC'S VIEW VS. REAGAN'S

Polls asking general questions turned up strong support for the broad outlines of Reagan's plans of cutting the budget, boosting defense and reducing the role of government. But when questions dealt with specific programs and policies, the answers showed strong differences in views between Reagan's and those of the public. For example, the *Time* poll previously mentioned reported that while 63 per cent favored tax incentives for business, only 51 per cent wanted an across-the-board income tax cut of 10 per cent per year, as promised by Reagan. That was a surprisingly small percentage in view of the self-interest of people in cutting taxes. On the matter of wage and price controls, which were opposed by Reagan, 46 per cent favored them against 39 per cent who did not. People were apparently even willing to pay for environmental controls, in contrast to Reagan's view that many were unnecessary burdens. When asked whether some such controls should be eliminated in order to reduce the costs of consumer products such as cars, 46 per cent disagreed against 40 per cent who agreed.[9]

While most people agreed with the general aim of reducing federal spending, 55 per cent did not want those cuts to hurt programs for health, education, housing. And while 57 per cent favored balancing the budget, a goal that Reagan apparently will not accomplish, 57 per cent opposed cutting the budget by reducing social programs, another finding contradicting Reagan's actions once in office. People also seemed willing to pay extra for product safety standards opposed so strongly by business and the Reagan team. The poll indicated that 58 per cent of those responding said they favored such standards even if they made consumer goods more expensive.

LIMITED EVIDENCE OF MANDATE

Polls showed other contradictions between the public's views and Reagan's. They included indications of strong public opposition to abortion curbs favored by Reagan and equally strong support for gun controls, which Reagan opposed even after he was shot by a deranged youth. Most people, however, seemed to agree with his support of public prayers in schools, federal aid to private schools and the death penalty. On energy matters, a poll commissioned by the White House Council on Environmental Quality in 1980 showed strong support for development of alternative fuels such as solar. A solid 61 per cent said solar was the energy source which the nation should "concentrate on most."[10] Nuclear energy was the source preferred the least. A strong 73 per cent agreed that "an endangered species must be protected even at the expense of commercial activity," while 65 per cent felt that marshes and swamps should be preserved instead of drained for development.

Although not too much reliance should be put on polls, they showed considerable differences between the public's views and Reagan's reading of them. The only mandates that could be supported by the polls were vague ones to improve the economy, trim the federal budget and restore American prestige around the world.

For Reaganites to claim that voters also were demanding huge slashes in taxes for both individuals and business, a deficit higher than Carter's own projections for Reagan's first full fiscal year in office, gigantic boosts in military spending at the expense of almost every other government program and wholesale cutbacks in health and safety protections was reading a lot more into the election results than appeared to be justified. To claim further that voters wanted to open up government forests to commercial development, stop promoting human rights around the world, increase nuclear arms shipments and reduce Social Security benefits also appeared to be stretching the message of the elections. Further, there was no evidence that voters wanted to slash environmental regulations.

Only a master politician could get away with making such claims in behalf of private business and at the same time appeal to the typical blue-collar worker whose interests were often at odds with the business world. Professor James Q. Wilson of Harvard University helped explain the apparent contradiction in a book review. "Mr. Reagan," he wrote, "has managed to capture perfectly the mood of the American populist conservativism; a belief in traditional virtues and a hope for economic progress, expressed in a criticism of government, bureaucracy and regulations in the abstract, with little attention to the particular programs that must be changed if these abstractions are in fact to be altered. Every bit of poll data we have shows a nation composed of persons who object to the pace but not the direction of change, who complain about the welfare state in general but support almost every component of it in particular . . . who are fed up with the United States being 'pushed around' overseas but who are skeptical of any increased American involvement in international affairs . . . "[11]

However, Reagan officials proceeded to interpret the election results as they saw them regardless of the conflicting evidence.

They also wasted no time setting forth what they wanted to change. So much happened so fast that even the most percep- tive observers of the American scene were diverted from recognizing the contradictions.

VOICE OF DOUBT

Among the first to say "wait a minute" was columnist Richard Cohen of *The Washington Post*. After reviewing the changes of the first two months, he commented: "I don't think most people voted for this. What they voted for was a change — not a revolution. They voted for a bit more backbone in our foreign policy and maybe a little toughness in the budgeting process. They wanted someone to get hold of the economy and do something about inflation, and if that meant making some hard decisions, that was fine with them. But they did not vote against poor people, and they did not vote to repeal the lessons we learned in blood in Vietnam . . . If there was a statement [in the election results], it was that Carter lost, not that Reagan won — certainly not that he won big and certainly not that he won with a mandate to fundamentally change the relationship of the government to the people. What was expected was some minor changes, some tinkering, less liberalism, maybe, but not a crash course in conservatism. You knew with Reagan that there would be less government, but not, I think, less heart."[12]

Cohen was a lonesome voice of dissent. The press as a whole appeared to be a captive of the new Administration. Reporters found themselves so busy finding out what was happening that they had little time or inclination to find out what the changes meant to people and what their reactions were. And most commentators seemed reluctant to question what ap- peared to be the prevailing mood of widespread approval. Democratic legislators who survived were especially reluctant to raise questions for fear of going against the tide. And citizen groups, apparently still shell shocked by the election, were too stunned to act.

The traditional "honeymoon" accorded new Presidents by the press and opposition politicians was especially happy for Ronald Reagan and his partners. They made the most of their electoral victory, continually referring to a "landslide" and "mandates" for almost everything they wanted. They even began referring to a "revolution" and "a call for national renewal." They merchandised the "mandate" idea with resounding success.

MERCHANDISING THE MANDATE IDEA

By taking action quickly once in office, the Administration gave the impression that it had a widely endorsed answer to the nation's major problems. And by focusing on broad strokes — such as the record budget cuts and military spending increases — it kept the focus of attention on the big picture rather than on the more controversial details. The big news each day was essentially dictated by the White House, since it determined when and what to announce. Presidential addresses to joint sessions of Congress and other public occasions were planned to take full advantage of the euphoric situation.

Reagan himself — an extremely affable man — was built into a popular figure to unify a divided nation. But early public opinion polls did not indicate as much public acceptance as headlines indicated, showing Reagan with a lower performance rating than Carter after two months in office. As the details of the budget and tax cuts became known, voices of criticism began to be heard.

Then, on March 30, the shots rang out, and Reagan fell to an assassin's bullet. Although it was a traumatic occasion, much more dangerous than first news reports indicated, the attack on the President wound up sending Reagan into an unexpected "second honeymoon" of public approval. As he recovered from the effects of the shooting, the public mood and impressions improved, too. A poll by Yankelovich, Skelly & White Inc. for Time Inc. in late May showed that 51 per cent of the public felt that things were going well in the country, compared to only 26 per cent who felt that way in January. Patrick Caddell, former President Carter's pollster, also reported a rise in long-term optimism, from late 1980 to the spring of 1981.[13]

White House aides sought to exploit the euphoria of Reagan's recovery in his first public appearances after the shooting. Deliberately avoiding controversial aspects of his program, he spoke at West Point of a "new spirit" in the country: "There is a spiritual revival going on in this country."

Referring to Carter's lament in 1979 about a "crisis of the American spirit," Reagan proclaimed: "The era of self-doubt is over."

At this point, he had the best of all worlds. He was able to generate optimism without getting specific. The upbeat mood grew in the absence of any calamity and may have been enhanced by the slackening of inflation due to leveling off of oil prices. As reporter Hedrick Smith noted: "Reagan has managed to tap and nurture a budding mood of national self-confidence even before his major policies have had enough time to achieve real practical impact or to be properly tested."[14]

CONTRASTS GROW WIDER

As time went on, however, contrasts between his actions and public views grew wider. His plan to make El Salvador a symbol of American confrontation with the Soviets soon turned into a welter of public worry about a new "Vietnam." And the Administration ran into a set of restrictions imposed by a Congressional committee on further aid to that Central American country. Public polls began to show strong opposition to sending military advisers there. Reagan's bold attempt to cut into basic Social Security benefits for early retirement, despite campaign promises not to do so, also ran into Congressional opposition, resulting in a rare 96-0 rejection by the Senate. His effort to name hardliner Ernest Lefever to the human rights post at the State Department created such resistance even among Republicans that Lefever was forced to withdraw. Meanwhile, numerous citizen groups, labor organizations and others began to stage demonstrations and campaign against his policies. Perhaps most ominous of all was the mood of uncertainty on Wall Street over whether Reagan's economic program would work.

The bumps on the road to his "new beginning" got steadily worse because so many traditional ways were being uprooted in Washington. Administration officials and their counterparts in Congress took the risk of generating a powerful backlash by pushing so intensively to reverse the course of government and society itself with such little evidence of popular support. They also took a big chance that their formula for economic improvement would not work despite the strong confidence of supporters. And in foreign affairs, they risked the loss of powerful allies with policies designed more for the 1950s than the 1980s.

QUESTIONABLE ASSUMPTIONS

Reagan and his crew also were operating on some questionable assumptions. The main one was that the federal government—in the form of taxes, spending and regulations—was the chief cause of the nation's economic problems. Another assumption was that Americans wanted to repeal all major social programs and laws adopted since Franklin Roosevelt. Still another was that spending a lot more money on the Pentagon would increase the nation's military strength, and that in turn could increase prospects for peace. A further assumption was that challenging the Soviets everywhere on earth could bring a more stable world. Also assumed was that increasing government secrecy and boosting the power of intelligence agencies would strengthen a democratic society.

To solve the nation's economic problems, Reagan turned to the *laissez-faire* theory, on the assumption that business, once freed of government restraints, would bring prosperity and equity to all.

Reagan did not seem aware that *laissez-faire* had died a natural death nearly a century before. It died because it had failed to meet demands for economic justice, a concept that had scarcely been raised during the heydays of the Industrial Revolution. The idea of the postal fraud statues of 1872 was to protect the public from the unfairness of uncontrolled business. Creation of the Interstate Commerce Commission in 1887 and the Sherman Antitrust Act of 1890 were attempts to tame the industrial robber barons before they destroyed the country. The increased role of the federal government over the years reflected a growing concern for economic and social justice as well as demands by business for economic aid such as import quotas or price supports.

PROBLEMS OF MARKETPLACE

Reagan also seemed unaware of the problems of the marketplace which had given rise to the consumer concerns of the 1960s and early 1970s. Having become accustomed to a life of luxury far removed from the grubby chores of sweating out supermarket lines and putting up with surly store clerks and trying to get expensive products repaired properly at a reasonable cost, Reagan had no reason to add his voice to those of angry consumers. The increase in the complexity of products, the reduction in product quality in a throwaway society, the hidden hazards inside fancy packages and the difficulty of comparing the values of fractionated packages simply passed him by. In the same way, life on his isolated Rancho di Cielo far from the madding crowds and polluted highways left him with no burning desire to improve an environment that appeared so sublime from his vantage point. He tended to associate the struggle for clean air and water with the disheveled young people who started the movement.

In addition, he seemed unconcerned about the serious social problems that were suddenly injected into the nation's consciousness by the riots of the 1960s. There is no doubt now that many of the social programs created to cure these problems raised hopes too high and did not work as planned. It is also true that most of the programs continued to grow despite dubious results. But the problems themselves did not go away. Most only became worse. Meanwhile, millions of Americans came to depend on government assistance for survival despite a national level of affluence unprecedented in history.

ESSENTIALLY UNINFORMED

As a frequent speaker and commentator on the national scene, Ronald Reagan occasionally showed recognition of major problems other people face, but he remained essentially an uninformed bystander rather than an advocate for improving conditions for less fortunate people during the period of huge social changes. Throughout the national upheavals and reassessments that altered the views of many Americans, he continued to cling to the political and social views that shaped his thinking in the 1950s. His basic political aims did not go much beyond reducing taxes for the well-to-do and making life easier for large corporations.

As governor of California from 1966 to 1974, his main concern and that of his principal backers was controlling costs of state services. Although he was successful in reducing welfare rolls to some extent, he was unable to prevent state budgets from doubling, along with the taxes to pay for them. Although his own rhetoric continued to be anti-environment, his overall record as governor was not as bad as he sounded. On many controversial issues, he seemed not to know the historical background or future consequences, only to be rescued by a fortuitous intuition to make the politically safe decision. Lou Cannon, a reporter who knows Reagan as well as any, observed that "this combination of ignorance and intuition worked reasonably well for Reagan as he struggled to understand the intricacies of government."[15]

Despite the realities of California politics, Reagan continued to cling to the beliefs he held before becoming governor. The fact that he signed one of the most liberal abortion bills anywhere did not stop him from taking a strong position against abortion in his quest for the presidency. The fact that he blocked some environmentally damaging water projects in California did not prevent him from ridiculing environmentalists in the campaign. The fact that he failed to reduce the size of the state government or lower taxes did not make him waiver from his position that the federal government was much too large and its taxes were too high.

He has consistently viewed the world from the corporate towers where his best friends run their fiefdoms. In his view, there is no conflict between what is good for business and what is good for the general public. They are one and the same, because workers need jobs and the public needs the fruits (and taxes) of their labor. This uncluttered view of society has allowed him to dismiss nearly all concerns about marketplace abuses and environmental problems as trivial or unjustified in view of the overall benefits of a "free enterprise" system.

RUNNING DOWN WASHINGTON

He has never understood the necessity of having government protect the public from the abuses and excesses of private business. To him, whatever excesses and abuses exist are generated by the government. He also has never fully accepted the role of government as a provider of benefits to those who cannot help themselves. As one who attained success from a humble background through luck and hard work, he sees no reason why anyone else cannot do the same.

Like his big business friends, he opposed many of the new laws and programs enacted during the 1960s and 1970s to cure social wrongs. And he fully supported the concerted campaign of business interests to reverse the trends in Washington. In fact, he became an enthusiastic advocate of the movement and he repeated the anti-Washington line wherever he went.

The clever catchwords of "big brother" and "big government," as well as the perennial complaints about taxes, helped persuade Reagan and many others that Washington was indeed their main enemy. Among those thoughtlessly repeating the slogans were retirees getting government checks, business executives receiving federal contracts and subsidies and average citizens who did not realize how numerous laws and rules hated by business benefited their health and pocketbook.

By the time Reagan entered the primaries in 1980, the anti-Washington campaign was in full flower. Deregulation, started by Carter, was flourishing with a gradual phaseout of some regulatory agencies such as the Interstate Commerce Commission and the Civil Aeronautics Board. The Federal Trade Commission, the country's principal consumer protection agency, was being whittled down by influential friends of business in Congress. And an all-out assault of federal regulations, taxes and many social programs was underway, spearheaded again by business lobbyists. Big business was in the catbird seat in the nation's capital.

Reagan laced his stock campaign speech with jibes at Washington. He also uttered numerous exaggerations. In speaking about "over-regulation," he inferred that almost all government rules and laws were strangling the economy. He spoke of "tens of thousands of unnecessary regulations" hampering the auto industry, though he later found only about three dozen deserving of review by his Administration. He vowed to "free farmers from unnecessary and counterproductive regulations," but once in office, he found that most regulations affecting farmers were designed to prop up prices, which farmers wanted.[16]

UNCRITICAL OF BUSINESS

To industry audiences, which the candidate frequently addressed, he never spoke a critical word or took issue with their complaints about government rules. To reform transportation regulations, he suggested formation of a task force made up of truckers and their clients to "work out a fair elimination of some regulations and the retention of others." He suggested that OSHA "consult with, advise and assist businesses in coping with regulatory burdens before imposing penalties." He supported efforts to relieve the textile industry of "regulatory burdens" such as cotton dust standards, waste-water and air pollution controls. He even invited the coal industry to help rewrite clean air rules. He apparently saw nothing wrong with cozy relationships between regulators and the regulated.

He showed little understanding of why the rules and laws had been enacted in the first place. And, like many business executives, he showed little concern about the injuries and deaths which safety regulations were designed to reduce. He seemed to miss the basic purpose of many regulations. As author Mark Green pointed out in *Village Voice*, "The appropriate framework to discuss the issue of regulations is not whether Americans want more or less regulation, but whether they want more or less cancer."[17] As much as 90 per cent of cancer cases have been attributed to environmental causes. Reagan spoke often about violent crime on the streets but never about the violence perpetrated on the public by insensitive corporations whose toll of injuries and diseases far exceeds those of street criminals.

INACCURATE ALLEGATIONS

At a time when assaults on the environment and human health were growing steadily, Reagan and other conservative politicians were claiming that efforts to control such hazards had reached "overkill." And when acid smoke from Midwest industrial plants was killing fish and other wildlife in the Adirondacks, when illegal use of a growth hormone by Iowa and Texas cattle growers was putting carcinogenic residues in meat served throughout the country, Reagan and some others were advocating weakening controls and handing them over to states whose failure to control the problems in the first place had led to federal involvement. At a time when carcinogenic PCBs (polychlorinated biphenyls) had become regular ingredients of mothers' milk and when carbon dioxide from motor vehicles and industrial plants threatened eventually to alter the earth's temperature and flood the coastal areas, Americans were being told — and convinced — that business should be given more freedom from government controls.

Some inaccurate claims of over-regulations were repeated so often that they became accepted as facts. One was the allegation repeated by Reagan and others in the 1980 election that federal regulations cost $100 billion a year, or about $1,800 per family. The figure was first floated by economist Murray Weidenbaum in 1976 and repeated in that campaign by President Ford. Weidenbaum calculated that business compliance costs were 20 times government costs of administering every regulation. Actually, however, only about $5 billion of the budget is spent on federal health and safety regulation. The Congressional Research Service concluded that Weidenbaum's figures were based on a dubious rationale, but he went on to become chairman of Reagan's Council of Economic Advisers. Weidenbaum continued to use the figures without adjusting them to inflation or calculating the benefits of regulations, which could far exceed their costs according to a Ralph Nader study.[18]

Inflation was also blamed entirely on Washington. Although the government played a role in inflation, particularly through interest rates, business played a much larger role through its power to raise prices. Actually, business likes many regulations because they tend to increase profits. These include food marketing orders and crop supports which allow producers to virtually control supplies and prices of most agricultural products. Other regulations allow trucking firms and insurance companies to set rates with antitrust immunity.

Reagan talked as though American business were still as competitive as it was many years ago. Yet in the key industries of automobiles and steel, there was so little price competition among domestic firms that they had lost much of their markets to lower-priced imports. He did not mention the major role of such price setters in the nation's inflationary spiral.

In view of the gap between Reagan's views and those of the public, how could Reagan have won the election and then succeeded in changing the government so drastically?

There were three major factors: moralists, money and the media. Reagan not only built up an effective political organization to run the campaign but he won the backing of many powerful groups that were not traditional supporters of Republican candidates. Leading the pack were religious moralists. The bottom line was money, big money, mostly from business and conservative interests. He also used the news media in a masterful way both during the campaign and after taking office. (See the next chapter for more on the media's role.)

Reagan had no trouble winning the support of traditional Republicans despite some leftover resentment from moderates afraid of another conservative debacle like Goldwater's in 1964. But he knew he would need much broader support and set out to win over blue-collar workers and ethnic groups that usually lined up with the Democrats.

WITH GOD'S HELP

One of the most effective forces corralled by Reagan was the network of religious fundamentalists best known for their nationwide television hookups. Their ultra-conservative views with a moral tinge dovetailed almost perfectly with his and those of many conservative candidates for Congress in both parties. Reagan happened on the scene at just the time this large and growing wing of the New Right in American politics was rising in influence.

Reagan and the Republican National Committee began courting religious conservatives more than two years before the 1980 election. Among Republicans of the New Right who started meeting with evangelists then, according to author Frances FitzGerald, were Howard Phillips, director of the Conservative Caucus; Terry Dolan of the National Conservative Political Action Committee (NCPAC); Robert Billings, president of the National Christian Action Coalition; Paul Weyrich of the Heritage Foundation, a right-wing thing tank; and Richard Vigueries, the direct-mail specialist for conservative causes.[19]

The television evangelists included Jerry Falwell, a founder of the Moral Majority; Ed McAteer and James Robison, leaders of the Religious Roundtable; Robert Grant of Christian Voice; and Pat Robertson, director of a religious network based in Virginia Beach, Virginia.

One result of the continuing talks was a series of planks in the 1980 GOP platform arranged by evangelists. They included opposition to abortion and taxation of religious schools, many of which were created primarily for racial purposes, as well as support for prayers in school and tuition tax credits for

private schools. So happy was Falwell with the platform that
he told CBS it was "exactly what we believe."

Falwell claimed to have more than 2 million members in his
electronic church with 681 television and radio outlets and an
annual budget of $60 million a year. Robertson claimed to have
150 TV stations and 3,000 cable outlets with annual revenues
of about $50 million. Jim Bakker, head of the PTL Club, made
similar claims. Altogether, these and other evangelists claimed
a weekly audience of some 50 million Protestants and 30
million Catholics. But writer William Martin checked with the
A.C. Nielson Company, the TV rating service, and found that
the total audience was about 13.7 million.[20]

Whatever the actual figures, these television moralists
represented a substantial block of voters. Their combined
power was enough to change the traditional political balance in
a major way. Falwell claimed that he and other televised
preachers had added at least 3 million new voters to the rolls in
1980, not to mention millions more whose votes might have
been influenced by the message that "born-again" Ronald
Reagan was somehow more moral than the other two leading
candidates for President, Carter and Anderson, who were also
"born-again" Christians.

Most of the evangelists were careful not to endorse Reagan
directly, since that would risk losing tax exemptions. But they
managed to get their views across in equally powerful ways, including direct mail campaigns, fund raising and special events
featuring appearances of the favored candidate and his wife.
The day before the key Iowa primary, Falwell held an "I Love
America" rally attended by 10,000 people and featuring Nancy
Reagan. Reagan himself was the star at a Religious Roundtable "National Affairs Briefing" in Dallas attended by
another 10,000 people, mostly preachers and businessmen.
Each received a pamphlet entitled, "Ronald Reagan: A Man of
Faith." It was there that Reagan tossed off one of his more
quotable verses: "I know that you can't endorse me. But I
want you to know that I can endorse you."

He was apparently willing to go far beyond that. According
to one report, he met privately with Roundtable leaders after
the applause died down and agreed to give them the right to
review top Administration appointments in exchange for their
campaign help. Robison claimed that the meeting "could easi-

ly turn out an extra 5 to 10 million voters." Ed McAteer, founder of the Roundtable, added: "This movement will put Ronald Reagan in office."[21]

It may have. It certainly gave him a big push, not only in votes but money. One group alone, Christians for Reagan, raised $6 million for the candidate. Reagan was the main recipient of huge funds raised by PACs, most of which were conservatively oriented. By spending money independently of the candidates, the PACs did not have to conform to contribution limits set by the Federal Election Commission. Most of the PACs which helped Reagan and Bush indirectly also helped conservatives win election in Congress.

POWERFUL JESSE

One example was the North Carolina Congressional Club, a creation of Senator Jesse A. Helms of that state, which spent $7.8 million to help elect candidates that fit the narrow Helms image, including Ronald Reagan who was given $4.5 million. Others were NCPAC, which spent $7 million and the Fund for a Conservative Majority, which spent about $3 million. Still other PACs of the same stripe were sponsored by the National Rifle Association, Citizens for the Republic (which Reagan set up with funds left over from his 1976 Presidential bid), Conservative Victory Fund, Business Industry PAC and Americans for Constitutional Action.[22] Corporate PACs heavily favored Reagan and fellow conservatives.

Helm's organization funneled large sums into campaigns of other Congressional candidates. One of its successes was the Senate election of John P. East, a disabled person considered so much like his benefactor as to be called "Helms on wheels." Fund-raising letters followed the new-right pattern of using fear and exaggeration plus a strong dose of patriotism and piety. "Nearly every one of the 10 to 20 million letters mailed from the club each year," reported *Time*, "warns of the growing dangers of communism and government social spending." Said Helms in one letter: "In the face of the growing Soviet war machine, the ultra-liberals have virtually disarmed America." In another mailing, he said "liberal pressure groups are at work, organizing to flood Congress with mail demanding that liberal food stamps and welfare giveaways not be cut . . .

the Lord may well be giving us one last chance to save America. God bless you always. Sincerely, Jesse."[23]

At times, Helms and East were capable of being extremely personal and vicious. Anyone who criticized tobacco supports risked receiving their full venom, as several Congressional colleagues found out in September. When asked by a reporter for a Raleigh newspaper about some criticism of tobacco supports by Rep. Fred Richmond, Helms was quoted as saying: "I'm not going to yield to any blackmail from some loudmouth Congressman from Brooklyn ... one who has a curious lifestyle, I might point out." The reference was to a homosexual charge faced by Richmond a year earlier. At a press conference, East lit into fellow Senator Thomas Eagleton, who was sponsoring a bill to reduce tobacco supports, by saying: "Now, he was George McGovern's running mate, you know, in 1972, and then dropped out because it turned out he had mental problems..."[24]

LIES AND HIT LISTS

Even more controversial was NCPAC because of its use of "hit lists" and "negative" campaigning (going after an incumbent before any opponent has appeared). NCPAC Director John T. (Terry) Dolan once said: "A group like ours could lie through its teeth and the candidate it helps stays clean." Indeed, the group was caught in so many falsehoods about Congressional voting records in 1981 that Dolan was forced to revise mailing materials and adopt a policy of allowing his targets a chance to review his charges before they were mailed to the public. For example, NCPAC accused Senator Henry Jackson, a noted "hawk," of being against military spending because he had opposed a minor spending increase while favoring more important spending bills. Republican Party Chairman Richard Richards, whose party benefited most from much of Dolan's activities, condemned NCPAC for "creating all kinds of mischief." Nevertheless, by May, 1981, Dolan had already targeted 21 Senators as villains in the 1982 elections based on their alleged stands on six topics: school busing, abortion, prayer in schools, the Panama Canal treaty, defense spending and tax cuts.

Most of the success of right-wing appeals was due to the superior fund-raising techniques of Richard Vigueries. By combining the latest direct-mail techniques with letters of innuendo and exaggeration, he built up the largest political fund-raising operation in the country, all for Republican and ultraconservative causes. Victor Kamber, a Washington political consultant, estimated that Vigueries had put Republicans at least six years ahead of Democrats in direct-mail fund-raising abilities.[25] By early 1981, the GOP was already sending out appeals to 2 million regular contributors to raise money for the 1982 elections. In contrast, the Democrats had only 100,000 names on their list.[26]

Trade associations were also extremely instrumental in fashioning national Republican victories in 1980. The biggest by far was the U.S. Chamber of Commerce, which had a budget of nearly $70 million in 1980 and some 165,000 member companies. Its "non-partisan" PAC, the National Chamber Alliance for Politics, took sides in 126 electoral contests, favoring Republicans in all but two cases. Through its numerous publications and broadcast activities, the Chamber indirectly but effectively helped the Reagan-Bush ticket by promoting similar economic policies.

After the Inauguration, the Chamber turned on the full force of its lobbying power to persuade Congress to approve the new Administration's program. Reagan's chief lobbyist, Max Friedersdorf, told *Fortune* writer Richard I. Kirkland Jr. that the Chamber's efforts were "crucial" to the program's success. With its 2,700 Congressional Action Committees around the country — each containing about 20 business executives claiming personal influence with a legislator — the Chamber was able to generate at least 12,000 phone calls to legislators within 24 hours, plus countless thousands of letters and telegrams. Other business groups, such as the National Association of Manufacturers and Business Roundtable, also pulled out all the stops to help the Republicans before and after the election.

These powerful groups and huge sums tipped the political balance in favor of Reagan and other conservatives. By doing this so decisively, they also may have thwarted the popular will in the election. Although there is no way to prove such a point, it was clear that big money made a big difference in the 1980 election and in Congress's consideration of his program.

3

The Deciding Factor

It's no different, really, from the days of the muckrakers and Tammany Hall, when the boys would sit around and pick the nominee. It's still a small group of guys, only now they're the political reporters who come up here from Washington.

Hugh Gregg
Former Governor of New Hampshire[1]

During the 1980 election campaign, Walter Rodgers of the Associated Press was covering a speech by Ronald Reagan to an audience of coal operators in Youngstown, Ohio. Unlike some reporters, he followed the candidate's text closely. As he listened, he gradually began to feel that the message was alarming. As Rodgers described it in June, 1981, to an Associated Press radio editors' conference, Reagan seemed "willing to give everything the coal operators wanted in environmental matters." Yet Rodgers said none of the broadcast journalists there got the point of the speech in their initial reports.

"I was the only reporter who caught the story," he told the radio editors, "so I went to the other reporters. I convinced them. Finally, some started writing the story for the next cycle, being the following morning." Rodgers was not trying to appear superior. After all, paying attention to a major Presidential candidate was not above and beyond the call of a reporter. He recited the incident only to illustrate the lack of alertness and aggressiveness of many reporters, particularly toward Reagan. Based on his experience, he concluded that Reagan escaped the tough scrutiny given President Carter.

Many reporters would have to agree with Rodgers that Reagan had an easier path in the press during the campaign

36

than President Carter did. For one thing, Reagan faced fewer questions because he was less accessible. That was not the way the campaign started. Reagan began taking questions freely from reporters until some of his off-hand remarks began to boomerang, and his close advisers put him under wraps for the rest of the campaign.

At the White House, it was a reverse situation. Carter started out with the proverbial "Rose Garden" strategy, limiting his accessibility to formal occasions under a controlled environment in order to appear Presidential. By the time this started to backfire and Carter took to the road, Reagan had retreated to his less-accessible mode, leaving the President more vulnerable in the final, crucial months of the campaign. After the election, Carter's press secretary, Jody Powell, charged that reporters had been easier on Reagan in questionings and tended to skip over controversial actions and statements of his in the past.

THE COOL ONE

Differences in press treatment of the two major candidates were perhaps the key factor in the final result. But also important was the difference in the way the two appeared to millions of people watching via television. As a former movie actor and veteran on the speech circuit for General Electric and the Republican Party, Ronald Reagan had learned to be at ease before cameras and microphones. He also had a natural affability that television conveyed well. Although Jimmy Carter had developed a keen ability to articulate his views before the camera, he never was able to rid himself of a certain nervousness and lack of humor. The old movie cowboy did not have those problems. He also knew better than Carter that political campaigns in the television age are not won with factual presentations but with a few simple points repeated over and over. Reagan knew how to advertise himself better than Madison Avenue could. In the jargon of Marshall McLuhan, Reagan was "cool" and Carter was "hot" when coolness was the key to political success.

These differences between the two leading candidates showed up clearly in the second TV debate. As Carter tried desperately one more time to zero in on unfavorable aspects of Reagan's record in California, the former governor broke in

with a big smile and said: "There you go again." He offered a
few calm denials, knowing that the truth could not be decided
at the moment. Reagan knew what Carter did not, that the
debates were not going to be decided by facts and debating tactics but by images and impressions.

Toward the end of the campaign, Carter saw what was happening and began to complain. In an interview with ABC's
Barbara Walters, Carter said the press "sometimes has failed
to cover major issues" and appears more concerned with "how
the campaign was run, the so-called tone of the campaign, the
personal foibles or misstatements of the candidates."[2]

THE BOTTOM LINE

Most members of the news media had heard similar complaints in other campaigns and had made valiant efforts to improve coverage. But they were hampered by the accessibility
of candidates and the difficult logistics of a national campaign
as well as the media's own bottom line: the need to sell papers
and attract audiences with interesting fare.

That old bottom line kept popping up in the 1980 campaign,
and so did the usual criticism afterward. One of the more prominent dissenters was author David Halberstam. "In an important year," he wrote in *Parade* magazine, "when grave
questions confronted the nation on how it would retool itself to
face a changing world and deal with a changing economy, we
had a trivial process trivially covered, a shallow campaign
made even more shallow by the media's participation."[3]

The networks were particularly vulnerable to that charge
but blamed it largely on the lack of time given to news programs. For many years, Walter Cronkite deplored the inade-
quacy of 22 minutes for covering the day's news, yet he always
wound up each day's program with a claim that "that's the
way it is." Elmer Lower, former president of ABC News,
repeatedly called for one hour of network news each day. So
have many others. But even an hour's time for national news
would not remove the need for visual appeal and brevity. Because of the limitations of televised news, complex subjects are
difficult to cover. The emphasis on the visual especially
restricts treatment of the political process. In Halberstam's
words, the networks "do not in any real sense cover American

politics or, more important, the complicated on-going process of democratic society that takes place election year or not.[4]

To another observer, television coverage in 1980 was "a three-course menu for fluff." That is the way *Washington Post* reporter Robert Kaiser summed it up. He said the campaign on TV was not even good theater: "If this were a Broadway show, it would have closed unceremoniously in New Haven."[5] All TV news of the campaign, he added, could be lumped together into three formats: charge/counter-charge, a day in the life of the candidate and the handicapper's report on the horse race in some state.

FORMULA FOR FLUFF

None of these formats, as he pointed out, is designed to provide information to serious voters. They are designed primarily to fit the needs of television. The only format that comes close to serving a serious purpose is the charge/counter-charge, which at least gives the audience an opportunity to learn where a candidate stands on a fleeting point. But it is impossible to explain a serious controversy in a minute of time or less. Television producers know they give short shrift to serious matters, but they fear that to depart from the carefully designed format would risk losing viewers.

The 1980 horse race began well before the New Hampshire primary, with reporters and columnists assessing the chances of the various entries. The field of potential front runners was larger than usual, including Republican Bob Dole, Philip Crane, Howard Baker and John Anderson along with the heavy favorite, Ronald Reagan, on the Republican side, and with Teddy Kennedy threatening to give President Carter a real run for the Democratic nomination.

After it was over, *The Washington Journalism Review* asked the candidates and their aides for comments on news coverage. Everyone but John Anderson was critical, with losers implying that lack of media attention was the main factor in their defeat. As Anderson put it, "What is important is whatever was covered by ABC, NBC and CBS news last night. If the news media doesn't (sic) cover them, then the events never have any meaning."[6]

Those with the strongest complaints were Crane, Baker and Dole, each of whom said coverage was virtually non-existent.

Crane said that exposure on talk shows was the most important factor. Baker claimed that he never got on CBS News from Nov. 1 to March 8. Bush said the reason he was accused of not speaking on the issues was that "I was not perceptive enough to fail to answer all those questions about 'How well are you going to do next Tuesday?' " Dole complained that Reagan and Bush got the most coverage among Republicans. "It almost appeared that the media had decided Reagan should be opposed and the opponent should be Bush," he said.

It also looked as if the media had decided early that Barry Commoner was not a serious candidate as the nominee of the independent Citizens Party. After it was over, Commoner claimed that he, too, had been blacked out. As an example, he cited only one "substantive article" in *The Washington Post* during the last ten weeks of the campaign and virtually nothing on television.

KNOCKING OFF KENNEDY

On the Democratic side, the press also came close to running the whole show. Teddy Kennedy's decision to challenge President Carter followed many speculative stories that put pressure on him to rescue the Democrats from Carter's low rating in the polls. "We did it. The press drafted Kennedy," wrote columnist Richard Reeves in October, 1979, adding that "for better or worse, the press has more control than the politicians."[7]

The press also had a big hand in Kennedy's downfall, clearing the way for Carter, whom many considered the weaker candidate to oppose Reagan. The biggest blow to Kennedy was the TV interview with Roger Mudd, in which Kennedy had trouble answering such fundamental and predictable questions as why he wanted to be President and what role his estranged wife would play. Mudd seemed under orders to press especially hard on personal factors, including Chappaquiddick. The interview, taped on the day of the Iranian capture of the embassy, showed Kennedy to be surprisingly inarticulate without a prepared text, a weakness which had appeared before but not so dramatically.

Once that weakness became clear, he was through as a viable candidate. His image never came up to TV's expectations, therefore he was not Presidential material. Although Kennedy later tried to focus more on the issues, such as Carter's lack of leadership, the news media did not let him do so. One example occurred a month after the Mudd debacle. In an off-hand remark, Kennedy said that the Shah of Iran had run "one of the most violent regimes in the history of mankind" and had stolen "umpteen billions of dollars from his country." Although Kennedy was essentially correct, the first reaction of reporters and editors was that Kennedy had goofed. They, like many Americans, knew the Shah as a long-time friendly ally and were not aware of what he had done to Iran with U.S. help. Columnists and commentators clobbered him. News reports concentrated on Kennedy's lack of finesse, and treated his remarks as wild and insupportable without bothering to check them out.

POLITICAL ATTACKS

Then came a spate of "exposes" about Chappaquiddick, amounting to a massive political attack by *Reader's Digest*, Time Incorporated's *Washington Star*, and the *New York Times*. All long-time supporters of Republican politics, they apparently timed their attacks for maximum political effect, more than 10 years after the event. (The *Digest's* heavy promotion of its story led to a citizen complaint to the Federal Election Commission alleging that the magazine had effectively made an illegal campaign expenditure because of its unusually extensive distribution of the article, including videotapes re-enacting the 1969 tragedy for TV outlets.) None of the heavily played articles presented anything of significance that had not been reported earlier. But they were extremely damaging to Kennedy by calling attention again to unanswered questions about the affair.

When Kennedy later tried to talk about the economy and other major issues, news reports described it as a desperate strategem of a losing candidate. "Once the press had labeled Kennedy a loser," wrote Blair Clark, his manager for the primary campaigns, "as it began to do with increasing boldness after the Iowa caucuses, much of the reporting on him was slanted that way—the loser must win the next one, the loser won't quit. It was more the decline of the campaign than the campaign itself that got covered."

With Kennedy killed politically, with big assists from the

news media, Carter became a shoo-in for the nomination but under the worst possible circumstances for the Democrats. Almost every traditional Democrat was disappointed either in the loss of Kennedy or Carter's record. Thus, many Democratic votes were readily available for Reagan or the leading independent candidate, John Anderson, a career Republican who began to disavow his former conservative stands on many subjects in search of Democratic votes.

Polls indicated that Reagan was the main beneficiary of all these negative factors affecting his opponents.

Under the circumstance, personal factors had become more important than political views and experience. It was charisma alone that determined the victory of Ronald Reagan, according to media analyst Gerald Goldhaber, writing in the journal, *Campaigns & Elections*. "Issues have nothing to do with an election's outcome," he said. "What is important is the image projected when a candidate deals with an issue, but not the issue itself." With his charisma test, he predicted Reagan's victory in May of 1980.

But to say that the 1980 election was determined by this factor was inaccurate. Like previous elections, this one was decided by a shifting mixture of factors, some of which were unique to it. The two most powerful issues were inflation and the Iranian hostage situation. In the final analysis, they both worked against Carter. But the net effect was largely determined more by the media than the candidates.

ECONOMIC NEWS

It is not easy for any medium to report economic news in an interesting and understandable way. It is particularly difficult for television to translate statistics into sound and pictures. Newspapers and magazines thus had an inherent advantage in tackling inflation and other aspects of the economy in a serious and imaginative way. They also had reason to believe that the election itself might hinge on economic issues.

In the first place, Carter and Reagan viewed them from opposite perspectives. Carter had little interest in drawing attention to negative developments such as a rise in the Consumer Price Index or interest rates. Reagan, however, showed from the outset that he considered the nation's economic situation the main battle ground of the campaign. He tried to portray the situation as negatively as possible. At times, he spoke of the economic "crisis," even a "calamity." Surely, the double-digit inflation, the record high interest rates and the depressed auto and housing industries pointed to some difficult times. Whether they amounted to the worst crisis since the Depression, as Reagan claimed, was debatable. But the issues were important to almost everyone in a deeply personal way.

In spite of that, a study of media coverage by a team of American University students showed an extremely spotty performance. For two weeks before the New Hampshire primary, when increases in living costs were hovering around 18 per cent and interest rates were around 20 per cent, such economic news consumed only two of 24 campaign stories on NBC, three of 28 on ABC and three out of 27 on CBS, according to the students. Coverage was found to be equally spotty in *Time*, *Newsweek*, and five of the seven daily newspapers surveyed. A case in point, said the students, was the *Boston Globe*, which ran 217 stories during the height of the New England primaries, only 18 of which dealt primarily with economic issues.[9]

In interviews with 80 editors and reporters, the students found many who called economics either too dull to report, too difficult for the reader to understand or too remote from the political news to cover.

Asked why the candidates' economic views were not given more coverage, one reporter said: "People don't want to read that dull, serious stuff. They want a little tinsel town, the sports analogy . . . like a talk show. They don't want some bald chrome-dome with glasses talking about the supply side or the demand side or all that heavy stuff."

In reporting on their survey in *The Columbia Journalism Review*, the students questioned this prevailing attitude of the printed press, the one medium most capable of handling such a difficult subject in an understandable way. "Obviously," they said, "the press *can* make significant contributions to the economic debate — by compelling candidates to think through their positions, by checking up on their figures, by examining their records. An activist press could also inject new ideas into the flow of the campaign."[10]

Also obviously, newspapers and magazines chose not to provide such leadership or attempt innovative approaches. The only exception among general newspapers surveyed was *The Los Angeles Times*, whose occasional hard-hitting articles were picked up by other publications to fill the gaps. When economic reporters did seek outside opinions, said the students, they would "round up the usual suspects" whose opinions were well known and predictable.

ADVANTAGE REAGAN

Whatever deficiencies the media had on economic matters redounded to Reagan's advantage. He barely had to say anything as the news told of increased living costs and depressed industries. In the absence of any real discussion, every item of bad economic news was good news to Reagan. Adding to his advantage was the failure of reporters to question him more about how he would improve conditions. He thus was able to score points by saying he would cut government spending without having to say which programs he would cut. And he was able to say he would "turn the economy around" without explaining how he would do it.

Lost in the verbiage was the fact that Carter tried to reduce government spending, even reaching a balanced budget on paper for a brief period, and he tried hard to improve the economy but was thwarted by Republicans in Congress. Reagan also was able to claim ownership for the ideas of curbing regulations and increasing the military budget, both of which Carter had done. Reagan's reliance on the "supply side" or "trickle down" theory of economics was not reported fully until after the Inauguration despite plenty of evidence during the campaign. More incisive reporting on these matters could have changed the election results. Barring that, it could have prepared the nation better for Reagan's economic program. As it was, he had clear sailing on this, the biggest issue of the campaign.

The sameness of Carter and Reagan on many economic matters helped account for the lack of coverage and discussion. But a lively debate was available if coverage had extended to another candidate, Barry Commoner, nominee of the Citizens Party. Ironically, he was the only candidate to raise basic issues, just what the media claimed to want, yet he was virtually ignored by the news media. One of his main topics was the extent to which big business controlled society itself as well as the government. To him, the biggest cause of inflation was not government spending but manipulation of prices and supplies by monopolistic corporations. By bringing him into the discussion about the nation's economy, the media could have been assured of considerable newsworthy copy. By leaving him out, they showed more interest in picking winners than reporting the issues.

HOSTAGE HOOPLA

Another major issue of the campaign was the capture of American hostages in Iran. According to David Altheide, author of *Media Logic and Bureaucratic Propaganda*, more media attention was paid to the hostages than any single event in recent history, including Vietnam, civil rights, moon missions and the most comparable event, the capture of 82 crew members of the USS Pueblo in 1968. In a three-month survey of television coverage, Altheide found that each network presented at least one report on Iran almost every day, plus a large number of specials. ABC led in specials by a wide margin, transforming its half-hour *Nightline* program to *America Held Hostage* in March, 1980, and kept it up to the release of the hostages in January, 1981.

But quantity did not bring quality of coverage. According to Altheide, only seven of 368 reports on all three networks featured the Iranian revolution itself, which brought about the hostage situation. Not only were most reports superficial, but they tended to indicate that the only issue was the unwarranted taking of the American embassy. "The message repeated on all networks," said Altheide, "was that the Iranians were either confused, insane, or just plain stupid," an emphasis hardly conducive to public understanding of the historical and cultural background of U.S. involvement in Iran.[11]

Not mentioned by Altheide was another important factor in the election campaign: the counting of days — totalling 444 — the hostages were held at the end of each day's regular network evening news program, even when there was no news to report. These daily reminders, plus the daily half-hour specials by ABC, combined to put incalculable pressure on the Carter Administration to do something, anything, to get the hostages freed before November 4. The saturation coverage undoubted-

ly had a substantial effect on Carter's decision to send the ill-
fated rescue mission as well as his other actions and statements on the matter. That was the conclusion of Frederic B.
Hill, a correspondent on leave from *The Baltimore Sun*, reporting in *The Washington Journalism Review*[12] on a study of TV
news, public opinion polls, and other factors.

In fact, television's role went back much further. American
news media came in for considerable criticism for failure to
portray the whole revolution in Iran more clearly. Nearly a
year before the hostages were taken, Professors William A.
Dorman and the pseudonymous "Ehsan Omeed" complained
in *The Columbia Journalism Review* that American news
coverage of Iran was almost always from the Shah's perspective. The American press, they said, "by and large accepted
the Shah's implicit argument that the best his people can
muster in the way of ideological resources are religious
fanaticism and communism." The authors cautioned that
unless the false stereotypes of 26 years were corrected, the
United States might be led by the media into another
quagmire like Vietnam. Much of the impetus and acceptance in
Iran of the embassy takeover apparently came from a feeling
among Iranians that the United States had misunderstood
them and their country. The frequent use of American television cameras by the hostages' captors was largely an effort to
correct what they perceived to be incorrect images of
themselves in the United States.

Because of the inaccurate view of Iran presented by the
media, the American public was unprepared to understand the
Iranian revolution. By becoming participants as well as
reporters in the Iranian crisis, the news media helped put the
whole country into a no-win situation.

Hodding Carter, the chief spokesman for the State Department, was among the crtics of the press after the election. In
an article in *The Columbia Journalism Review*, he said, "Some-
day somebody's going to do a piece on how much of policy and
coverage was actually based on any kind of understanding of
the dynamics at play in Iran. I'm talking about the critics as
well as the policymakers and all forms of press. The basic
underlying realities of what was going on in Iran were ignored . . ."[13]

Ronald Reagan knew enough to stay in the background on

this matter, especially after it became apparent that Carter was clearly on the defensive. All Reagan had to do to score heavily with many voters was to allude, as he did repeatedly, to the need to stop being "pushed around" in world affairs. By referring frequently to a perceived American "weakness," Reagan was able to imply the need for shoring up the nation's international prestige without having to say specifically how it could be accomplished. Thus, there was no real debate over American policy in the Third World at a time when the fate of the world was increasingly dependent on it.

THE MILITARY MUDDLE

Another issue neither covered well nor discussed fully was military power. Candidate Reagan scored points by saying he would not allow the country to be "second best," implying that Russia could defeat the United States in a nuclear war. Since Carter did not want to appear opposed to a strong America, he did not argue that the nation already was more powerful than the Soviets. Reagan was thus able to preempt the whole issue of national strength without having to say how he would have done it differently.

He also benefited as right-wing propaganda outlets rushed in to fill the void in the discussion. Without bothering to check on the source of many studies and pronouncements, the media served the conservative cause by repeating many of them as legitimate news. An example was the *Newsweek* cover story, *"Is America Strong Enough?"* the week before the election. Citing a number of "defense experts," the article said Russian missile strength "threatens to subject the United States to nuclear blackmail, if not a Soviet first strike, as early as 1982."[14] Almost all sources for the article were from right-wing think tanks financed by ultra-conservative Richard Mellon Scaife, heir to the Mellon fortune.[15]

Failure of the media to cover these issues adequately, not to mention stimulate public debate, undoubtedly had a big influence on the election. As Commoner wrote afterwards, "Journalists had two options: they could have expanded the debate to other candidates or experts capable of addressing the issues fully and intelligently; or, at the least, they could have forced the major candidates to answer tough questions on the issues. They did neither. And so the media must take

some responsibility for a campaign which, in a year that certainly did not lack critical issues, once again became an
issueless popularity contest."[16]

What was probably more surprising was Commoner's
naivete about the press. He was surprised by its innate conservatism and control by business interests. He learned the hard
way that news is big business and, like other businesses, is run
primarily for profit, not public service. Few industries are as
concentrated in ownership. Less than two dozen cities now
have competing daily papers; chains have gobbled up more
than two-thirds of the rest. In the broadcast field, the three
commercial networks dominate what goes onto the television
screen. And news outlets depend on only two wire services for
non-local news.

At the same time, non-media businesses have been moving
increasingly into control of news organizations. And owners of
media companies, in turn, have been moving into directorships
of non-news businesses. The heavy business influence is felt
right down the ranks, from publisher to reporter, though few
along the line acknowledge the chain publicly.

Through the appointment process, owners can assure that
editorials and commentaries reflect pro-business, conservative
Republican views in many cases. During the 1980 campaign,
editorial endorsements of Ronald Reagan were printed in nearly twice as many newspapers as endorsements of Carter,
according to *Editor & Publisher*.[17]

ENTER MADISON AVENUE

An added benefit to Republican candidates in 1980 was a
whole new wave of advocacy advertising begun in the
mid-1970s by large corporations and business associations.
Largely in response to consumerism and adverse publicity
from disclosures about bribery in foreign business deals, many
firms began advertising and public relations programs to improve their public image. Disappointment with treatment in
the news media was also a factor. Network television was the
only place these ads did not appear, because of network
policies against accepting "controversial" advertising, but few
individual stations had such restrictions.

So pervasive had these advertised viewpoints become that
columnist Mark Shields, surveying the scene in April, 1980,

observed: "The fact is that the ideas of business are virtually the only ideas in circulation this election year." Noting that "whichever side in a campaign dominates the dialogue of the campaign almost invariably wins the election," Shields pointed out that "the issues these business ads are presenting so persuasively and attractively — the balanced budget, the need to cut the size, scope and spending of the federal government — are the very issues that Ronald Reagan has been championing for the past 16 years."[18]

Typical was an ad appearing the same month in numerous newspapers announcing "Growth Day 1980," an event designed to counteract the 10th anniversary of "Earth Day." Proclaiming that "we have something good to say about America," the long list of conservative and business leaders asserted that "We are Americans who believe the 'zero-growth' policies advocated by Ralph Nader, the radical environmentalists and other anti-business extremists would guarantee a bleak economic future for everyone . . ."[19] Another widely circulated ad in the same month was by Union Carbide, reporting a poll which allegedly showed that "Americans reject no-growth future, see technology and business as forces for growth." [20] The ad also claimed that "58 per cent of the public thinks that government is at least somewhat larger than it should be." The net effect of these ads, like the editorials and commentaries, was to help Reagan's chances for election.

THREE CHEERLEADERS

After the election, Reagan received unusually favorable treatment by nearly all facets of the news business. Many publications were so happy he was in office that they began cheerleading exercises. Leaders were Time Inc., *Reader's Digest* and *U.S. News & World Report*, which altogether cover most households in the country.

Time Inc. alone claimed an estimated readership, including pass-on copies, of 68 million for its seven magazines, with more revenue than any other publishing firm. It also set out to be the biggest cheerleader. It ordered 100 employees to produce 23 articles for publication the month after the Inauguration on the theme, "American Renewal," almost identical to President Reagan's Inaugural theme of "national renewal." "Our chief

purpose," wrote Editor-in-Chief Henry A. Grunwald, "is to
dispel the notion that nothing can be done" to correct national
problems. He did not explain why seven news magazines
devoted months of effort producing so much non-news fitting
so closely into the Republican themes for the campaign and
new Administration.[21]

Many journalists at *Time* magazine also wondered why, according to an article in *The Wall Street Journal*. It quoted Otto
Friedrich, a *Time* writer, as calling the project "more than
preaching." Later, Grunwald announced that the project had
had "enormous appeal," leading *Time* to produce a 160-page
compilation in book form at special discount prices for bulk
distribution. Whatever the real purpose, the effort served to
support the new Administration with a huge political boost in
literary form and helped to rally Americans behind the deep
budget cuts and other drastic changes with calls for vision and
sacrifice.

Similar biases filtered down through Time Inc. to its
magazines and now-defunct newspaper, *The Washington Star*,
which showered the Reagan crew with adoring headlines and
supportive stories. William Boot, a pseudonym for a former
employee of the *Star*, wrote in another publication: "In a
general sucking up to the Reagan Administration by the press,
the *Star*'s slurp was probably the loudest of all."[22] Across the
top of the front page the day after Reagan presented his
economic program, the *Star* ran an excerpt beside a waving
American flag: "The people ... don't demand miracles, but
they do expect us to act. Let us act together." The lead story
used Reagan's own words — bold, revolutionary, most ambitious program ever attempted — without any quotation marks
to describe the budget and tax proposals. The *Star* was not
alone with its biased treatment of the new Administration.
Many other papers let their editorial favoritism permeate their
news columns despite journalistic tenets to the contrary.

Reader's Digest, reportedly the President's favorite
magazine, was particularly supportive of Reagan. In addition
to running numerous articles during the campaign promoting
the views of conservative candidates, the magazine followed
the Inaugural with more pro-Reagan articles explaining
"supply-side economics," "the pitfalls of talking to the
Soviets" on arms control, and the series, "It's Your Money,"

backing up Reagan's attempts to cut funds from government programs. It bought the State Department's controversial "White Paper" on El Salvador hook, line and sinker.

U.S. News & World Report ran a steady stream of articles slanted in favor of the Republicans both before and after the election. One sample in the September 22, 1980, issue carried a large headline on the cover saying, "Rebuilding America: It Will Cost Billions." Inside were pieces on "Carter's Big Gamble" (in not debating with Reagan and Anderson), "Carter's Promises . . . and His Performance," "A Firsthand Look at What Ails the Navy" and "Reagan's New Plan for Taxes, Spending." Score: Four negatives for Carter, two pluses for Reagan.

After the election, the magazine presented a special section: "How to Get America Back on Track," taking a leaf from Reagan's campaign book with interviews with nine conservative Reagan advisers and none with contrary views.

By June, 1981, the editors of *U.S. News* detected "an upbeat mood across the land — a freshening of patriotic faith in America, a belief that the nation can rally from hard times." Their cover story, "We're Rallying: America's Springtime Mood," was based on interviews with mostly middle class members in seven cities. The effect was to help sell Reagan's drastic changes even though they may hurt many people, few of whom were represented in the interviews.[22] Next was an interview with Ben Wattenberg of the conservative American Enterprise Institute: "Reagan Can Exploit Public Mood to Political Advantage," followed by an article on the improved economy.

REAGAN 136, PRESS 0

Altogether, the new Administration led a charmed existence in the news media during its first five months in office. At the panel discussion for Associated Press radio editors and broadcasters mentioned earlier, panelists made two major points: (1) reporters were not doing a good job covering the White House, and (2) the White House was doing too good a job managing the news.

When asked by a member of the audience how well the press corps was covering the new Administration, AP's Walter Rodgers summed it up with a score: "Ronald Reagan, 136

[representing the number of days Reagan had been in office];
White House press corps, 0." He added: "We have failed, I
think, to convey accurately the vast gulf between Ronald
Reagan's ideas and Ronald Reagan's personality." To another
question, Rodgers said: "We fail to point out that Ronald
Reagan still has no foreign policy, that we are wallowing in the
vacuum of political leadership which has yet to produce an
American president who can effectively reduce the potential
for nuclear war."

When asked why these points did not get into his own daily
news reports, he said that, as a reporter, his job was merely to
present the facts. He added that the Administration was making it extremely difficult to obtain news: "There is a conscious
policy of this Administration to control our access to the news,
to limit our access to the President, who is our news. I think
they have a deliberate and very skillful and successful policy of
keeping us in the dark on as many issues as possible." He
quoted the poet Swinburne to sum up Administration policy
on the press: "One who is not we see, but one whom we see not
is; surely this is not that, but that is assuredly this." [23]

The Reagan Administration already has gone further than
previous ones in managing the news. It has stepped up the
policy of inviting groups of editors from other parts of the
country for periodic briefing and "photo opportunities" with
the President, all designed to develop closer ties with editors,
publishers and broadcasters. It also has emphasized the policy
of establishing comraderie with invitations for journalists to
White House social functions. A surprising number of on-the-
line journalists have had no problem in taking on these potential conflicts of interest. Columnists George Will and James J.
Kilpatrick even entertained the President and other top Administration officials in their homes without qualms and
without much criticism from colleagues or papers receiving
their columns. And the papers that print *London Sunday
Times* columnist Henry Brandon did not bat an eye when his
wife became Nancy Reagan's social secretary.

Through contacts with journalists and their ultimate bosses,
Administration officials dangled exclusive interviews with the
President as bait implicitly in return for favorable treatment.
Through these contacts, they also managed to "leak" tidbits
with which to influence Congress or "punish" those who got

out of line. Presidential political adviser Lyn Nofziger, a former Nixon campaigner, blended press and politics by planting negative stories about legislators who refused to go along with certain Reagan programs. He also helped plant hostile questioners in press conferences and meetings back home between legislators and their constituents, and arranged visits to Congressional districts by big-name Republicans, in an operation nicknamed the "Southern blitz," to get negative publicity in local news outlets.

INCREASING SECRECY

In their efforts to prevent unfavorable news, Administration officials reversed the openness of earlier Administrations. By June, there was a concerted campaign to impose more secrecy on national security matters. The former practice of having top-level officials of the National Security Council in the White House and the Central Intelligence Agency brief reporters on unclassified matters was quietly ended. At the same time, regular briefings of reporters at the Departments of State and Defense and the White House were rendered less informative because of a policy prohibiting publicists from discussing topics for which they had no official position paper. At the Pentagon, officials were warned ominously by Deputy Secretary Frank A. Carlucci against disclosing "even unclassified matters when they relate to sensitive internal deliberations." At the Pentagon's request, Rep. Sam Stratton introduced a bill in Congress proposing that "no declassification on the nation's most vital secrets can be made by any single official — even the Secretary of Defense." The bill would also "prevent, by the establishment of appropriate penalties, the publication of such secrets or . . . require that any publication of such information by the media be accompanied by the name of the source of such information."

"This pernicious proposal," said columnist Jack Anderson, "would instantly make every editor in the country eligible for a stretch in the slammer. Not only would editors be unable to expose military misspending unless the government itself chose to enlighten the populace, but they also could print no more than the government wished them to report about the military budget, which consumes so much of the taxpayers' money."

With these moves, the new Administration fell into an old trap, believing that it could control the news with punitive measures that never have worked except in war time. As Anderson explained: "When the government keeps a tight nozzle on the news, the official pipelines spring multiple leaks." And the leaks become all the more newsworthy because of the restrictions.

DISTORTING THE FACTS

El Salvador became a dramatic example of both poor media coverage and the adverse effects of government news management. The story began only three days after the Inauguration with a newspaper column by Cord Meyer, a former CIA official. He wrote that he had seen "damaging proof" that the Soviets were shipping arms to El Salvador rebels through Cuba and Nicaragua. The charges, which may have been leaked to Meyer, did not set a fire in the news corps, perhaps because such accusations were familiar in the world of Latin American politics. Virtually the same story was published two weeks later in *The New York Times*, which said it had "obtained" secret documents captured from the rebels proving the Communist connections. An avalanche of similar reports followed, with bits of information added by State Department officials ready to help.

With the stage thus set, the Department released an eight-page summary of the "secret" papers, which was gobbled up by a largely unquestioning press. While editorial writers and commentators were reacting with predictable horror at the "news," few reporters attempted to check the authenticity of the government documents. It was not until April that John Dinges of the Pacific News Service, a small independent organization, did so. He reported numerous errors in translation and other information refuting State Department statements. Similar revelations were reported by Christopher Wenner of *The Times* of London, who found that the alleged Communist weapons were barely enough to supply one brigade for a week and were largely home-made or relics of World War I. *The Los Angeles Times* picked up Dinges's story, but it did not get wide play.

It was not until June 8 that this side of the story finally received widespread attention. It came when *The Wall Street*

Journal quoted the State Department author of the original summary, Jon Glassman, as acknowledging numerous "mistakes" in translation and some "misleading" statements by American officials.

The State Department defended Glassman's summary but did not dispute the essential elements of the *Journal* story. Department officials became bitter at the press corps, accusing it of having overplayed the story which they themselves had sought to play up in the beginning for political purposes. The news media were also attacked by right-wing groups and individuals, who claimed that the *Journal* and others had been victimized by Soviet "disinformation" supplied by ex-CIA agent Philip Agee.

It had taken four and a half months for the news media to inform the public that there had been virtually nothing of substance to the original charges by the State Department. In the interim, Secretary of State Haig and Presidential aides Edwin Meese III had threatened to invade Cuba to stop the alleged flow of arms. They eventually backed off because of public fears of another Vietnam, not because of press diligence in checking the facts.

4

Putting the Foxes in Charge

Running the government is like running General Motors... And that's where our background comes in... We're going to sur- round Ronnie with people of experience, the very best people in America... the ones we'd hire for our own business.

Alfred S. Bloomingdale[1]

To understand what Ronald Reagan and his helpers are do- ing for — and to — the United States, it is necessary to look at the people closest to him. From his movie roles to his political career, he has been promoted and managed more by others than himself. He owes virtually everything in politics to the small group of self-made millionaires who propelled him into the governorship of California.

After the 1980 election, it was only natural for Reagan to turn once again to these trusted advisers and managers for help. And once again, they sprung into action, ready to help select those who would be running the federal government for the next four years.

From the 47th floor of the Arco Plaza Tower in Los Angeles, more than a dozen members of his "Kitchen Cabinet" volun- tarily pitched in to help pick a federal Cabinet and lesser government officials as well as offer advice to the President- elect. "Our biggest value," Alfred Bloomingdale told *Washington Post* reporter Martin Schram, "has been in get- ting names. I'm not talking about a few. I'm talking about thousands of names, from our business and social contacts throughout the United States. We each called our friends."[2]

These wealthy, gray-haired, conservative, Republican, white businessmen and lawyers thus set up and ran the principal screening process for the new Administration, and they did it by merely calling their business and social contacts.

They claimed they made an attempt to get minorities and women into key posts. According to Bloomingdale, "Ronnie asked us to consider minorities. Well, we got Hispanics. We got blacks. We got ladies. But if they're not right, we didn't take them. We are after quality first.

"Running the government," Bloomingdale told Schram, "is like running General Motors ... The Cabinet Secretaries will be like the presidents of Chevrolet and Pontiac. Competition is good. But their competition stops at what is good for General Motors. Because that is the greater good — just like what is good for the United States of America. That, too, will be the greater good."[3] Bloomingdale seemed unaware of how a similar attitude expressed by Defense Secretary Charles (Engine Charlie) Wilson made him the laughing stock of the Eisenhower years.

For these men, the search for quality and "the greater good" was taken seriously, within the confines of their own circles. But in practice, the final decision often came on another level: whether the prospective nominee for office worked for Ronald Reagan, contributed to his campaigns and shared the conservative mind-set. "Democrat" was such a dirty word that when one was proposed, according to Schram, crusty old Justin Dart interrupted: "The hell with the sonofabitch. He wasn't with us when we needed him."[4]

In general, the people named to Cabinet and other high posts reflected the conservative, corporate character of the Kitchen Cabinet and Reagan himself. In fact, the new Chief Executive reached into this group for several key appointments. They included Casper Weinberger as Defense Secretary, William French Smith as Attorney General, Charles Wick as director of the International Communication Agency and Theodore Cummings as Ambassador to Austria. The only Democrat to make it to Cabinet level was a woman, Jeane J. Kirkpatrick, who was named Ambassador to the United Nations. The only black, Samuel Pierce, was another millionaire Republican. He became Secretary of Housing and Urban Development.

Notable was the absence in the Cabinet of any representative of the far right wing and the burgeoning single-issue political groups which had worked hard for Reagan and were demanding something in return. Nor was the brash reactionary, William Simon, chosen for Treasury Secretary despite strong pressure from the Kitchen crew. The first selections surprised critics with the overall quality of experience and knowledge represented by most despite the narrow confines of their backgrounds and some large potential conflicts of interest. The absence of zealots, with the exception of Interior Secretary James Watt, reflected the hard-nosed business advisors who had no stomach for them. Watt was accepted because he was so business-minded.

POLITICAL LOYALTY UPPERMOST

But sub-Cabinet appointments fell even below these modest marks. Like the topmost group, those nominated and approved were also predominantly well-to-do businessmen with strong conservative views and a record of donating money or time to Reagan campaigns. Qualities like competence, independence, imagination, even expertise in the particular field involved, became so secondary to political factors that they often were not considered.

To help find sub-Cabinet officials and draw up policy guidelines for the various areas of government, there were a dozen transition teams under the direction of Edwin Meese. On numerous occasions, he made it clear that the first requirement in personnel selection was loyalty to Reagan and his political views. Members were from private business or academic circles indebted to corporate clients. Among them were advocates for far-right causes and single-minded individuals determined to wipe out government programs and regulations they disliked.

The most influential person in this process was Meese, a man who had worked so closely with Reagan in Sacramento that he had been dubbed "deputy governor." He not only approved key personnel for the teams themselves but laid down the ground rules that guided their activities. In this way, he was able to shape the new Administration precisely in his own image and that of the President-elect.

It was only natural for the 49-year old "deputy governor" to move into a similar job in the Reagan White House. From this pinnacle, the former prosecutor and retired Army officer came to supervise the President's Cabinet, the Domestic Council and National Security Council as well as coordinate Administration policy.

With Reagan's habit of working less than a full day and taking long vacations and weekends, Meese wound up as more of an acting President than assistant to the President. He soon became known as the "prime minister" among underlings. In most policy matters of Presidential importance, Meese called the shots, and Reagan simply went along, doing what Meese recommended and not bothering with matters not brought up by his chief aide.

The tough, hard-line Meese was a perfect gate-keeper for the easy-going Reagan. From his days in law school to the White House, Meese showed a love for administrative work and long hours. He was especially interested in law enforcement, having won Reagan's praise for his personal leadership in quelling student riots with mass arrests at the University of California campus at Berkeley in 1969.

For other top staff spots, Reagan chose two political veterans of the same stripe, James A. Baker III and Michael K. Deaver. Baker, a Houston lawyer, became chief of staff with responsiblity for Congressional and press relations, while Deaver, the former publicist, became deputy chief of staff and manager of Reagan's personal schedule. In many matters, however, the three worked as equals, sharing White House responsiblities.

THE SCREENING PROCESS

To direct the White House talent hunt for department and agency posts, they chose the deputy director of the controversial Nixon loyalty operation, E. Pendleton James, a professional "head hunter." His superior and mentor under Nixon was Frederick Malek, who had been accused of politicizing non-political jobs. With this key appointment, the Reagan Administration showed that it was not only insensitive to the meaning of Watergate but was determined to use the same type of loyalty tests pioneered with such fateful results at that time.

It was James' job before, during and after the transition period to round up names of possible nominees for high office, then submit them to the inner circle. After the Inauguration, he included key Congressional conservatives as reviewers.

About 20 arch conservative Republicans on Capitol Hill, led by Jesse Helms of North Carolina, also submitted their own names for high government posts. As a result, nominations came from many directions, and many were caught in a crossfire, leaving some vacancies unfilled for months. By mid-April, the Helms group even decided to hold up confirmations of several dozen State Department assistant secretaries and ambassadors in order to get their own ultra-conservative nominees approved. The mutiny began while the captain of the ship was in the hospital recovering from gunshot wounds.

To further complicate the screening process, part of the Kitchen Cabinet set up shop after the Inauguration for the same purpose but without portfolio in the Executive Office Building, just across an alley from the Oval Office. Their boldness and obvious influence with the boss soon caused tensions with the official staff at the White House. The final blow for the inner circle came when several corporation executives complained to the White House about being pressured to contribute large sums for an advertising campaign and regional forums to sell the Administration's program to Congress and the general public. The confidants had set up a "Coalition for a New Beginning" for this purpose, apparently in cooperation with Lyn Nofziger who had an adjoining office and who was a close adviser to the President. Top aides Baker and Meese finally told the powerful squatters that they would have to leave or comply with federal conflict-of-interest laws. They left in a huff.

CONFLICTS OF INTERESTS

Under the 1978 Ethics in Government Act, people appointed to government office are required to disclose their financial investments. If there are any potential conflicts of interest, they must dispose of their holdings or put them into a blind trust. The law also prohibits appointees from dealing with matters involving their previous employer for one year after taking office. However, the law does not apply to informal groups set up by a candidate or by a President-elect for guidance. Thus, the transition groups became filled with people with substantial conflicts.

For example, people chosen to guide the recruitment and policy planning for the Department of Agriculture included officials from food manufacturing organizations with strong interests in reversing labeling regulations requiring disclosure of key data to food buyers, and the people in charge of programming the Energy Department included representatives of energy companies determined to changes rules they did not like. The chief person in charge of reviewing the Consumer Product Safety Commission had led a "consumer" group secretly financed by business and had advocated the reversal of many key Commission actions. Even lawyers involved in pending cases accepted appointments to positions where they could alter the government's conduct of the cases. On almost every team were enemies of the government activity involved.

The ethics law was part of an effort to close the so-called "revolving door," which had allowed many people with built-in conflicts to move in and out of previous administrations with impunity. In most administrations, it was not unusual to see many appointees from regulated industries join the ranks of the regulators, then return to waiting jobs after government service. Likewise, many government employees seeking private jobs deliberately took actions favoring a prospective employer in hopes of gaining employment in the future.

The Carter Administration made a substantial effort to reverse these practices. For the most part, its appointments to regulatory bodies were from sources other than the regulated industries. But Reagan officials made no pretense at following the Carter example. In fact, they began reversing the pattern in a sweeping manner while complying technically with the law. They even sought to change the law to ease its requirements.

BUSINESS TAKES OVER

This brought strong criticism from David Cohen, president of Common Cause, a citizen lobby in Washington. "On a regulatory body," he told a reporter (for *The Wall Street Journal*) "you should have some sense of building in balanced outlooks and varied experiences, but (Reagan) isn't doing it. The appointment process is part of the missionary zealotry in the Reagan Administration." In effect, Reagan turned the chicken house over to the foxes. As a result, business and industry took over their own regulation in most offices.

The mere presence of a potential conflict of interest does not

62 One Sweet Guy

guarantee that a person given public responsibilty will not exercise it properly. Many representatives of regulated industries have proven to be competent, fair-minded public servants, often because of their special knowledge. But such appointments increase the risk of favoritism and scandal. And they give the appearance of conflicts even if none exists.

Among the more visible examples of potential conflicts in the new Administration was James G. Watt, the Secretary of the Interior, who had jurisdiction over most publicly owned land. President Reagan named him to the post even though Watt for three years had headed the Mountain States Legal Organization, a group funded largely by petroleum, lumber and mining firms. A leader of the so-called "Sagebrush Rebellion" in the West, Watt's group had filed numerous court challenges and petitions against federal rules restricting grazing on public lands and the use of motorized rafts on the Colorado River. It even opposed decreased electric rates for the poor and elderly and use of tax funds to assist school dropouts. Watt told one reporter that environmentalists were "the greatest threat to the ecology of the West." His elevation to the Cabinet post marked a complete reversal of previous government policy of protecting, rather than exploiting, publicly owned lands. It also reflected Reagan's own view that environmentalists were "extremists."

CONTROVERSIAL APPOINTMENTS

Other Cabinet members with potential conflicts included Treasury Secretary Donald T. Regan, whose Wall Street firm championed tax shelter programs considered illegal by the Internal Revenue Service, a subdivision of the Treasury. Another was William French Smith, the President's personal lawyer who became Attorney General. Smith assured Senators that he would be able to run the Justice Department without letting his personal dealings with the President interfere. A further problem for him was his prior legal work for subsidiaries of American Telephone and Telegraph Company, the target of an antitrust suit started by the Nixon Administration. He also served on the board of directors of numerous large corporations with potential legal problems with the federal government.

Among the more controversial appointments was that of

Energy Secretary James B. Edwards, an oral surgeon and former governor of South Carolina, whose only visible qualification was as a nuclear proponent. While governor, he promoted nuclear energy as "the only answer" to the country's energy shortage. He said he did not even mind storing the nation's nuclear wastes in his state because the alternative would be slavery in Siberian salt mines. Edwards freely acknowledged having difficulty managing the $10 billion Department of Energy. "You know," he told a reporter for *The New York Times,* "when you run for an office and you get elected, all during the campaign you're planning what you're going to do when you get there. But a Cabinet post like this sort of falls on your head unexpectedly, and it all comes at once ... It's a little bigger challenge than I thought."[5]

As Secretary of Agriculture, hog farmer John R. Block also ran into potential conflicts because of his prior opposition to government efforts to restrict sodium nitrite in processed meat and government dietary guidelines urging people to cut down on fat and cholesterol. He aroused a storm of protest when he said in confirmation hearings that he thought food exports ought to be used as a "weapon" to get other nations to do what the U.S. wants them to do. As a wealthy farmer, Block had a further potential problem in balancing his own interests in agribusiness and his responsiblities to administer food policies for the benefit of all members of the public.

FOREIGN AFFAIRS APPOINTMENTS

Among the earliest appointments was that of Richard Allen, Reagan's National Security Adviser, the same post he held during the campaign. Allen served in the Nixon Administration as a member of the National Security Council, a post he later lost reportedly because Kissinger considered him too far to the right and too friendly to South Africa. In those days, Allen had urged the State Department to lift sanctions against the white-controlled African nation. He also had had mysterious dealings with Robert Vesco, Lockheed and the CIA while shuttling between White House jobs and private consultanies.

One of Allen's contributions to the Republican campaign in 1980 was a position paper advocating further curbs on Congressional overview of, and press access to, intelligence agencies. He favored further recruitment of reporters, ministers and business people as spies with immunity from lawsuits that might develop. In a long review of his record, *Mother Jones* magazine called him "the most dangerous, deceptive man in the Reagan camp . . . Reagan's all-in-one Ehrlichman, Mitchell and Kissinger."[6] In his high post with the campaign and Administration, he had an opportunity to make sure that other officials in the foreign policy area were as far right as he was, from the Secretary of State on down the line.

One of his first recommendations was to hire Jeane Kirkpatrick, a Georgetown University professor, after she wrote to Reagan during the campaign. Describing herself as a Democrat, she said she subscribed to the Reagan-Allen view of the world. Despite her lack of experience, she was named Ambassador to the United Nations. She quickly showed her inexperience when she met secretly with some South African generals, including the head of intelligence, in violation of U.S. policy. She explained that she had not known who they were. When that explanation failed to silence criticism, she said it was her personal policy of "being open to people and being willing to listen to almost any point of view." On the other hand, said columnist Mary McGrory, she had refused to meet with relatives of several American nuns who had been murdered in El Salvador by unknown assailants. She contended that "the nuns were not just nuns (but) political activists" aligned with revolutionaries in that strife-torn country. Neither she nor anyone else offered evidence to prove the point.

William Clark brought even less experience in world affairs to the State Department as the No. 2 official there. At confirmation hearings, the California Supreme Court Justice failed to answer correctly numerous elementary questions about geography and foreign affairs. At one point, Senator Charles Percy, Republican chairman of the Foreign Relations Committee, said that he would vote against confirmation of the close Reagan friend. But Percy later changed his mind, adding that "the President has told me how much he wants Bill Clark for this job."

An even more controversial appointment in the foreign relations field was that of Ernest Lefever. He was named Assistant Secretary of State for Human Rights even though, as a consultant, he had opposed elevating human rights in foreign policy. In his writings, he had dismissed evidence of widespread torture by right-wing governments in Latin America as "a residual practice of the Iberian tradition." The Ethics and Public Policy Center, which he headed before his appointment, had received $25,000 from the Nestle Company and coincidentally published several attacks on critics of the sale of baby formula by Nestle and other companies in the Third World where the lack of pure water caused widespread infections in infants who would otherwise have been breastfed. Lefever later withdrew his name after being rejected overwhelmingly by the Senate Foreign Relations Committee, only to be hired later as an aide to Haig without portfolio.

To head the Arms Control and Disarmament Agency, Reagan chose Eugene V. Rostow, a former Kennedy Administration official. Although he was a staunch advocate of greater American military power and strong critic of reducing arms, he did not win the approval of Jesse Helms, who thought him too soft on communism. To appease Helms, Reagan agreed to name Lt. Gen. Edward L. Rowny, a strong critic of the 1979 SALT (Strategic Arms Limitation Talks) treaty as chief negotiator of the agency. Rowny had been one of the SALT II negotiators until he resigned to campaign against the treaty because he felt it gave the Russians an unfair advantage in heavy missiles and bombers. Reagan, who also had spoken out strongly against the treaty on numerous occasions, thus filled the top positions in the arms control agency with two of its most ardent critics.

One of Reagan's first acts was to fire Robert E. White, Carter's ambassador to El Salvador and a career foreign service officer, after White publicly disputed the new team's analysis of that country's situation. Even though White was not alone in his criticism, he was summarily dismissed without even a normal debriefing to find out what he knew. To replace White, Reagan named Deane Hinton, who had served in the U.S. embassy in Chile during the overthrow of Allende, a bloody affair that the CIA was accused of engineering. As Assistant Secretary of State for Inter-American Affairs, Reagan chose Thomas O. Enders, a career foreign service officer with no Latin American experience.

No appointment was more controversial than that of Alexander Haig as Secretary of State. Reagan appeared to ignore or not know of Haig's questionable role with Nixon during the Watergate period. Nor was Reagan aware of how ambitious and impetuous the general was. What apparently impressed Reagan officials the most was Haig's performance as commander of the North Atlantic Treaty Organization (NATO) where he generally had gotten good marks for his dealings with European member nations. (For more on Haig, see Chapter 10.)

A strong record of denouncing communism and Soviet Russia was a decided advantage for anyone wishing to serve in the new Administration, even in positions apart from foreign affairs. Also a help was to be a strong advocate of big business and conservative politics. Almost every person named to a sensitive post dealing with public issues fitted that mold. That was largely because the screening process itself was corporate-oriented, all the way from Reagan's close friends through the transition teams and final checkpoints in Congress and the White House.

SUB-CABINET OFFICIALS

Among key appointments fitting the pattern were:

● Anne M. Gorsuch, an attorney for Mountain Bell Telephone Company, named to head the Environmental Protection Agency despite a record of opposing controls over hazardous waste and auto pollution control devices. She was recommended by millionaire brewer Joseph Coors and James Watt, fellow campaign workers in Colorado.

● James R. Harris, an Indiana State senator appointed to direct the Interior Department's Office of Surface Mining, who had bought land worth millions of dollars from two mining companies at bargain prices, according to *The Wall Street Journal*.

● Richard E. Lyng, former president of the American Meat Institute, who was appointed Under Secretary of Agriculture for Marketing and Consumer Affairs.

● Mark S. Fowler, a lawyer for broadcasting companies, named to head the Federal Communications Commission.

● John S.R. Shad, vice-chairman of E.F. Hutton and Company, one of the country's largest brokerage firms, named to head the Securities and Exchange Commission.

● Richard T. Pratt, a finance professor, formerly an

economist with the U.S. League of Savings Associations, appointed to head the Federal Home Loan Bank Board, which regulates savings and loan associations.

● J. Lynn Helms, former chairman of the General Aviation Manufacturers Association and former president of the Piper Aircraft Corporation, named to head the Federal Aviation Administration, which regulates air safety.

● James L. Malone, an attorney who represented Taiwan Power Company and two Japanese power companies that operate nuclear generators, named Assistant Secretary of State for Oceans and International Environmental and Scientific Affairs, which deals with nuclear nonproliferation policies. Senator John Glenn (Ohio Democrat) temporarily held up Malone's confirmation because of alleged discrepancies between his testimony before the Foreign Relations Committee and his registration statements to the Justice Department as a foreign agent. Malone was also questioned about a transition team report he co-authored which said that there should be "no concern" about proliferation to "industrialized nations with substantial and expanding commitments to nuclear electric power." The report cited West Germany and Taiwan, where Malone's clients were located. He was confirmed.

● James Hendrie, named acting head of the Nuclear Regulatory Commission even though his performance as chairman during the TMI crisis was so severely criticized that Carter had removed his as chairman.

● Thorne Auchter, named to head the Occupational Safety and Health Administration though as a Florida contractor he had said the agency's rules and enforcement should be cut back.

● Robert Burford, a Colorado legislator who favored further commercial land development, to direct the Bureau of Land Management.

● C.W. McMillan, former lobbyist for the National Cattlemen's Association, as Assistant Secretary of Agriculture for Marketing and Transportation in charge of meat labeling and other regulations.

● Raymond Peck, a coal industry lobbyist, to head the National Highway Traffic Safety Administration.

● Philip F. Johnson, a lawyer for the Chicago Board of Trade and director of the Futures Industry Association, named to chair the Commodity Futures Trading Commission.

• Reese H. Taylor, Jr., a lawyer for various trucking interests whose appointment was reportedly in return for the Teamsters Union's campaign support, named to head the Interstate Commerce Commission with jurisdiction over rail, bus and trucking transportation.

• Robert N. Broadbent, a pharmacist from Nevada, named to head the Water and Power Resources Service, formerly known as the Department of Interior's Bureau of Reclamation.

• James A. McAvoy, named to the Council on Environmental Quality although roundly criticized by environmental groups for the job he did as head of the Ohio Environmental Protection Agency.

• James C. Miller III, who led the Administration's efforts to weaken the Federal Trade Commission, picked to head the Commission, the government's main consumer protection agency.

• Nunzio Palladino, a strong supporter of the nuclear power industry, named chairman of the Nuclear Regulatory Commission.

At the Pentagon, Reagan officials followed tradition by filling many posts with executives of defense contracting firms. An example was Thomas K. Jones, who left the Boeing Company to become Deputy Undersecretary of Defense for Research and Engineering for Strategic and Theater Nuclear Forces, where he had jurisdiction over deciding whether to purchase Boeing military equipment.

FORMER NIXON AIDES

Reagan officials seemed to show no qualms about appointing controversial figures from the discredited Nixon Administration to sensitive positions, even in the White House. In addition to Haig, Allen and James was Fred Fielding, who served as an assistant to John Dean. Fielding was appointed as White House counsel where one of his duties was to administer the Ethics in Government Act. At the State Department, Secretary Haig named as a traveling emissary General Vernon Walters, former CIA deputy director who had acceded to a Nixon request to warn acting FBI Director Patrick Gray not to pursue the Watergate case because it might expose CIA operations in Mexico which Walters knew did not exist.

Other former Nixon aides in the Reagan Administration in-

cluded Robert C. Odle, Jr., a former supervisor of James Mc-
Cord at the Committee to Re-elect the President, named
Assistant Secretary of Energy for Congressional, Intergovern-
mental and Public Affairs, and Constance Stuart, a former
press secretary to Patricia Nixon, named Assistant to the
Secretary of Energy for Public Affairs.

MASS DISMISSALS

To make room for all the apostles of business and the right,
the new Administration resorted to wholesale firings in some
areas of government. Political appointees from previous administrations are naturally expected to leave when a new administration takes over, since they have no tenure. But the
Reaganites went far beyond the norm by firing clerks as well
as professional staffers in numerous offices. Reasons were
rarely given, leading to the feeling that they were entirely
political.

Among the first to receive dismissal notices were some 51
lawyers and clerks in the Interior Department's solicitor's office, which handles violations of federal regulations regarding
public lands. Secretary Watt claimed that the previous administration had hired more than the authorized number for
the office.

But one lawyer, who vowed to fight the actions, called it a
"budget smokescreen for a political purge." A House civil service subcommittee immediately announced that it would investigate whether a law was violated requiring budget cut approval before staff cuts were made.

Another target of mass firings was the relatively small
White House Council on Environmental Quality. All members
of its professional staff, which administers environmental impact statements so roundly disliked by polluters, were given
dismissal notices to make way for new people, who would
presumably be less conscientious about environmental regulations.

Still another mass firing was conducted in the Department
of Education. Nearly three-fourths of the 955 student loan col-
lectors were dismissed despite an "impressive record," said
Secretary Terrel H. Bell, who turned the task over to private
firms.

JOB FREEZE

In order to dramatize his determination to sweep out the "deadwood" in Washington, President Reagan announced a job freeze on the day of his Inauguration, retroactive to Election Day. The sudden move caught approximately 20,000 people in a bind. All had received notices saying they were hired during that time, but few had actually gone to work. Some had even moved and purchased homes or leased apartments. Many of the "deadwood" filed suit, charging Reagan had acted illegally.

The following August, an appeals court agreed but sent the matter back to the district court for final determination of each case. In a unanimous decision, the higher court ruled that the government had "played hide-and-seek with job seekers" by rescinding hiring commitments with "apparent... indifference to the consequences of its actions..." The court also ordered the lower court to decide whether the freeze had violated a 1974 Watergate-reform law prohibiting a President from refusing to spend funds appropriated for a specific purpose.

The Administration also showed its willingness to knock off individual officials. One was Anthony Robbins, who had built a distinguished record as head of the National Institute of Occupational Safety and Health, an agency thoroughly disliked by many businesses. He was fired by Richard S. Schweiker, Secretary of Health and Human Services, in "the public interest" after Schweiker received an article from a Chamber of Commerce periodical attacking Robbins as a "social activist" with a "radical, antibusiness posture." His commission in the Public Health Service also was revoked, an action almost never taken except in cases of gross misconduct.

Even the selection of federal judges was targeted for change. A program created by Carter to reduce political considerations was replaced by one featuring "the traditional procedures" which allowed Senators to veto or name candidates. A memo released in March by Attorney General Smith said the Administration was "firmly committed to the principle that federal judges should be chosen on the basis of merit and quality," but it left open to Senators how those values would be determined for any candidate. The change ordered by Carter had been designed partly to make it easier for minorities and women to win appointments in states where Senators had exercised their "blue slip" veto powers in the past to block certain appointments. Smith said the new prodecures would also apply to the selection of U.S. attorneys around the country.

CONSERVATIVE ALLIES IN CONGRESS

Republican Senators helped convince the Administration to take this action, another example of the muscle-flexing enjoyed by the new powers in Congress. The election left the conservative combination of Republicans and Southern Democrats more firmly in control than before. In the Senate, Republicans took over chairmanship of all committees, with ultra-conservatives taking charge of some key panels. They included Jesse Helms, who headed the Agriculture Committee; John Tower, Armed Services; Jake Garn, Banking; Pete Domenici, Budget; James A. McClure, Energy and Natural Resources; Strom Thurmond, Judiciary; and Orrin Hatch, Labor.

As a result of this wholesale shift, some issues and causes that rarely had obtained more than a few lines in the Congressional Record suddenly were propelled into headline status. While the White House was trying to get Congress to give the economic program first priority, ultra-conservatives in the Senate were introducing bills and planning hearings designed to protect Americans from abortions, sex education, family planning and other matters deemed by them to be "anti-family."

Most of the more conservative Senators had their own pet projects. Thurmond began a new push for restoring the death penalty in criminal cases. Laxalt and Helms jointly led the fight against abortions. Tower continued to advocate a higher military budget. A newly arrived Republican conservative, Jeremiah Denton, prepared to bring back teenage chastity. Others in the forefront of efforts to raise the moral level of the nation through legislation included Senators Gordon Humphrey and Rudy Boschwitz.

The informal leader of the ultra-conservatives was Helms. Once known as "the voice of free enterprise" on the radio in Raleigh, N.C., he stood well to the right of the traditional conservatives such as Barry Goldwater and Ronald Reagan. The

1980 election transformed Helms from a somewhat isolated spoiler in the Senate to what *The Los Angeles Times* called "the godfather of New Right politics across the country."[7] With a larger campaign kitty than any other legislator in the nation, he developed a network of campaign groups and tax-exempt foundations that helped elect a number of similarly minded legislators and defeated a flock of liberal Senators. What made Helms and his followers differ from the traditional conservatives, in the words of former Senator George McGovern, one of the victims, was "their zealotry, self-righteousness and vindictiveness."[8] As head of the New Right and chairman of the Agriculture Committee, Helms was able to control approximately 15 Senate votes on many issues, making him a power to reckon with in national politics.

Although he and his fellow crusaders were in the Senate and not officially a part of the new Administration, they became an integral part of the Reagan revolution. Most of their causes were Reagan's causes. More important, these legislators were in a position to implement passage of Reagan measures and approve key appointments. Although there were some differences in views between the White House and its friends in Congress, they were less important than the fact that conservatives controlled both ends of Pennsylvania Avenue.

5

Unleashing Big Business

*I would ask a task force made up of members of
the industry and of clients of the industry to sit
down with the regulations and work out between what they thought was a fair elimination of some and keeping of others.*

Ronald Reagan[1]

For most business executives and owners, Ronald Reagan
was a dream come true. From his first utterances on the campaign trail, the former General Electric publicist made it
crystal clear that he was on the side of corporations on every
point of difference with the public and the government. He
bought all the slogans of the Chamber of Commerce and helped
make them appear to be those of all the people rather than a
small, powerful segment. With such phrases as "get the
government off our backs," Reagan hit some extremely responsive chords in the voting populace.

In trying to turn the public against its own government, he
had considerable help from over-zealous bureaucrats and
misguided regulators through the years. The unpopular auto
ignition interlock, the standards for toilet seats and reams of
trivial paperwork provided plenty of ammunition for politicians taking pot shots at Washington. The fact that previous
administrations had begun to deregulate the government in
earnest and reduce the inevitable excesses of big government
was lost in the political rhetoric.

Also lost in the campaign talk were the main reasons for
government regulations: to protect everyone, including business executives and stockholders, from economic abuses and
health hazards of industrial society. It was no liberal plot that
built up the panoply of laws to curb business excesses. They

were created with bipartisan support and signed by presidents of both parties over a century of time after much negotiation and compromise.

NATION BESET WITH PROBLEMS

While business interests generally feel that the rules are too restrictive, others feel that many of the laws and regulations are too weak to be effective in protecting the public. Many also came long after much damage was done. It was not until the late 1960s and early 1970s that the nation discovered what the influx of toxic substances was doing to people and the environment. It was not until automobiles had killed more people than had been killed in World War II that Ralph Nader pointed out that thousands of lives could have been saved and many disabling injuries prevented with simple design changes in vehicle and highways. It was not until pesticide residues and other chemicals had begun killing whole species of birds and small animals that Rachael Carson reported that the basis of all life was being destroyed. And it was not until cancer had moved up the ladder of leading killers to the Number Two spot below heart disease that scientists began to realize that most carcinogens were man-made and that millions of slow, painful deaths could have been avoided. During this same period, a national study commission determined that accidents related to consumer products other than motor vehicles were injuring an estimated 20 million Americans a year, and that many injuries could have been avoided with simple design changes or more information for users.

At the same time, changes in the marketplace were upsetting the ability of consumers to compare values and hazards of competing goods and services. The task was made especially difficult by the growing technical sophistication of products and the tendency to hide essential information about quality and quantity inside deceptive packages. Adding to the problems was the finely tuned skill of Madison Avenue to create demands for products that never existed before and persuade people to buy new models before old ones were used up. Little attention was paid to the effects of a "throw-away" society until supplies of some natural resources began to be depleted. Even water and farmland began to disappear at alarming rates in the intense drive to build new housing and commercial development without concern for the limits of growth.

Suddenly, it seemed, the country was beset by problems that had not seemed apparent only a few years before. As new laws were passed, members of the establishment found themselves threatened by forces they did not understand and had never encountered before. At first, they tried to dismiss the complaints and paint the leaders of these movements as misfits, malcontents or worse.

But the hazards only got worse, posing an increasing threat to all life on earth. Numerous polls showed that most Americans came to agree with the demand for controls. The big question was how to correct the problems. They far transcended the ability of private organizations or state and local governments to handle, with their limited powers and finances. It became increasingly clear that only national and international bodies had sufficient clout to do the job. Yet all efforts so far have failed to make much progress. Much more remains to be done, particularly at the federal level.

UNDOING PUBLIC PROTECTIONS

But that is not what the Reagan Administration had in mind when it took office. The President himself acted as though such problems did not exist. For him, the only problem was what his business friends told him: that virtually all regulations were useless and cost too much. Ignoring opinion polls showing that the public backed health and safety regulations, he established a process of reviewing nearly every regulation on the books, with a view to eliminating as many as possible. He appointed officials who felt the same way he did, that the marketplace itself can correct the problems eventually if freed from government restrictions. He felt that whatever hazards existed were a small price to pay for the benefits of the "free enterprise" system.

Deregulation never was pushed harder. But instead of applying it with selectivity, Reagan applied it across the board, except where rules boosted business profits. Examples were rules of the Interstate Commerce Commission allowing trucking firms to fix rates with immunity from antitrust laws. Similarly, marketing orders of the Agriculture Department allowed growers of many fruits and vegetables to restrict supplies and thus fix prices rather than allowing competitive forces to set the rates.

Despite its advocacy of more business competition, the Reagan Administration wanted to keep such regulations. In response to demand from the Teamsters Union, which is made up largely of owner/drivers who strongly supported the Reagan campaign, the ICC was told to slow down the deregulation process begun under President Carter. As a result, prices for food and other products shipped by truck may go higher than they otherwise might. Reagan officials also prepared to relax ICC rules governing household moving firms, which were considered too onerous by the industry.

In other words, the new Administration was more concerned about getting government "off the backs" of business than "off the backs" of average people.

THE MAIN CRITERION: COST

The guiding principle was merely cost, the alleged cost to business of complying. The value of benefits was not considered except in relation to costs. Whether regulations were to be kept, dropped or revised was determined by a cost-benefit analysis, which compares the estimated costs to society against the value of benefits, or avoidance of costs.

The theory had been used to some degree in previous administrations, mostly for economic regulations, where costs and benefits are relatively easily calculated. But matters of health and safety do not lend themselves well to such simple answers. For example, in estimating the cost of an air pollution limit, it is not difficult to determine the cost of scrubbers and emission controls. But is is not possible to determine the hidden benefits, such as the long-range costs of medical care avoided.

The biggest problem is measuring the cost of human life. The most common method is to estimate the average amount of lifetime earnings remaining at each particular age, then adjust for other factors such as sex and race. The Labor Department developed such a table in 1976. It showed, for instance, a value of $328,475 for a 30-year-old white man compared to a value of $131,076 for a non-white woman of the same age. But putting a dollar value on human life is offensive to many people because it does not measure more important factors.

Calculating the cost of injuries is also difficult. A study done for the Senate Committee on Government Affairs reported: "There is no appropriate way to put a dollar value on the cost of pain and suffering endured throughout a lifetime by a child who is the victim of a sleepwear fire." In such a case, said the study, medical expenses would tell only part of the story. The study, done by the Center for Policy Alternatives at the Massachusetts Institute of Technology, reviewed 350 documents and reports pertaining to health and safety regulations. It found that the net effect was a saving of thousands of lives. Worker safety regulations alone, said the report, prevented 40,000 to 60,000 accidents and 350 deaths in 1974 and 1975. It concluded that "to adapt a strict cost-benefit approach to federal regulation . . . would not be advisable."[2]

But Reagan officials were unmoved. They set out to eliminate regulations without any apparent qualms about the lives and injuries that might occur as a result. The process started even before the Inauguration. Incoming officials pressured outgoing officials to hold back on numerous rules disliked by business. In response, the Environmental Protection Agency decided to cut back proposed limits on truck emissions for 1985 and reconsider proposed water pollution standards from industrial sources. The Consumer Product Safety Commission decided to consult with formaldehyde manufacturers before calling a public hearing on alleged safety problems. And the Federal Trade Commission, already hampered by reduced authority imposed by Congress in 1980, withdrew some of its proposed rules and requests for industry data in major antitrust cases.

PENDING RULES FROZEN

Once in office, the Administration's first act was to make good on a campaign pledge and decontrol fuel oil and gasoline prices, a move not scheduled to occur until the following September. The announced purpose was to stimulate more exploration, but the net effect was to raise prices and create a glut of supplies because of consumer resistance to the higher prices.

Next came a 60-day freeze on several hundred pending regulations. The action was taken so hastily that it caught up some rules favorable to business, including one by the Food and Drug Administration extending industry exemptions from a ban on the use of 23 food colors and rules already approved by courts after legal challenges.

The main thrust came from a Task Force on Regulatory Relief set up by President Reagan with Vice President Bush as chairman to screen out any "unnecessary rules." It succeeded the Regulatory Council set up by Carter for the same purpose. Claiming to have a "mandate to achieve the regulatory relief our economy desperately needs," Bush listed more than a hundred regulations for review, revision, or further freeze beyond the original 60 days. He said the Administration was determined to eliminate all that were not "cost effective."

However, he did not explain how the rules in question got onto his list. He did not really need to, for it became obvious that nearly all changes would financially benefit a business or professional group. In fact, many such groups had already made their demands privately. Some of the rules had been going through the regulatory mill for years, complete with comment periods, public hearings and court challenges.

In addition to ordering reviews, Vice President Bush issued an appeal for help in finding other rules to change or kill. He disclosed copies of form letters to business firms and other organizations asking for suggestions. The Administration, he said, wanted to strike a "balance between safety in the work place and environmental protection and at the same time eliminate from our economy unneeded regulations so that we can grow and increase our nation's productive capacity."

But his appeal was not heard by the general public, except via some news items, most of which did not mention his request. In effect, his appeal was negative in notifying only special interests with their own reasons for opposing regulations affecting them. Groups that had failed to get exactly what they wanted during formal rule-making proceedings were thus given another opportunity to derail rules they did not like for any reason. The public interest was hardly considered.

WHOLE PROCESS IN LIMBO

The net effect was to put the whole regulatory process into political limbo. Like ducks in a shooting gallery, regulations were lined up to be shot down regardless of their relative merit. Reverberations were heard down the line of government authority. And the message was loud and clear: Don't push any regulations that might be disliked by commercial interests under pain of displeasing the White House. In the business world, it was open season on rules protecting the public.

In many cases, deregulation became delegislation — avoiding the painful, public process of getting approval from Congress. An example was the detouring of auto safety rules. The effect was to negate the basic auto safety law by ending its implementation.

The closest thing to a master plan for deregulation was an outline of action from the right-wing Heritage Foundation. At another time in history, this fount of anti-government researchers might have been passed off as a harmless fringe element. But the Reagan Administration, lacking any detailed plan of its own, followed the Foundation's recommendations almost to the letter.

Paperwork was reduced dramatically. In announcing the first round of changes, Vice President Bush already claimed results. He said the number of pages in the *Federal Register*, the official chronicle of rule changes, had been sliced in half.

NEW LAYER OF BUREAUCRACY

But a funny thing happened along the way. By setting up a system of regulatory review in the White House Office of Management and Budget, the Administration wound up with a whole new layer of bureaucracy and red tape, just what it had campaigned against. It even ran into charges that the new system was illegal. (See Chapter 6 for more.) These problems, however, did not slow down the bandwagon. In August, the Vice President announced another bundle of rules for possible change or elimination.

In addition to its wholesale review and revision of regulations, the Administration had other devices with which to reduce the regulatory burden on business:

● Appointing regulatory officials who essentially disagreed with the laws they were supposed to enforce. As discussed in Chapter 4, nearly every regulatory agency was put in charge of such people.

● Shifting the burden to the states. The often repeated theory was that the best government was close to the people. Reagan aides chose to ignore the history that showed few states with the interest or capability to handle additional duties and the fact that many problems were national in scope, needing national solutions.

• Switching to voluntary compliance. Some of the new agency heads came into office advocating more emphasis on voluntary compliance without realizing that such a goal can be achieved only if a threat of enforcement is continued. In the Nixon Administration, the Food and Drug Administration tried for years to get cosmetic manufacturers to voluntarily register their products and label the major ingredients. The effort eventually failed because companies knew they were not required to comply.

• Cutting the budget so much that an agency could not carry on its regular functions.

Some of the major areas of regulations affected by cutbacks were:

WORKER SAFETY

Government efforts to protect American workers from serious hazards to health and safety were particularly disliked by business firms. The Occupational Health and Safety Administration (OSHA) became a symbol of alleged over-regulation and was Number One on business hit lists. So it was natural that the Reagan Administration took early action to strip it of much of its power and effectiveness. First, the White House appointed Thomas G. Auchter, a Florida contractor who had been critical of the agency, to direct its operations. He was immediately ordered to put all regulations and proposed regulations to the cost/benefit test.

Then the Administration took an unusual step. It asked the Supreme Court to stop considering a legal challenge to an OSHA limit on cotton dust in textile mills. The rule was designed to reduce the incidence of byssinosis, known as brown lung disease, which the AFL-CIO said affected 150,000 of the 800,000 workers exposed to cotton dust. The Supreme Court case had arisen when textile manufacturers brought suit to oppose the rule, which required vacuum equipment rather than less expensive individual respirators. The case, which had already been argued before the Court, involved the question of whether costs must be weighed against benefits in government safety regulations. In opposing the Reagan move, textile unions said: "The tremendous burden that illness and disability imposes on our society far outweighs the relatively minor costs of cleanup of the industry."[3]

In a surprising decision, the high court ruled against the manufacturers and the Reagan Administration, saying safety, not cost, must be the determining factor in setting standards for cotton dust. The ruling was seen as a major defeat for the Administration's insistence on cost/benefit analysis as the basis of safety regulations. OSHA Director Auchter, however, vowed to continue using what he called "the most cost-effective" means of protecting worker safety.

In a similar case, OSHA officials asked the Supreme Court to set aside a lower court ruling upholding standards for workers exposed to lead, a powerful poison if breathed or swallowed. But the Court decided to let the ruling stand, thus approving a requirement to transfer workers with high lead levels in their blood. Rather than putting this into effect, however, OSHA compromised by reducing the permissible level of lead and granting exemptions to 21 companies. The revised standard thus affected only about 1 per cent of the 800,000 workers exposed to lead.

CONCERN FOR BUSINESS

Auchter's concern for business interests came to the fore again in a bitter confrontation at a House hearing in July. At one point, he refused to leave the witness table to allow another OSHA official to tell his version of Auchter's role in removing a government warning that formaldehyde can cause cancer and in the firing of a scientist whose views agreed with the warning. Only after Rep. Albert Gore, Jr., chairman of the House Science Subcommittee, threatened to call the sergeant-at-arms did the OSHA director leave the table.

Under earlier questioning, Auchter acknowledged that he had withdrawn the label requirement after his top aide had met with two lawyers for the Formaldehyde Institute, an industry group. Auchter denied having fired the scientist, Peter F. Infante, after the meeting with industry lawyers, but the deputy who sent the dismissal letter told the hearing that he had acted on Auchter's orders. Infante called himself a victim of industry pressure. (One of the industry lawyers was John Byington, former chairman of the Consumer Product Safety

Commission, which had banned the use of the substance in insulation after he left the agency.) The dismissal letter was later withdrawn.

An estimated 750,000 people handle formaldehyde on the job, and millions of people are exposed to it through their handling of insulation, toothpaste, shampoo and other products. The action taken behind closed doors at OSHA illustrated the way many industry groups succeed in getting their own way in the government. It also showed how government officials profit from their expertise after leaving office.

RIGHT TO KNOW HAZARDS

An estimated 21 million Americans are believed to be exposed to serious health hazards at work. Illnesses and injuries such as cancer, kidney and liver disease and urinary dysfunctions kill about 100,000 workes each year. Yet many of the hazards are not known to workers. OSHA has estimated that as many as 15 million workers are exposed to toxic substances known only by meaningless brand names. Only about 20,000 of some 86,000 trade-name substances are subject to federal regulation as work hazards. This lack of information has led many workers to handle dangerous materials without proper precautions or protective clothing. It helps to explain why cancer cases have grown significantly in recent years. A task force of the Carter Administration estimated that 20 to 38 per cent of cancer cases were associated with hazards on the job.

The Carter Administration subsequently proposed that employers be required to identify and label such substances. The proposal was called "extremely important because it would allow employees to identify the chemical substances and know the workplace hazards to which they are exposed, thereby enabling them to take actions to better protect themselves." This was one of the rules pulled back by the Reagan Administration for review.

Auchter was especially determined to suppress information embarrassing to industry. He ordered the destruction of 50,000 government booklets designed to educate workers and employers about cotton dust and their rights and responsibilities relating to the government standard. He later explained to a reporter who discovered the incident that the cover photograph (of a strickened worker who later died) was too sympathetic to victims of the disease. He also ordered OSHA's 10 regional officers to stop showing three films on cotton dust and withdrew two slide presentations, one on cotton dust and another on acrylonitrile, a tumor producer, apparently because of business opposition to them. A press aide acknowledged that Auchter had not read the booklets or seen the visual materials before taking action.

EXCESSIVE NOISE

Excessive noise is not as serious a hazard as carcinogens, but it affects a large number of people. Government data indicate that some 20 million Americans have irreversible hearing loss due to excessive noise. As a result, the Carter Administration proposed that employers install hearing conservation measures for workers exposed to average noise levels of 85 or more decibels over an eight-hour period. This was another proposal held up for review by the Reagan Administration.

In August, OSHA issued a substitute regulation which the AFL-CIO called a "watered down version" of the Carter proposal. The revision relies on the use of ear plugs and ear muffs rather than engineering changes to reduce the noise level. The changes, which were pushed by the U.S. Chamber of Commerce, will affect an estimated 5 million workers exposed to more than 85 decibels of noise over an eight-hour shift.

Auchter also sought to disperse more of his agency's functions to the states and increase voluntary compliance. The law allowed states to operate their own safety programs if they were "at least as effective" as the federal one. By 1981, nearly half the states and territories had such programs in effect. Indiana's plan, however, had been challenged by former OSHA Administrator Eula Bingham because of what she called "a consistent pattern of poor performance in critical program areas." Auchter reversed her position and later approved a Virginia plan strenuously opposed by organized labor as defective.

Among other worker safety matters slated for review were comprehensive guidelines for protecting workers against cancer-causing substances. The guidelines were held up by the Reagan Administration because they did not include cost-benefit analyses in setting exposure levels.

POLLUTION CONTROLS

As a candidate, Ronald Reagan set the tone of his administration with some revealing remarks, including his view that air pollution had been "substantially controlled." In a speech to Youngstown steel workers, he said trees and plants were worse menaces. "Growing and decaying vegetation in this land are responsible for 93 per cent of the oxides of nitrogen." He added that Mount St. Helens, the Washington volcano, "probably dumped more sulfur dioxide in the air than 10 years of automobile driving or things of that kind." Neither he nor anyone on his speech writing staff caught the error of referring to oxides of nitrogen instead of nitrous oxide, a harmless gas. Nor did they realize that cars do not emit sulfur dioxide.

To direct the Environmental Protection Agency, which had authority over most pollution matters, Reagan belatedly chose Ann Gorsuch, a person with no experience in such work and with a record that caused environmental groups to vigorously oppose her nomination. The office had gone unfilled for months while Reagan officials reportedly sought someone willing to accept budget cuts and undo pollution controls. Even before she took office, the Administration relaxed air pollution rules to allow a so-called "bubble" policy, one long sought by polluting firms. It permits an individual plant to exceed the limit but not violate the law if it is grouped with other plants that pollute less.

The main issue she faced as administrator was what to do with the Clean Air Act, which expired September 30, 1981. Since the law was passed in 1970, there had been many missed deadlines and relaxations of standards for cleaning up major pollutants. The first deadline was 1975. It was eventually extended to 1982 (1987 for cars). Even the latter deadlines were not likely to be met because of the failure of many states to gear up their own plans, delays and court battles caused by business opposition and the unwillingness of federal regulators to push harder than political realities would allow.

Administration officials planned many changes in the law, but their plans were upset when a draft of them leaked into the news media. Upon seeing the proposals, Rep. Henry A. Waxman, chairman of the House Energy Subcommittee on the Environment, called them "a blueprint for destruction of our clean air laws." Thomas Austin, head of the California Air Resources Board, said they would double auto pollution and increase acid rain. On the other hand, the National Association of Manufacturers was delighted since the plan echoed suggestions made privately to the White House by the Association and other industry groups working in coalition.

Among the provisions were ones eliminating the need for polluted areas to show improvement toward reaching national standards, leaving to the states the authority to judge whether progress has been made or whether deadlines needed to be extended, making enforcement lawsuits optional rather than mandatory and eliminating a program to prohibit pollution of clean areas. The draft did not address the increasing problems of acid rain, toxic emissions from industrial plants, the worldwide threat from carbon dioxide or the effect of chlorofluorocarbons on the earth's ozone layer.

Stung by the adverse publicity, Administration officials regrouped and issued a series of guidelines, some of which pleased environmentalists. But they reversed course again in making later recommendations to Congress much like their earlier proposals. Clearly, the Reaganites were trying to give industry everything they could without suffering too much political damage.

They also chipped away at individual rules that sought to control specific hazards. One was a limit on the amount of lead additives permitted in gasoline in order to reduce harmful health effects. Refiners had complained that the rule was unduly expensive because it required the use of more crude oil in order to make up for the reduction in lead. This rule was held up in response to requests. EPA officials also relaxed auto emissions standards for carbon monoxide and diesel fumes at the behest of manufacturers.

In addition, Reagan officials also attacked clean water standards. In July, the EPA asked a federal court to excuse the agency from having to comply with most of a 1976 consent agreement with industry and environmental groups. The agreement had settled several lawsuits, including one accusing the agency of failing to enforce the Clean Water Act. The EPA said it wanted to be free to decide for itself which toxic substances to regulate, whether industrial effluent permits meet standards and be allowed to extend industry compliance deadlines up to 29 months. The agency explained that it could not handle the work involved because of budget cuts. Meanwhile the chemical industry went to court to get the entire agreement overturned.

One of the main problems in cleaning up water supplies is the pervasive existence of pesticides, chiefly from farm runoff. For years, the EPA tried to get a handle on the huge task of registering pesticides and reviewing their ingredients to make sure that they were not too toxic for the environment. The sheer volume of chemicals involved and the limited resources of the agency hampered this process before the Reagan cuts made the problem worse.

Instead of stepping up these efforts, the EPA decided to ease the rules regarding pesticides. It held up rules requiring pesticide manufacturers to test and register new products before selling them to the public and rules requiring chemical producers to report certain information about new products before marketing them.

RESCUING HERBICIDES

It even came to the rescue of Dow Chemical Company, producer of Agent Orange, the herbicide blamed for thousands of deaths and disabling injuries in the Vietnam War. The company's 2, 4, 5-T and Silvex weed killer, containing virtually the same chemicals, came into common household and commercial use in this country after the war. They also ran into increasing charges that they caused miscarriages, birth defects, cancer, liver disease and skin disorders in people exposed to the chemicals in crop or forest spraying programs. An unavoidable contaminant of the weed killers is dioxin, one of the most toxic substances in existence. Because of the danger, household uses of the chemical were banned by Carter officials. They proposed to ban most remaining uses of the herbicide but ordered public hearings before taking final action. The company wanted to settle the matter with a warning label. But Reagan officials called off the hearings for private negotiations with the firm.

They also decided to make it easier for chemical companies to comply with a 1979 law designed to control dangerous industrial wastes. The law, passed largely because of the disturbing revelations at Love Canal near Niagara Falls, N.Y., called for licensing of disposal sites and strict regulations governing the transporting and dumping of such materials at thousands of such areas around the country. But at the request of the chemical industry, Reagan officials agreed to relax previously proposed requirements, fitting them to the degree of hazard involved in each case. It soon became apparent, however, that this move would increase regulatory paperwork contrary to the new mood in Washington.

EPA also held up previously issued guidelines setting tougher limits on the amount of highly toxic industrial wastes that could be dumped into municipal sewage systems. Business firms had alleged that the limits were too expensive and were based on erroneous research. Raising the level of toxicity in sewage would risk polluting water used elsewhere for drinking. Meanwhile, Reagan officials made plans for resuming the dumping of such wastes in the ocean.

EXPLOITING NATURAL RESOURCES

Reagan's policy on natural resources was to develop them to the fullest and to relax environmental controls wherever they interfered with such development. Like previous administrations, this one continued to emphasize production of fossil and fissionable fuels despite dwindling supplies and rising costs in both monetary and environmental terms. Although the nation will eventually have to develop alternate sources, such as solar power, and conserve resources more, the Administration chose to reduce government efforts in these areas. The overall effect was to speed up the rise in prices of energy because of the dwindling supplies of fossil fuels and the steady demand for them.

In several ways, the Administration's energy policy violated its own principle of getting the government out of activities that could be handled by private business. For example, although the budget office wanted to reduce government subsidies to synthetic fuel production, the White House made some big exceptions.

Reagan officials also continued subsidies for the nuclear industry. Several stalled, controversial projects were included in budget requests, notably the Clinch River Breeder Reactor, which President Carter had tried to kill because of huge cost overruns and questions about its technical feasibility. Despite startup costs of $1 billion for the plant that had not reached production, Congress appropriated still more in 1981 toward a total cost expected to exceed $3 billion.

Production was also a rallying cry for the nation's chief conservator of natural resources, Interior Secretary Watt. Claiming to be doing the Lord's work as a "born-again" Christian, he offered virtually every acre under his jurisdiction to commercial exploitation regardless of location. He pushed so hard for oil exploration of offshore ocean tracts that several companies complained that they could not handle the volume, and he later had to pare down his plans. He argued that the nation's need for production, particularly energy, was more urgent than the need to preserve the environment. "No area should be excluded," he said in reference to development of public land.

Among policy changes announced by Watt were ones to:

● Relax strip mining requirements for restoring land;

● Open up wilderness lands to mining, thus virtually repealing the 1965 Land and Water Conservation Act, which had led to the purchase of some 5 million acres for federal and state parks;

● Offer national wildlife refuges to states that wanted them;

● Allow motorboats in the Grand Canyon's Colorado River and allow off-road vehicles in wilderness areas and beaches despite the environmental damage attributed to such vehicles;

● Resume construction of water projects, such as dams and canals, which had been discontinued by President Carter because of the costs and environmental damage caused by them.

Because of the scope and intensity of his actions, opposition soon became intense. The conservative National Wildlife Federation reported that its members overwhelmingly disagreed with his policies. But he was undeterred. When they sought to reason with him, he refused to make appointments. By summer, all the major environmental and conservation organizations were calling for his resignation. And Congress took steps to clip his wings by blocking some of his thrusts. Although the President seemed to back him — even urge him on with a flip "sic em" remark, according to columnist Colman McCarthy — the White House reportedly began to require Watt to clear major actions with it before announcing them.

Neither the Interior Department nor the Agriculture Department seemed worried about the steady loss of water resources and rich farmland. One might have expected that an administration so deeply rooted in the West, where water and farmland are precious assets, would reverse the course of neglect that has ruled many administrations. But that was not the case.

PRODUCT SAFETY

The principal agency dealing with the safety of consumer products became the focus of much attention in the battle of the budget cuts. Congress eventually approved just what the Administration wanted, a 30 per cent cut in funds for the Consumer Product Safety Commission, an action called "devastating" by Commission officials. Since the agency was one of the smallest in Washington, total savings amounted to only about $8 million, a proverbial drop in the federal bucket.

More important than financial savings was the history of opposition to the Commission by business interests. They did not like to have defective products publicized or recalled, actions which the Commission was authorized to require. Nor did they like the idea of the government setting safety standards which might raise prices to buyers.

One proposal was to eliminate the Commission entirely and transfer some of its duties to the Commerce Department. That idea did not make it through Congress at first, but Reagan officials tried later. They also had another ace up their sleeve through the appointment process. They named Nancy Harvey Steorts, a former aide to Earl Butz while he was Secretary of Agriculture, to head the agency. At her confirmation hearing, she told legislators she planned to emphasize education and information rather than enforcement. "The era of confrontation and adversity (sic) is past." she declared. "I will do everything in my power to keep it out of that agency." But at her first meeting with the rest of the Commission, fellow members rejected her concept, saying that enforcement must be continued with high priority in order for the agency to be effective.

Important products with safety problems outside of the Commission's jurisdiction include motor vehicles, medicines and nuclear power, all of which were subject to regulations that the Reagan Administration wanted to relax or eliminate in response to industry requests.

AUTO SAFETY PUT IN REVERSE

For the attack on vehicle laws and safety regulations, the Administration decided to cut funds in half for the National Highway Traffic Safety Administration and name a coal industry lobbyist, Raymond Peck, with no experience in the field to run the agency. He proceeded to stop the process of proposing new safety changes in cars, end the system of notifying the public about safety recalls, discontinue rating cars for "pass" or "fail" in crash protection tests and pull back nearly three dozen regulations for review and possible elimination.

"In effect," said Ralph Nader, "they have repealed the motor vehicle safety and emission laws." One study showed that safety regulations had prevented at least 37,000 deaths on the highway from 1975 to 1978.[4]

Among the regulations affected were:

● A proposal to require an automatic dash board warning when tire pressure dropped to unsafe levels, at an estimated cost of $4 per car;

● Rules to make seat belts more comfortable and convenient;

● A rule to require safety tests to prevent battery explosions and to warn buyers of the problem;

● Rules to improve the safety of multi-piece tire rims, many of which have suddenly exploded, causing numerous fatalities and injuries; and

● Rules to improve brake standards for vans, buses and trucks.

The stated reason for the changes was to save money for Detroit. Transportation Department officials claimed that the changes would save the industry $1.4 billion in capital costs and reduce consumer prices by $9.3 billion. But Clarence Ditlow of the Center for Auto Safety, a private research group started by Nader, estimated savings per car of only $150, which he said was "not a significant saving on cars averaging $9,500 in price."

In addition, Reagan officials decided to delay for one year the passive restraint rules that were to be phased in over a three-year period beginning with the 1982 model year. The rules gave manufacturers a choice of installing air bags or automatic belts. Here, too, the government accepted manufacturers' claims, alleging that air bags would cost a prohibitive $1,000 to produce and attach.

But Ditlow disclosed a confidential 1979 government memo quoting estimates from General Motors that air bags on 1982 models would cost only $206 on a mass production basis. Peck's response was to demand that Ditlow return the confidential memo under penalty of legal action.

GM's answer was to raise prices an average of $600 per car for 1982 models without air bags. Other manufacturers posted similar price increases.

PROTECTING DRUG PROFITS

Nothing comes closer to life and health than the safety of medicines. And no set of laws has a firmer basis for existence that those requiring that all drugs have proof of both safety and effectiveness before they can be sold to the public. But drug makers have fought a running battle with regulators for years with frequent delays, court challenges and other tactics designed to thwart government efforts to protect the public health.

As a result, hundreds of prescription and non-prescription drugs on the market still lack proof of safety or effectiveness. This means not only that billions of consumer dollars are wasted on useless products but that many people are subjected to unnecessary and dangerous reactions, adding further to costs and human suffering.

The main complaint of manufacturers has been that many regulations add unnecessarily to costs. Yet the drug industry has frequently topped all other industries, including the oil industry, in the annual listing of profitability by the Federal Trade Commission. Industry officials invested heavily in the Reagan campaign and moved quickly to cash in after the election. They found a sympathetic reception from Reagan officials. Among the government proposals pulled back for review were:

● A proposal to require drug manufacturers to include warning information in pill packages, starting with 10 of the biggest selling medicines. These "patient inserts" were to be similar to more technically written inserts advising doctors and pharmacists about important side effects and precautions. Industry representatives had lobbied hard for years against such a proposal even on a trial basis on the ground that it might "confuse" people.

● Regulations allowing lower-priced generic versions of patented drugs to be sold after the patents expire without the necessity of redoing all the clinical tests originally done for the patented drug. At the request of industry representatives, who were prominent on the transition team dealing with this area of government, Secretary Richard S. Schweiker of the Department of Health and Human Services told drug firms privately that he had withdrawn the long-established policy of automatic approval of generic drugs, despite his own record in Congress of favoring generic products. When the decision leaked out, several consumer groups filed suit alleging that his action violated the law. A Congressional hearing followed. Several weeks later, he returned to automatic approval of generic drugs. At the same time, however, he said he would advocate changing the law to allow patents to begin only after drugs are approved rather than when patents are granted. This would add billions of dollars to consumers costs by extending the period of monopoly pricing under patent protection.

At the same time, drug makers sought to reduce the lag time between when a new drug is submitted to the government and when it is finally approved for public sale. Schweiker hastened to assure them that the procedure would be speeded up. He said he would relax the rules requiring review of test data and reduce paperwork despite the fact that it was this review process that blocked the marketing of thalidomide and prevented the birth of many deformed babies in the early 1960s.

EASING NUCLEAR REGULATIONS

Nuclear power companies had similar demands. They blamed administrative delays for the high cost of new plants although the record shows that such delays accounted for only a small portion of the problems. Nevertheless, Acting Chairman Joseph Hendrie of the Nuclear Regulatory Commission (NRC) agreed with industry demands. He cited an "overwhelming need to speed up the licensing process" despite his knowledge that such reviews had not been sufficient to find the flaws that later became evident at Three Mile Island. He announced plans to cut eight months off the time required for granting operating licenses. And he decided to please the industry further by eliminating the right of the public to get key safety data from the NRC staff, prohibiting subpoenas of NRC staff for information, allowing the chairman to act without consulting other Commission members and issuing interim operating licenses before formal hearings on safety matters have been completed.

One of the rules had classified irradiated animal carcasses and some laboratory equipment as low-level nuclear wastes and therefore restricted to burial in a few designated places around the country. Relaxing the rule meant that these wastes could be disposed of in open city dumps and ordinary landfills at an estimated saving of $13 million a year. The Commission also increased by six-fold the acceptable level of radioactive tritium and carbon 14 acceptable in municipal sewage systems.

Other safety regulations held up for review and possible elmination included a set of rules establishing safety standards for mobile homes after an epidemic of fires had indicated that the design of many such structures prevented easy escape during a blaze.

ECONOMIC REGULATIONS

Among regulations held up by Reagan officials involving costs rather than safety matters were:

● Minimum standards of design, construction and "livability" of residential structures in order to qualify for government mortgage insurance and rent subsidy programs. These standards have served as assurances of quality for millions of home buyers and tenants over the years.

● Rules setting up lease and grievance procedures for tenants of public housing and regulations requiring local agencies to review hospital construction and equipment purchases in order to keep costs down.

● Standards requiring automobile bumpers to prevent body damage in a crash at 5 miles per hour. Some companies wanted the standard lowered to 2.5 mph, a difference which would cost motorists an estimated $400 million more in repair costs.

● Regulations relaxing eligibility requirements for low-interest subsidized loans to moderate-income families for buying homes. The regulations were considered too costly to the government.

● Requirements that labels on meat products disclose the existence of bone fragments resulting from mechanical deboning processes. Packers had fought this rule for years, finally losing out to the principle that meat buyers have a right to know whether they are getting granulated bone along with their protein. Packers claimed that the disclosure made sales impossible.

The Federal Trade Commission (FTC), the main agency policing economic abuses of the marketplace, had its budget cut. Budget Director David Stockman at first ordered a 30 per cent cut, but objections from small business interests and some Republicans in Congress forced him to shave his request to about 11 per cent for fiscal 1982. The reduction was expected to bring the closing of some regional offices which monitor the marketplace and do about one-third of the antitrust work.

The psychological effect of the political change in power had an even greater effect. The criticism of regulations and government antitrust efforts by candidate Reagan and his top aides made it clear to FTC officials that they should not push too hard for fear of their political lives. The Commission already was on a short leash as a result of Congressional action the previous year. The new atmosphere led it to water down some pending proposals and greatly reduce its overall efforts to curb deceptive advertising and fraudulent business practices.

NOBODY HURT, SAYS BUSH

Despite all these changes affecting the American people, Vice President Bush saw no loss to the public. After announcing the second round of actions in August, he said: "There is nothing in our approach destined to diminish the quality of life and the quality of the environment . . . We're trying to find a balance that has not been found in previous rules. There's an awful lot of people out there saying there's a better way to skin this cat." But almost all of those "people" were business firms, professional groups and local governments. Few others responded to his earlier proposal.

People most affected by the proposed changes neither participated nor knew what was happening. It was another example of the "overwhelm-them-with-details" approach of the Administration. Like the budget and tax proposals, the regulatory changes were presented in large packages for quick dumping and getaway. This meant news for only one day for everything rather than a separate item for each proposal. It not only cut down on public attention but reduced the possibility of a significant backlash. By emphasizing the "review" angle, Administration officials also helped fend off critics. "We're not prejudging whether everything in these regulations is bad," assured Bush. But any regulation that made his list for "review" was not long for this world. It was rare for one to pass muster and return to active duty.

WIELDING THE LEGISLATIVE BROOM

While individual regulations were being swept away *en masse* by the Administration, still more basic changes were being planned in Congress, along with some White House blessings. One bill, sponsored by Senator Paul Laxalt and co-sponsored by 80 other Senators, would give the President the authority to control the rule-making procedures of so-called independent agencies, which are not under direct Presidential control except for the power to appoint top officials. Independent agencies include the Consumer Product Safety Commission, Environmental Protection Agency, Federal Communications Commmission, Federal Trade Commission, Interstate Commerce Commission and Securities and Exchange Commission. All had refused Vice President Bush's request to submit their rules to the White House budget office for review, though some took similar action by themselves.

Another provision of the bill would even take away the historic presumption that regulations coming out of the government are legal, leaving the courts to decide that in each case. This would make it possible for business interests to block regulations until they are finally upheld or disapproved by the courts many years later.

Other provisions included Congressional veto power similar to that imposed earlier on the FTC, systematic reviews of all regulations every 10 years, a requirement that agencies calculate the cost of complying with regulations before adopting them or provide a formal explanation if the most "cost-effective" alternative were not chosen.

Laxalt admitted that "this is the kind of legislation that you wouldn't dare introduce 10 years ago. In those days, all we heard was 'How can you put a price tag on health and safety?' But we must. Maybe we don't want to pay for 100 per cent clean air.''[5]

In view of the overwhelming sentiment in the Administration and Congress for such proposals, it was clear that the regulatory process faced further restrictions.

The next logical step would be to have no regulation of business at all. Bizarre as that might seem, a Republican-oriented think tank was busily preparing such a proposal. The Reason Foundation of Santa Barbara, California, planned to publish a book, *Instead Of Regulation*, arguing that the "free enterprise" system could do what 11 major government agencies do to protect the public. When the Administration and its friends in Congress are ready to go that extra few yards, the Foundation will have a plan ready for implementation.

6

Undermining Law and Order

Observe the rules or get out.
Ronald Reagan[1]

Ten days after taking over as President Reagan's chief assistant, Edwin Meese III decided to heal an old sore. As a former prosecutor and retired lieutenant colonel in the Army Reserve, he had been smarting over efforts of the previous administration to prosecute some 140 FBI agents for burglarizing private homes in the name of national security but without court approval during the Nixon Administration. Meese was particularly incensed about convictions of two high FBI officers, W. Mark Felt and Edward S. Miller, for authorizing the illegal break-ins, also known as "black bag jobs."

Although the two officials had been found guilty, they were let off rather easily with no jail terms and fines totaling $7,500. One reason for the light sentence was the massive campaign by active and former intelligence agents who raised $1.5 million for legal expenses and conducted demonstrations to support all of the accused. Like Meese, they felt that no charges were justified because of the implied approval given by top officials for such illegal entries over many years, notably by J. Edgar Hoover, former FBI director.

Unlike the accused agents and officers, however, Meese had a neat way to wipe the slate clean. He could get a Presidential pardon. All he needed was a written request from the convicts' lawyers. Meese did not bother to go through the formal Justice Department procedure for seeking pardons, nor did he notify the prosecutor in the case. He simply circumvented the federal laws and regulations governing official pardons.

In April, President Reagan went along with Meese and readily issued the pardons, which eliminated the convictions and the fines. Afterwards, Reagan issued a statement

97

equating the action to the lack of prosecution of draft evaders in the Vietnam War. "Four years ago," he said, "thousands of draft evaders and others who violated the Selective Service laws were unconditionally pardoned by my predecessor. America was generous to those who refused to serve their country in the Vietnam War. We should be no less generous to two men who acted on high principle to bring an end to the terrorism that was threatening our nation." He was referring to the fact that the burglaries condoned by Felt and Miller were for the purpose of seeking information on the radical Weather Underground, a group suspected of several bombings.

Prosecutor John W. Nields vehemently criticized the pardons, the secrecy in which they were prepared and the failure to go through normal channels. "The central proposition of democracy," he told a reporter, "is that government is second to the people, and its powers are limited by the Constitution. The jury and the court collectively affirmed this proposition. But the Executive Branch pardoning the Executive Branch for violating the rights of the people strikes at the heart of this proposition."[2]

It also illustrated the "law-and-order" stance of Reagan and Meese. It showed how far they were willing to go beyond the law to promote their own political philosophy. To them, loyalty to right wing political concepts sometimes has to supercede strict adherence to the laws of a democratic society. To them, the law is a means of combatting street thugs and curbing those who disagree with established authority rather than restraining authority itself.

On the campaign trail, Ronald Reagan frequently complained about the way the courts interpret the law. He accused the Supreme Court and other federal courts of making new rules for society, of siding with social activists rather than holding strictly to basic laws. In a campaign appearance at Amarillo, Texas, he said he not only disagreed but would not support the Court's decision banning prayers in public schools.

Earlier in the campaign, he told *The Washington Post* that he would seek to halt what he called the Court's "unprecedented grasp for power" in refusing to block the use of federal funds for Medicaid abortions.[3] In a formal statement in February, 1980, he had vowed to "make the Supreme Court learn that just as the American people will not tolerate

Presidential wrong-doing or Congressional corruption, so too will the United States not accept any judicial usurpation of the power that would threaten our system of self-government.''⁴

After becoming President, he obviously saw no contradiction between his campaign statements and his own refusal to abide by the decision of a court and jury which convicted the FBI officials.

POLICE AND MILITARY UPPERMOST

Nor did Meese. No man was a stronger advocate of law and order than he. According to reporter Martin Schram, Meese was "a man of two overriding professional passions: a love of police and law enforcement operations and a love of the military ... He was the law school student who preferred sketching military reserve organization charts to outlining contracts and torts. He was the assistant district attorney who spent his off hours riding in police patrol cars. He was the governor's executive assistant who liked to relax at home while listening to police radio chatter.'' Schram also noted the Meese collection of porcelain pigs, symbolic tributes to the police who were denounced as pigs by street demonstrators in the 1960s.⁵

Meese found it difficult to find anything to criticize in the way police handle their jobs, especially in view of what he felt were excessive legal restraints imposed on law enforcement officers by the courts. He saw no justification for an organization such as the American Civil Liberties Union, calling it "the criminals' lawyer" because it often sought to protect the civil rights of criminal suspects and people who disagreed with the establishment. In his opinion, common criminals should be punished severely, but white collar criminals should be treated with sympathy and tolerance.

CURBING RIGHTS TO FIGHT CRIME

The Administration's response to the campaign talk about violent crime was to appoint another task force to study the problem. It was the fifth national commission charged with finding solutions to the steady rise in crime. The statistics themselves served as a reminder of how ineffective previous attempts have been to control a problem that is essentially a local matter.

This one was no exception. Its major recommendation was to build $2 billion worth of new prisons, despite a prediction by Meese that such funding was "very unlikely." And it advocated changes in the laws along the lines Meese had long advocated. One was to deny bail to defendants considered dangerous to the community. Another was to allow prosecutors to use questionable evidence if they have a "good faith belief" that it was obtained legally. This was an effort to get around the "exclusionary" rule that prohibits use of evidence obtained without a warrant to convict a person.

The latter recommendations had been made in other administrations without success, but the prospects of enactment were much greater under the Reagan Administration. A week before release of the report, Meese told the American Bar Association that the White House was already preparing legislation to incorporate such changes in federal law. And Assistant Attorney General Rudolph W. Giuliani informally endorsed the concepts when the report was presented publicly. Criticism came immediately, however, from the ACLU which contended that such changes would undermine the constitutional rights of private individuals.

Another recommendation was to set up stricter controls over handguns by requiring a waiting period before purchase and requiring owners to report lost or stolen weapons to authorities. Mild as these suggestions were, they were given no chance of enactment in view of the power of the gun lobby to squelch virtually all previous efforts to impose such restraints. President Reagan's continued opposition to further controls over handguns, even after his own near-tragic confrontation with a gunman, further doomed such suggestions.

A month later, the White House decreased the chances still further by recommending elimination of the Treasury Department's Bureau of Alcohol, Tobacco and Firearms, which administers weak restrictions on guns and maintains a system of weapon identification that helped trace the gun involved in the shooting of Reagan himself. The move caused Rep. Peter W. Rodino, chairman of the House Judiciary Committee, to say: "It makes no sense for the Administration to dismantle the federal agency responsible for tracking illegal guns and enforcing firearms laws at a time of heightened national concern over violent crime."⁶ The National Rifle Association had demanded the agency's elimination.

CONDONING CORPORATE BRIBERY

While Reagan officials were pushing hard to crack down on street crime, they launched an effort to ease a relatively new law against bribery by business firms. In 1977, Congress had passed the Foreign Corrupt Practices Act following revelations that more than 400 American corporations had secretly bribed foreign officials. The law was designed to curb a growing practice of bribing foreign purchasing agents in order to make sales. The Securities and Exchange Commission had launched legal actions on the grounds that the secret bribes were unfair to stockholders and customers of the firms involved.

Stung by the publicity and prosecutions, business leaders began a campaign to get the law watered down or eliminated. In response, Republican Senator John H. Chafee introduced a measure to reduce SEC authority and remove most of the accounting requirements of the law. His legislation would prohibit payments only where there was "reason to know" that the money would be used to bribe a foreign official. Democratic Senator William Proxmire, who had sponsored the original law, called the Chafee bill a "disaster" that would prevent any major prosecution for bribery.⁷ Business leaders claimed that the law's restrictions had caused them to lose business to competitors who were free to offer bribes. But American exports had increased after the law went into effect.

Nevertheless, the Reagan Administration decided to support Chafee's bill. But before presenting testimony, the White House transferred the chief law enforcer at the SEC, Stanley Sporkin, to the CIA and appointed John S. R. Shad as chairman, a man more in tune with the demands of business than his predecessor. Shad endorsed most of the Chafee bill.

While the revisions were being debated, Associate Attorney General Ralph Giuliani met with officials of McDonnell Douglas Corporation, the big defense contractor which had been accused of bribery and mail fraud, without informing the prosecuting attorneys in the Justice Department. The meeting was arranged by Senator John Danforth, Missouri Republican, whose brother was a company director. The company, which

Danforth said was the state's "leading corporate citizen," and four executives were charged with paying $1.6 million to Pakistani officials in return for airplane sales. When the two prosecuting attorneys learned of the meeting with Associate Attorney General Giuliani, they quit the Department. Giuliani said he did not know about the charges before the meeting with the aircraft executives although Senator Danforth said he had informed Giuliani of the purpose of the meeting.[8] In September, three months later, the Department dropped the criminal charges against the four company executives in return for a guilty plea by the Corporation and payment of $1.2 million in fines.

EASING THE RULES ON ETHICS

Another law that got in the way of Reaganites was the Ethics in Government Act, passed after the Watergate revelations. It set up requirements for high government appointees to disclose their financial holdings in order to prevent conflicts of interest and established a mechanism for handling charges against officials in the Executive Branch through appointment of a special prosecutor independent of the Justice Department.

Among those seeking to have the law watered down was Fred Fielding, former aide to John Dean in the Nixon Administration, who was given the job of administering the law at the White House by Reagan officials. Fielding wanted personal financial disclosures to be made only to Congressional committees, not to the public. Reagan officials had complained a number of times that the disclosure provisions had prevented them from hiring qualified people for public service, presumably because of something they did not want known. Attorney General Smith, a lawyer who always had worked behind the scenes, was one of those who objected to the law. He particularly disliked the special prosecutor provision and suggested changes.

Still another Watergate reform law that did not sit well with Reagan officials was the one setting up the Federal Elections Commission. Created in 1974, the Commission sets limits on the amounts that can be contributed to candidates in federal elections. It also requires contributions to be reported to the Commission. The purpose is to prevent recurrence of the campaign spending excesses of the 1972 election and reduce the influence of powerful special interests in government.

The Commission's restrictions were especially irritating to Republicans, the traditional party of wealthy contributors. Particularly galling to them were the limit of $29 million for Presidential nominees and the $1,000 limit on the amount that individuals can contribute to Congressional candidates in a primary or general election. When word leaked out in August that the Commission was preparing to release a report charging the Reagan campaign committee with violating the law during the 1980 campaign and owing the government $1.5 million, the GOP went to court to block release of the report on the grounds that it would cause "irreparable damage, loss and injury to certain individuals."[9]

MORATORIUM FOR FRAUD AND WASTE

One of the Watergate reforms that the Reagan forces might have been expected to keep was the network of Inspectors General in each agency for the purpose of rooting out the old bugaboos of "fraud, waste and abuse." But before the sun set on Inauguration Day, these crusaders for clean, lean government all had dismissal notices. So sudden was the move that the Office of Management and Budget did not find out about it until sometime later. No reason was given for the dismissals in the rush to find room for campaign workers and others fitting the conservative mold.

The news provoked a flood of criticism, particularly from Congressional supporters of the system. They pointed out that the offices had been designed to be immune from such actions in order to ensure impartial investigations and prosecutions. Before any hearings were held, however, on the possibility of illegalities in the dismissals, Reagan officials reappointed some of the dismissed officials and claimed their budgets would be increased. They also were made members of the President's newly created Council on Integrity and Efficiency. But Rep. L.H. Fountain, the North Carolina Democrat who had sponsored the Inspectors General law, said the total Reagan staff of 5,000 to monitor some $400 billion in public funds was "less than the number of persons employed by the Los Angeles County sheriff."

All these efforts to undo reforms instituted after Watergate raised the specter of more lawlessness like that of the Nixon Administration. Particularly upset was Common Cause, a citizen group which had led the fight for enactment of many of these laws. In a magazine commentary in June, the organization asked: "Is this Administration planning to return the government to a pre-Watergate mentality?"[10]

BRINGING BACK WATERGATE

Few leaders of the new order seemed to understand the meaning of Watergate or the dangers they were risking by their actions and attitudes. Reagan himself seemed to miss the point of Watergate when he said as a candidate: "The traditional immorality of politics is no defense of Watergate. It's obvious, though, that the press wouldn't have been as interested in Watergate if the Democrats had been the culprits, which in itself is an indictment against the morality even of those who ferreted out the Watergate immorality. They weren't objectively ferreting out immorality; they were trying to prove that the faction they disagreed with had played 'dirty tricks' on the faction they supported."[11]

Such a view shows ignorance of the basic issues beyond the actual break-in of Democratic headquarters: the concerted White House efforts to spy on opponents, tap telephones of colleagues, steal private records, destroy campaign data, use contributions illegally, use tax returns for political purposes, destroy official records, withhold potential evidence from Congress and the courts, commit perjury, hand out government contracts on the basis of contributions and many other illegal acts. The ultimate effect was to subvert the democratic process on a wide scale.

With such a misunderstanding of Watergate, Reagan ran the risk of stumbling into a similar debacle, particularly with his attempts to undo the reform laws. His disregard for laws he did not agree with fitted into his general view of government itself as a lawless, profligate, evil monster that had gotten out of control and had to be "cut down to size." Throughout his campaign, he repeatedly denigrated the very government he wanted so much to run, blaming it for everything from family problems to high prices. It is only a short step from such contempt for government to disrespect for the laws which form the basis of civilized society.

BUILDING NEW BUREAUCRACY

These misconceptions were particularly apparent in Reagan's approach to government regulations, the rules set up to implement the laws protecting the public from physical and economic abuse. In his haste to undo regulations disliked by business, he set up another layer of bureaucracy of questionable legality in the White House itself. In establishing the Task Force for Regulatory Relief headed by Vice President Bush, no mention was made of the Administrative Procedure Act, the law which had been passed by Congress to govern the regulatory process. That law calls for publication of proposals for public comment, including public hearings, with detailed guidelines for regulatory agencies to follow in order to assure that all views have a chance to be represented and issues are handled fairly.

Before setting up the new super-regulatory office, the White House asked for a legal opinion from the Justice Department. The Department responded with a statement saying Presidential powers were broad enough to authorize such an order. But a detailed analysis of the Presidential order the following June by Morton Rosenberg of the Congressional Research Service of the Library of Congress strongly disputed that opinion. He saw in the order a possible violation of the Constitutional separation of powers, since the Executive Branch thus was able to circumvent agencies and procedures established by Congress. Rosenberg said in effect that the new super-bureaucracy created by Reagan to review regulations amounted to an unprecedented and unauthorized grab for power. He was particularly critical of the circumvention of the existing law and the opening of a "new access point to the agency decision-making process without providing safeguards against secret, undisclosed and unreviewable contacts by government and non-government interests seeking to influence the substance of agency action."[12]

But the analysis did not phase Reagan officials. When asked about it, James Miller, executive director of the White House regulatory task force, fell back on the approval provided by the Justice Department. "If you were involved in litigation," he asked, "would you want to be represented by the Department of Justice or the Congressional Research Service?" He in-

dicated that the White House would continue reshaping
regulations regardless of legal opinions to the contrary.

CONDONING CORPORATE MURDER

There was a more fundamental issue, however, that Administration officials did not address. It related to the effect of
regulations on people. In their fervor to undo rules because of
allegedly unnecessary costs to business, advocates of such
changes ignore the human factors. To fail to protect people
from harm is excusable if done through ignorance or
carelessness. But to deliberately set out to increase hazards to
people with full knowledge of the consequences is something
else. .

Paul Savoy, professor of law at Southwestern University,
calls it "profit-oriented murder." In an article in *The Nation*,
he said: "When we speak of crime and violence, we immediately think of shootings and stabbings ... But when people are
needlessly crippled or killed by their working and living conditions; when working men and women die of brown lung disease
caused by exposure to cotton dust in textile mills; when innocent children are killed in automobile accidents from injuries
that could have been prevented by automatic safety systems;
when people could have been rescued from conditions of in-
tolerable deprivation but are left to the silent killers of hunger,
cold and sickness — their pain and loss is no less attributable
to human action. Yet we shrink from recognizing this infliction
of human suffering as a form of violence."[13]

Nor do most citizens think of such things as crime. They
don't picture government officials or corporate executives
deliberately setting out to kill people. But if one accepts the
traditional meaning of "intent" (as noted by Professors Wayne
LaFave and Austin Scott in their *Handbook on Criminal Law*)
as including knowledge of the consequences of one's action,
then deliberately exposing people to damage or death can be
just as much of a crime as pointing a gun with knowledge of
what the bullet can do.[14] Tire companies that knew about the
potential dangers of polyvinyl chloride effectively sentenced
countless workers to cancer and premature death by
withholding what they knew, just as Ford executives knew
that failing to install an inexpensive baffle to prevent rear-end
fires in Pintos and failing to warn purchasers would result in

needless deaths. In what could have been a precedent-setting case, Ford was acquitted of criminal liability for murder in one case after the judge excluded from testimony company analyses stating that the cost of the safety device exceeded the cost of probable law suits resulting from an estimated number of rear-end collisions.

By relaxing protections designed to save lives and prevent injuries, Reagan officials shared responsibility for the consequences. By participating in cost/benefit analyses, they demonstrated their knowledge of the human costs of their actions, just as ordinary street criminals calculate what a gun or knife will do to human flesh. But the "crimes" of federal officials are incomparably larger because of the vast number of victims and the power of government to prevent harm by changing societal patterns.

PAVING THE WAY FOR PRICE-FIXERS

One of the biggest tests of the new Administration's attitude toward crime came in its policy toward monopolies and mergers in the business field. One might expect that people dedicated to free market principles would be especially interested in fighting any anti-competitive acts they could find. At the least, one might expect them to uphold the applicable laws to the letter. All the patron saints of the Reagan economic policies — such as George Gilder, Milton Friedman, William Simon — preached the value of competition. They all believed, as did Reagan, that removing government restrictions and taxes on business would bring the economy into better balance through the forces of competition.

But big business is not interested in more antitrust activity. It wants to be free to grow further. Many big business executives contributed heavily to Republican campaigns in 1980. Now they wanted to cash in their chips by demanding a slowdown of antitrust activities.

Reagan showed his sympathy with their demands on the campaign trail. While in Michigan, the home of the breakfast cereal industry, he echoed that industry's criticism of the Federal Trade Commission's test case against the top firms, the first government attempt to prosecute a "shared monopoly."

His remarks put the Commission under pressure to slow

down its efforts in all antitrust cases, pressure which was multiplied by Reagan's election. With the pattern thus set during the campaign, White House budget cutters aimed at the Bureau of Competition of the FTC. Their plans to eliminate it were temporarily thwarted only when some influential legislators and small business interests, the main beneficiaries of the Bureau, objected. But the FTC got the message and cut back on much of its antitrust activities. It also got James Miller, the Administration's chief deregulator, as chairman.

Setting the pattern at the Justice Department was especially important, since it was the government's main enforcer of the law. Much depended on the type of person named Attorney General, the head of the Department. To solve that problem, Reagan went no further than his personal secretary, William French Smith. Known as a society lawyer, Smith practiced entirely on behalf of large corporations and wealthy individuals. With that choice, Reagan signaled big business that it had nothing to fear except fear itself from antitrust enforcement.

Smith soon flashed the same signal. "We must recognize," he told the District of Columbia Bar Association, "that bigness does not necessarily mean badness and that success should not be automatically suspect. In some industries, competition yields a large number of competitors, in others only a few, depending upon the economies of scale, distribution costs and other factors." He said the Department of Justice would be "rethinking past policies" toward mergers, a clear indication of reduced concern about the trend toward increasing business concentration. In addition, he said the Department had begun to review more than 1,200 judgments and decrees "to determine which might profitably be modified or vacated." He added that the government should not prevent competing American firms joining together for foreign business. All of these moves, he assured his audience, were being done to foster competition.[16]

At the Securities and Exchange Commission, the merger trend got an even more enthusiastic boost. In his first meeting with reporters, Chairman Shad said mergers generally resulted in a "net economic gain" to the country, because they cause "a substantial premium for the shareholders' equity." His views contrasted sharply with those of Harold Williams, his predecessor, who doubted that mergers would produce the expected benefits. A number of studies have shown that bigness in business does not necessarily bring the cost economies expected. Nevertheless, Shad made it clear that he considered many previous government efforts to preserve competition as unnecessary intrusions into the marketplace.

As the outlines of Administration attitudes became evident, the merger trend picked up spectacularly, topped by the $7 billion bidding war for Conoco by Dupont and Mobil Oil. And members of Congress began to blame Administration officials. Peter Rodino, chairman of the House Judiciary Committee, charged that the Attorney General's remark about bigness and badness "seems to have been a signal to many in the business world that enforcement of the Clayton Act will be relaxed."[16] In the Senate, Republicans showed less concern, having abolished the Subcommittee on Antitrust and Monopoly, a long-time fixture on Capitol Hill.

Failure to enforce antitrust laws was itself a law violation, in the eyes of Ralph Nader. Pointing to the anti-merger law's wording that "all mergers — horizontal, vertical and conglomerate" are illegal, he said failure to prosecute them violates the Constitution's requirement that "laws be faithfully executed." By refusing to enforce the law, he added, "the Administration is spitting in the eyes of Congress who wrote them, the courts who interpreted them and millions of American consumers and honest businessmen."[17]

SUBVERTING DEMOCRACY

Meanwhile, other high officials of the Administration set out to undermine the democratic system by disregarding laws governing the legislative process. One of the laws that got in their way was the Budget and Impoundment Act of 1974, another reform of the Watergate period. Its purpose was to prevent Presidents and their aides from refusing to spend money appropriated by Congress except in an emergency. It also set up an elaborate process of Congressional budget review, giving Congress more say in that process and reversing the trend toward more Presidential power.

A concerted assault on the law was led by Budget Director David Stockman, a hard-line economic conservative who had worked extensively on budget matters while a Congressman.

He knew the budget process well and how it could be turned around to work for the Executive Branch. Under the law, Congress was directed to establish broad goals in the spring, let various appropriations committees slice up the pie during the summer and consolidate everything in a "reconciliation" budget in early fall.

But Stockman and his Republican/conservative Democrat allies on Capitol Hill managed to get Congress to reverse the process by passing the "reconciliation" budget in the spring with all the major budget cuts locked into it. The committees thus had no choice but to go along. This maneuver caused critics to charge that the Administration and its friends in Congress had distorted the whole budget-making process. "We are dealing with more than 250 programs with no hearings, no deliberation, no debate," said Democratic Rep. Leon E. Panetta, a member of the Budget Committee. "It's a terrible way to legislate," admitted Republican Rep. Barber B. Conable, "but we have no alternative unless we're going to lie down."[18] To make matters worse, some non-budgetary legislative bills were tacked onto the budget measure, also contrary to the intent of the law.

LOBBYING FROM THE WHITE HOUSE

Another part of the Administration strategy was to push through the economic plan before potential critics had an opportunity to learn all the details and mount a substantial counterattack. Other elements of the campaign included personal contacts by the President and a "grassroots" drive led by White House political operatives working under Lyn Nofziger. As a result, Congress was flooded with letters and phone calls, not so much from ordinary people as from large contributors who carried more weight. Editorials and broadcast commentaries were predominantly favorable, adding still further to the momentum built up around President Reagan. Technically, it is against the law for the White House to lobby Congress, but all administrations have done it to some extent. However, none did it with such flourish and intensity as the Reagan Administration.

Through Nofziger's office, the White House drew on a vast network of Republican and right-wing organizations to engineer the contacts to Congress. Some business firms contributed by sending letters not only to Capitol Hill but to employees and stockholders. Each legislator with a key vote was analyzed by Nofziger for vulnerability to pressure. Then the pressure was applied.

In the final analysis, President Reagan himself cut some political deals. In order to win the votes of legislators from Louisiana and other states, he agreed to back costly price supports for sugar producers that could add $2 billion a year in prices paid by the public. In order to get votes in the Texas delegation, he agreed to more breaks for the oil industry. In order to get the votes of Georgia legislators, he agreed to leave peanut subsidies alone. Nobody dared suggest that the President was offering bribes, since he was following an old custom, but it is doubtful that any President had offered so much to so many. One Representative, when asked if his vote had been sold, said cynically that it had only been "rented."

One of the more questionable methods of pressuring legislators by Administration allies was to play a tape recording of a politically damaging radio ad to a legislator with the threat that the ad would run if he did not vote the "right" way. This was the ploy used by the conservative National Tax Limitation Committee in seeking votes for the Reagan economic program. One of the Congressmen on the receiving end told reporters about it and charged that it amounted to blackmail and reverse bribery. For those reasons, said Rep. Bill Nelson, a Florida Democrat, he would vote against the Reagan plan.[19]

Although these tactics may not have violated any laws, the end result was a subversion of the democratic process. Members of Congress are elected to represent the voters of their districts and states. It is doubtful that many voters back home would approve of having their interests traded or "rented" in a game almost always won by the interests with the most money, not the most popular support.

CURBING THE FLOW OF INFORMATION

One of the best deterrents to political crime and subversion is full disclosure of information to the public. The fear of exposure in the press probably does more to keep office holders relatively honest than the entire body of federal laws. On the other hand, it does not keep them from trying to limit press access to information that may be embarrassing to some party.

In 1966, Congress finally drew some lines in this constant battle between those who want information and those who want to hide it. The resulting Freedom of Information Act tipped the balance in favor of public access by directing the government to disclose everything with certain logical exceptions such as matters dealing with national security or personnel data. "Sunshine" laws added later were designed to force more meetings into public view. The Carter Administration pushed these concepts further than they had ever been on the theory that open government is better government.

The trend, however, was reversed by Reagan officials. They became less accessible to the press. They closed more meetings. They held fewer press conferences, following the President's example of only four in nine months, one of the lowest rates in history. And they reduced the amount of information for public distribution.

One of the main reasons apparently was to protect business firms from exposure of unfavorable details. That was apparently the reason why the National Highway Traffic Safety Administration stopped issuing public announcements about vehicle recalls for safety purposes. It was not until August that the news media began to realize the change in policy. By that time, there had been 101 recalls involving millions of cars and tires, only a few of which had been announced by manufacturers. Raymond Peck, head of the agency, told a reporter: "The purpose of this agency is not to create publicity . . . and not to excoriate or condemn the manufacturers."[20] Yet it is the fear of adverse publicity that helps to keep manufacturers on the alert for safety problems. And it is often a news story that alerts the owner of a defective vehicle in time to get the defect corrected before it leads to injury or death on the highway.

The main target was the Freedom of Information Act. Reversing a Carter doctrine, the Justice Department announced new guidelines declaring that when an agency does not know whether to release a document, it should always opt for secrecy. Both the FBI and CIA asked to be exempted entirely from the law, claiming that they had been hamstrung by unnecessary requests from people seeking their files. "As a consequence," said the Justice Department, "informants are more reluctant to share information with enforcement agencies, foreign intelligence services are more reluctant to share information with U.S. intelligence agencies, companies are reluctant to provide reliable information to the government, and other impediments to effective government are created.''[21] Yet the Department offered no evidence that any release of information had ever damaged intelligence-gathering.

BLOCKING PUBLICATIONS

At the Office of Management and Budget, the move for greater secrecy came in the form of new restrictions on publishing. The ostensible purpose was to cut down on waste, but critics claimed that the real purpose was to reduce confrontations with business interests that did not like what they read. Among the first publications put into mothballs were the Department of Transportation's "The Car Book," which compared crashworthiness characteristics of cars by make and model, not the kind of analyses to please Detroit; and a monthly newsletter of the Energy Department entitled "Energy Consumer," one issue of which allegedly was biased against the nuclear power industry. Over a million copies of these publications and others mentioned in Chapter 5 were withdrawn from public sale and distribution.

In the international arena, Reagan officials went all the way back to 1917 to find a law allowing them to block publications entering the United States from Cuba. When the Trading With The Enemy Act, which bans trade with certain countries during a national emergency, was invoked in 1962 to embargo trade with the island nation, periodicals were not included. However, Reagan officials quietly decided to seize periodicals and publications as they entered the country at Boston. Only when the pile reached more than 30,000 items and was reported to the press did they explain that licenses would be required of subscribers before they could receive any literature. They added, however, that no license would be granted if any money is paid to Cuba, making it highly unlikely that many licenses would be granted.[22] By fall, the pile of Cuban publications reached 100,000.

Although the tactic was obviously designed as another means of retaliating against Cuba for its role in supplying arms and aid to dissidents in various areas of Latin America, it also made the United States look as if it were afraid that Cuban literature would have a harmful effect on the population. And it risked violating the First Amendment guarantee of a free press, a high price to pay for a relatively minor provocation of Fidel Castro. By not even announcing the move in the first place, the Administration seemed unaware of the larger issues involved.

At the CIA, Director William Casey decided to simply shut down the agency's public affairs and information office on the grounds that "the difficulties of the past decade are behind us." Shortly after making that claim, however, Casey and a top aide ran into some ghosts from their own pasts, to the dismay of the Reagan Administration. First came a report in *The Washington Post* saying that Max Hugel, Casey's hand-picked aide to run all of the agency's covert operations, had been involved in improper stock trading practices while he was in business seven years earlier. Hugel, who boasted of having learned to cheat and deceive on the streets of Brooklyn, resigned the next day while professing his innocence.[23]

SKIRTING THE LAW ON DISCLOSURE

On the day of Hugel's resignation, came news reports of a federal judge's decision that Casey himself had misled investors in an ill-fated attempt to raise $3.5 million with an agribusiness firm that went bankrupt in 1971. Casey, chairman of the SEC in the Nixon Administration, had earned the gratitude of Reagan when he straightened out campaign finances. Hugel met Casey while serving as a campaign organizer. The double embarrassment grew out of the Administration's failure to obtain enough information about both men before they were appointed.

Added embarrassments arose within weeks as reporters dug into Casey's background, which a Senate committee was also investigating. As the pile of clippings grew, it became clear that the millionaire lawyer/entrepreneur had been involved in numerous civil suits and business firms that he had not disclosed as required by the Ethics in Government Act. The law authorized the Justice Department to file a civil suit against any appointee who "knowingly or willfully" fails to list holdings in excess of $1,000.

To resolve the matter, the White House decided to allow Casey to amend his January filing in August on the grounds that the omissions had been unintentional. His amendment listed 10 holdings totaling $472,000 and one direct liability of $18,000 listed earlier. The White House said none of the firms on the list had any "current" relationship with the CIA.[24]

The importance of a free flow of information in a democracy was attested to by a recent American President. "Fundamental to our way of life," he said, "is the belief that when information which properly belongs to the public is systematically withheld by those in power, the people soon become ignorant of their own affairs, distrustful of those who manage them and — eventually — incapable of determining their own destinies."

The speaker was Richard Nixon in 1973.[25]

7

Rights and the Righteous

In insuring the security of the people and the nation, there may come times you have to spy on your own people.

Ronald Reagan[1]

When former Secretary of State Cyrus Vance suggested on *Meet the Press* in early summer that the Reagan Administration did not appear serious about pursuing arms control talks with the Russians, he soon found himself accused of being a dupe of Soviet propaganda. When *The Wall Street Journal* disclosed damaging errors in the State Department's White Paper on El Salvador — based on the author's own admissions, no less — the paper found itself accused of having fallen for Soviet "disinformation." Other pillars of the American establishment have felt the sting of similar accusations after finding fault with Reagan's handling of foreign affairs. The usual method is for a high official to leak the charges to right-wing columnists who gratefully repeat them without identifying their sources.

When it eventually became clear that the late Senator Joseph McCarthy could find no documentation for his flurry of charges and innuendoes against innocent people, he became discredited and died in ignominy, leaving only the shame of a new "ism" to denote a type of vicious, false accusation of un-Americanism against people who disagreed with his concept of the world.

The new Administration, however, is reviving McCarthyism under other guises. "Disinformation" is only one of them. Another is to imply that people who fight against oppressive dictatorships are *per se* Communists. That is what the Reagan State Department has set out to do around the world, starting in El Salvador. Like Joe McCarthy, Secretary Haig sees the world divided between Communists and non-Communists. There is no middle ground..

HUMAN RIGHTS VS. TERRORISM

With such a view, the struggle for human rights is reduced to merely a struggle between communism, where rights are suppressed, and democracy, where they are not. But such a view greatly oversimplifies the world. It fails to recognize the fact that many people trying to improve their lot under an oppressive, anti-Communist regime are not dupes or agents of Moscow. Secretary Haig thus considered terrorism a bigger problem than threats to individual freedom from oppressive governments. Soon after taking office, he announced that "international terrorism will take the place of human rights" as the top concern of the Reagan Administration. In a speech to the Trilateral Commission, Haig said the greatest danger for human rights was "totalitarian aggression" and terrorism by the Soviet Union.

The shift in views from one administration to another even brought a shift in supporting data. The issue of terrorism began to hit the headlines before the case for its importance was made. To help make the issue credible, the CIA revised its own figures to fit the needs of the new bureaucrats. Before 1981, the CIA had never counted more than 413 terrorist attacks a year in the world. Suddenly, it found 760 in 1980 alone, plus more than 2,000 others which it had not included in totals for previous years, according to *Washington Post* reporter George Lardner.[2]

Responding to the escalating evidence, Congress prepared to investigate the new menace. Under the control of Reagan-Haig style conservatives, the Senate set up a new Subcommittee on Security and Terrorism chaired by Jeremiah Denton, a retired admiral. Denying that he was bringing back McCarthyism, he lost no time in opening hearings on "Soviet and surrogate support for international terrorism." In the House, conservatives sought — unsuccessfully — to recreate the Internal Security Committee, once known as the House Un-American Activities Committee.

The Center for Constitutional Rights warned that the Terrorism Subcommittee had "the capability and support to move this country back to the dark ages of McCarthyism." How-

ever, Denton said he was doing everything possible to avoid
violating anyone's rights. After all, said John East, also a
member of the Subcommittee, "the greatest threat to civil
liberties in the world today is terrorism.".

BOOKS FAN THE FLAMES

Helping to fuel the fires were two new, popular books. One
was *The Terror Network*, a recitation of alleged connections
between various terrorist groups in other countries. The
author, Claire Sterling, was a former newspaper correspondent
who was frequently quoted as a top authority on the subject.
Secretary Haig sent copies of her book to all members of the
Senate Foreign Relations Committee. The other book was *The
Spike*, a novel by Robert Moss and Arnaud de Borchgrave. In
Moss's own words on a promotion pamphlet, "It is the story of
how our news media have been used by the Soviet KGB and its
satellite intelligence services to manipulate public opinion in
the West in order to achieve Moscow's expansionist objec-
tives."[3] The fictional plot was turned into a non-fictional tool
to silence Reagan critics as dupes of Soviet "disinformation."

Another publication apparently behind the hunt for terrorists on Capitol Hill was a report by the Heritage Foundation, the conservative research group that supplied much of
the background and guidance for Reagan policy makers. It
suggested a number of organizations and individuals that
ought to be investigated in a crackdown on domestic radicals,
including Tom Hayden's Campaign for Economic Development, the Institute for Policy Studies and *Mother Jones*
magazine.

CIA DISCOUNTS MOSCOW'S ROLE

The atmosphere became so inflamed that Sterling tried to
cool it down. She told *Washington Post* reporter Henry Allen
that she disagreed with the way Reagan, Haig and their
friends in Congress were using her work. "I'd like to know, "
she said, "do Reagan and Haig mean to use the extreme right
to clobber the left on this issue?" If so, I part company with
them." Although citing the book as evidence of Moscow's
direction of world terrorism, she said that she had no proof of
that.[4]

The CIA agreed with her. In a report to government officers, it rejected the theory that the Soviets were directing terrorists around the world. In its National Intelligence Estimate, the agency said there was circumstantial evidence of Soviet involvement but no proof. At the same time, the FBI told a Congressional committee that terrorist incidents had declined so much in the United States that the agency had reduced its staff investigating them. Speaking on NBC's *Meet the Press*, FBI Director William H. Webster said there was "no real evidence" of Soviet-sponsored terrorist activity in the United States.

Ironically, however, there was evidence that Americans have trained terrorists both here and abroad. Newspaper and television teams reported in March that Latin American exiles were being trained in guerilla tactics in Florida and California for the purpose of returning to their own countries and overthrowing the governments there. It was no secret that Cubans have been training commandos in this country ever since the ill-fated Bay of Pigs even though federal law prohibits such activity. Apparently, terrorism was all right if aimed at foreigners.

Other reports told of as many as 50 Americans training terrorists on Libyan soil. According to *The Boston Globe*, the Americans included members of the U.S. Marine Corps on leave under the supervision of former CIA agents. The paper quoted a confidential report which said: "The United States, in effect, has become a major supplier of (military) hardware and technology in support of worldwide terrorism. Former CIA personnel, military Special Forces personnel and U.S. corporations combined to supply products and expertise to whomever can pay the price."[5] Secretary Haig promised an investigation.

Congressman David E. Bonior also sought an investigation. "If we are to have a litmus test to illustrate our commitment (against international terrorism)" he told the House Subcommittee on Inter-American Affairs, "then I would suggest that the first international terrorists whom the Secretary (of State) and appropriate law enforcement officials should bring to justice are those who are operating unlawfully right here in the United States."

About a month later, Haig took action. He ordered Libya to close its mission in this country, referring to "Libyan provocations and misconduct, including support for international terrorism." But the State Department refused to provide any details in response to questions from reporters. In September, the Justice Department sought indictments against two former CIA agents mentioned in news stories.

DISINFORMATION

Denton was particularly concerned about the wave of "disinformation." In his first hearing on terrorism he claimed that the Soviets had had a "measure of success" in deceiving a "story-hungry and sometimes gullible press." The contention gained currency when Secretary Haig, a friend of Moss and deBorchgrave, told a press briefing that "the Communist countries are orchestrating an intensive international disinformation campaign to cover their intervention while discrediting the Salvadoran government and American support for their government."

Haig's implications angered *Washington Post* columnist Stephen S. Rosenfeld, a former correspondent in Moscow. "It is mischievous," he wrote, "for an official with access to intelligence to suggest that the news is being polluted by a hostile intelligence agency."[6] Rosenfeld challenged Haig to "show his cards" or let the people wonder "whether he has any better purpose than to manipulate public opinion himself." Haig took the bait and allowed that the American press was "the best in the world" but offered no specifics.

Later, *The Wall Street Journal* borrowed a McCarthy tactic in commenting on a vote of the House Foreign Affairs Committee to impose some requirements to protect human rights before American aid could be sent to El Salvador. Under a headline calling the vote "a Communist victory," the paper said: "Communist forces are not winning the war in El Salvador, despite a continued flow of arms from Cuba and a capacity to shoot up the American Embassy now and then for sport. They are, however, having a modicum of success in the U.S. Congress."[7]

Some conservatives even saw Communist influence in the news reports about Secretary Haig's behavior following the shooting of Reagan. Right-wing columnists Rowland Evans and Robert Novak, who had many inside contacts at the White House, said there was an "anti-Haig campaign" with ideological roots "that have nothing to do with his conduct . . . Its origin is his hard anti-Communist policy, especially his move to save El Salvador." Further, they said, the campaign "has many earmarks of past attacks on any high official in any administration willing to condemn Communist aggression."[8].

RETIRED SPIES ENTER POLITICS

One reason for the sudden upsurge in attention given to terrorism and disinformation was a mass movement of retired intelligence officers to the Reagan camp as a result of Carter's downgrading of the CIA and FBI and upgrading of human rights issues. Reagan's victory opened up new vistas for them, with many moving into the White House and State Department while others took over key posts in Congress. Among the architects of the Senate hearings on terrorism were a former FBI agent who took over as the subcommittee's chief counsel and an author of the Heritage Foundation report, who joined the staff of Senator John East, a member of the Subcommittee.[9] Vernon Walters, the former deputy director of the CIA surfaced again in April as a close aide to Haig.

Meanwhile, a task force of intelligence experts from the CIA, FBI and Defense Department began meeting secretly with White House aide Edwin Meese III to draw up comprehensive plans to eliminate restrictions imposed on the CIA and FBI because of abuses disclosed during the Watergate period. Among the proposed changes they wanted was the elimination of President Carter's curbs on surreptitious entry and infiltration of domestic groups as well as the reduction in the Attorney General's authority to veto certain intelligence operations. The group, headed by CIA General Counsel Daniel B. Silver, focused on changes in the rules that could be implemented without legislation.[10]

The report in the press caused CIA Deputy Director Bobby Ray Inman to hold a rare on-the-record briefing on the matter. He confirmed that the CIA was seeking more freedom in which to operate and said President Reagan would issue an executive order to implement the proposals. But he denied that the CIA was seeking authority to conduct spying or covert activities within the United States. He said plans had not been made formal or final.

He did say, however, that Carter's restrictions had become outdated by the "changing world we're dealing with." He claimed that terrorism had become "an international institution, although luckily we have not been in the center of it here." His remarks brought criticism from citizen groups, particularly the American Civil Liberties Union, which said the proposed changes "would place civil liberties in jeopardy." The ACLU asked Reagan for assurances that the President would not allow illegal entries ("black bag jobs") into private homes in the name of national security.

But Reagan replied through Fred Fielding, a former Nixon aide, that such activities were sometimes necessary. The White House had already asked the Foreign Intelligence Surveillance Court to exclude secret searches of private homes from its jurisdiction. The court had been set up by Congress in 1978 to grant or deny legal approval for wiretapping and electronic bugging by the FBI and the supersecret National Security Agency. In June, the court agreed, thus freeing the President and Attorney General from having to get court clearance before ordering break-ins.

MORE SECRECY SOUGHT

Another hole in the dike that intelligence experts wanted plugged was periodic exposure of CIA agents by the *Covert Action Bulletin*. The *Bulletin's* purpose was to fight abuses by the intelligence agencies by making it more difficult for them to operate in secret without concern for human rights. With Reagan in the White House, the intelligence community saw a new and better chance to obtain a legislative ban on such disclosures. The Intelligence Identities Protection Act, introduced in the Senate by John H. Chafee, a former Secretary of the Navy, would make public identification of an FBI or CIA agent punishable by fines and prison terms.

However, the bill was written so broadly that it would also have prevented private citizens from innocently passing on information obtained from others and would have punished the press for reporting abuses of any government intelligence agency. Even the exposure of CIA connections with the Watergate coverup and CIA payments to King Hussein of Jordan would have been subject to criminal prosecutions. The bill's prohibitions were not limited to names of agents but to

"information that identifies" an undercover operative or
source. A news story identifying a building used by CIA
agents could thus be considered a violation. Some members of
the news media felt such a law would be an unconstitutional in-
trusion on the First Amendment. But in testimony before
Senator Denton's Subcommittee on Security and Terrorism in
May, Richard K. Willard, counsel to the Attorney General,
disagreed.[11]

So sensitive was the subject that no representative of the
news media dared testify against the bill for fear of being labeled a Communist or worse. The only critics who testified
were two officials of the American Civil Liberties Union, Morton H. Halperin and Jerry Berman, who were taunted for their
efforts by Chairman Denton. Among those endorsing the bill
at the hearing was CIA Director William J. Casey, who said
Secretary Haig also endorsed better cover for CIA operations.
Halperin was one of the White House aides whose telephone
was tapped on orders of Haig while both were working for
Kissinger. "There is a possibility," wrote liberal lobbyist Mark
Green, "that we may be in for our once-every-30-years security
scare (Palmer Raids in the '20s, McCarthyism in the '50s)."[12]

The script this time appeared to be the Heritage Foundation
report which concluded that "the threat to the internal security of the Republic is greater today than at any time since
World War II." It went on to urge the President to attack "the
reality of subversions . . . and the un-American nature of much
so-called 'dissidence.' " Reagan kept in the background
although his record of public utterances in the past put him
squarely on the side of Denton, Casey, Haig, *et al.* On a hopeful
note, Green wrote: "Perhaps even he will now realize that we
hardly defeat our Soviet competitors by imitating them."[13].

MINORITY RIGHTS

One of the thorniest topics for Reagan administrators was
minority rights. Almost all groups championing the rights of
blacks, Chicanos, Indians and other minorities sided with
Carter in the election because Democrats had always been
more responsive to their needs. Their hunches proved correct.
After the election, despite Reagan's advice for them not to
worry, they became victims of a triple whammy. Civil rights
groups not only faced deep cuts in their government grants

and contracts, but the reduced funds also weakened their ability to prevent cuts in social programs. To compound their problems, they also faced prospects of losing regulatory and legislative protections.

Affirmative action programs were the first targets. In August, the White House announced an ominous review of hiring guidelines. And in Congress, Senator Orrin G. Hatch launched a drive to eliminate them. In a 120-page critique, he called them "an assault upon America, conceived in lies and fostered with an irresponsibility so extreme as to verge upon the malign." One of his first acts in 1981 was to hold hearings by his Judiciary subcommittee on the constitutionality of affirmative action. The idea of requiring a proportion of employees to be from minorities was developed through regulatory actions and court decision, not through legislation. And the Republicans appeared determined to turn the whole program around or kill it. Hatch's bill would prohibit state and federal governments from issuing any requirements based on racial, color or national factors.

Voting rights were also beseiged. Although the Voting Rights Act of 1965 was not due to expire until August 6, 1982, conservatives in Congress began holding hearings on the law in April, 1981. The leading critic, Strom Thurmond, was in an excellent position to make drastic changes in the law as he had promised, since he was chairman of the Senate Judiciary Committee. Southerners who disliked the law were in control of key committees in both houses, leaving the law little chance to survive without a major revision. The biggest thorn in the side of Southerners was the "pre-clearance" requirement which forces states to get clearance from the federal government before making any changes in election laws or rules.[14] On the other hand, civil rights leaders said the law had proven to be one of the most effective in history, because it had brought black voter rolls up from 2.8 to 4.2 million since 1964.

In late May, the Justice Department announced a major turn in government policy, saying it would no longer promote affirmative action programs that include racial quotas in employment matters or mandatory busing to achieve school desegregation. Calling both policies "ineffective" and sometimes unfair, Attorney General Smith said they would be replaced by a "more practical and effective approach." He described this as a "color-blindness" that would not be directed at any "previously disadvantaged" group but would bring remedies to fit the "resulting harms actually being suffered today." In school situations, remedies would include improvement in the quality of education. He denied that the government would not enforce the law on segregation or that it would allow the government to foster segregation. But the Administration's first settlement of a suit involving North Carolina state colleges was called "significantly worse" than plans repeatedly rejected by Carter officials. David S. Tatel, a former Carter civil rights official, said the settlement showed that the Reagan Administration was not interested in enforcing civil rights laws..

WOMEN'S RIGHTS

Reagan's election presaged a slowdown in the battle for women's rights. His party's platform not only downplayed the issue but omitted any backing for the Equal Rights Amendment, the leading legislative goal of female rights organizations. Although candidate Reagan said he had "no argument" with the goal of equal rights for women, he opposed the ERA as a means of reaching that goal. Seeing the signs, women voters did not swing to him the way men did, according to interviews with people leaving the polling booths.

Once in office, Reagan officials matched their advance notices by moving slowly in appointing women to key posts and even reversed the course of previous administrations in various programs of special concern to women. The White House chose not to continue Carter's practice of appointing a woman to handle these matters. Instead, it left them to several officials, including both male and female ones. The highest appointment gained by a woman during the first five months in office was that of United Nations Ambassador, which went to Jeane Kirkpatrick. By June, the only other woman to receive a major role was Anne M. Gorsuch, who became head of the Environmental Protection Agency. Both were considered antifeminist by women's rights organizations. In July, President Reagan broke precedent in nominating a woman, Sandra O'Connor, to the Supreme Court, thus fulfilling a campaign promise.

Women were also affected to a great extent by the massive

cuts in budgets and regulations effecting them: At a time when
working women were demanding more day care facilities, programs for them were cut 25 per cent and shoved over to the
states in block grants. The Administration proposed
eliminating $25 million for two programs designed to help
schools and colleges fight sex discrimination.

Reagan's transition team for the Equal Employment Opportunity Commission, which enforces the Civil Rights Act of
1964 and the Equal Pay Act of 1963, recommended a 20 per
cent cut in funds. Reagan halved that, but, according to
Senator Paul Tsongas, even the smaller cut would "virtually
stop" investigations of systemic discrimination, stifle the
mandate to end discrimination in government agencies and
allow the backlog of charges to mushroom. Tsongas also
criticized the proposal to eliminate free legal services, two-
thirds of whose clients were women.

On the regulatory front, women were directly affected by the
postponement of affirmative action guidelines for federal contractors, which included protections against sexual harrass-
ment and unequal pay, and the withdrawal of a rule prohibiting such contractors from paying membership fees to
clubs discriminating against women. The Administration indicated it would replace an executive order requiring
businesses dealing with the government to develop specific
plans for recruiting and hiring women and minorities.

INTIMATE AFFAIRS UNDER SCRUTINY

Perhaps the biggest effect of the election on individual
rights, however, was in the most intimate affairs of life, such
as abortion, sex education of youngsters, sexual preferences,
birth control and prayer in school. In the past few years, these
personal matters have been kindled into burning national
political issues by a host of fundamentalist preachers and
right-wing organizations. Ronald Reagan became an ardent
supporter of these forces, and they in turn promoted his can-
didacy with an intensity rarely seen in American politics.

In return for their support, Reagan endorsed their demands
without qualification. He even promised to appoint judges
"who respect traditional family values and the sanctity of innocent human life," the code words for opposing abortion.
When it was pointed out to him after the election that judges

should not be advocates for a particular viewpoint, he retracted his comments. When he later appointed a woman to the Supreme Court, some groups opposed her because of her alleged views on abortion. They were also miffed at Reagan because he had not questioned her or other judicial appointees on their views of abortion.

But he did not back away from his opposition to abortion, even in cases of rape and incest. In response to a question from a Yale student in 1975, Reagan was quoted as having said he could not agree that "a woman has a right to control her own body."[15] At a press conference after becoming President, he appeared to agree with members of Congress who had introduced a bill declaring that human life begins at conception instead of birth. If this bill became law, there would be no need to ban abortions, because abortions would become murder. In July, a Senate judiciary subcommittee passed the bill on a party-line vote of 3 to 2.

APPOINTING ABORTION FOES

Reagan followed through on his commitment to anti-abortion groups by naming "pro-life" people to posts where they could affect government programs dealing with abortion. One was Richard Schweiker, a former Senator who was named Secretary of Health and Human Services. Another was Dr. C. Everett Koop, a prominent surgeon who had become famous for successfully separating Siamese twins and for opposing abortions, homosexuality and women's liberation, all of which he termed "anti-family." His nomination of Koop as Surgeon General was opposed by the Public Health Association on the grounds that he lacked training and experience in public health and preventive medicine, the principal concerns of the office. It was the first time in 100 years that the Association had opposed a nominee for the post. Others questioned appointing such a strong advocate on these issues to a position with responsibility to treat all groups equally. When special legislation removing a technical age barrier to his appointment ran into temporary trouble in Congress, Schweiker named him Deputy Assistant Secretary.

Schweiker also played a behind-the-scenes role in helping to promote anti-abortionist sentiment at a public hearing in the Senate on the bill to date human life from conception. Several weeks after the panel's vote was taken, *The Washington Post* revealed that a switch of Department witnesses by Schweiker had prevented disclosure of a study citing numerous benefits from abortions. Dr. Willard Cates Jr., director of abortion surveillance at the government's Center for Disease Control in Atlanta, was prepared to present a 11-page report noting that legal abortions had produced a substantial decline in abortion-related illnesses, that abortion-related deaths in the nation had plummeted from 235 in 1965 to only two in 1976, three years after the Supreme Court decision legalizing abortions, and that new surgical methods had reduced the risk of death in abortions to one-seventh of the fatality rate in pregnancy and childbirth. The study also indicated that legal abortions had brought a drop in teenage marriage and illegitimate births.

Instead of presenting the report at the hearing as scheduled, however, Cates was replaced by another official who read only three pages, omitting most of the favorable references to abortions. Thus, the subcommitte did not have the full story before it voted. And the public did not learn of the findings at the time.[16]

Anti-abortion sentiment soared in Congress after the 1980 election results. In late May, the Senate voted, 52 to 43, to add an anti-abortion amendment to the comprehensive budget bill. It prohibited federal payments for all abortions to poor women except in cases where the mother's life was at stake. The House voted 253 to 167 to make the same prohibition apply to federal employee health insurance.

Most of the far right goals shared by Reagan were packaged into "The Family Protection bill," introduced in 1980 by Senator Paul Laxalt and in 1981 by Senator Roger Jepsen. The legislation would ban government money for abortions, sex education, contraceptives and family planning, all of which were considered to be "anti-family." In addition, it would deny civil rights to people with "perverse lifestyles" (code words for homosexuals), prohibit funds for treatment of venereal disease, prevent taxation of racially segregated academies, block federal programs to prevent child abuse and allow parents to review textbooks before their use in public schools. In addition, the bill would deny free legal services for abortion and divorce.

GETTING GOD INTO SCHOOL

The old controversy over prayer in public schools was also dusted off for a new round of hearings and legislative efforts. Ever since the 1963 Supreme Court ruling that holding prayers in public schools was a violation of the First Amendment, fundamentalist religious leaders had been campaigning to overturn the decision through legislation that would allow prayers in public schools. Rekindling the old fires especially bothered people whose faith did not coincide with the Christian sponsors and others who felt that religion belonged in home and church rather than in the public schools.

One of the goals of the religious right was more federal money for parochial and private schools, another issue that went to the heart of the First Amendment. Although the Supreme Court has repeatedly rejected direct government aid to private and religious schools, advocates of such aid have never given up. Buoyed by the election of Ronald Reagan, who backed the idea during the campaign, these advocates launched a campaign in Congress with new strength. Democratic Senator Daniel Moynihan took the lead with a bill to have the government grant tax credits of $500 per student in non-public schools.

Chief supporters of the measure were Catholics, with the largest system of non-public schools; orthodox Jews and evangelical Christians, also with their own school system. They contended that public schools had become inferior and "godless." Opponents said the move for tuition tax credits would set up a new system for educating the middle class while destroying public schools for those who cannot afford private ones.

One bone of contention was whether private schools created to avoid racial integration should be taxed. In 1978, the Internal Revenue Service removed the tax exemption of such academies on the grounds that they were primarily for racial purposes. So intense was the anger of religious leaders that Congress reversed the IRS action.

Equally sensitive was the subject of sex education. Most of the conservatives who felt that prayer belonged in school felt that sex education did not. They were convinced that it encouraged illicit sexual relations among young unmarried people and was therefore immoral. At a public hearing featuring a bland film on the subject, Senator Denton required observers to prove they were 21 or over before admittance. A fundamentalist preacher and member of the Moral Majority, he once advocated capital punishment for adulterers.

BANNING BOOKS

The election of Reagan and other conservatives in Washington also brought new life to censorship movements throughout the country. Book burning and book banning began to gain headway among far-right groups as they sought to purge what they felt were immoral influences on children in schools and libraries.

From November, 1980, to May, 1981, the American Library Association counted attempts to remove or restrict access to 148 different books in 34 states for bad language, pornography and other alleged evils. Mel and Norma Gabler, operators of the largest "textbook clearinghouse" in the nation, claimed that inquiries had increased 50 per cent after the election, according to a report in *The New York Times*. It said that in the town of Onida, South Dakota, birth control information was removed from the high school guidance office, and the word 'evolution' was banned in advanced biology. *Brave New World* and *Catcher in the Rye* were dropped from classes in literature, and the award-winning children's book, *Run, Shelley, Run,* was banned from the library. The newspaper also reported that in Des Moines, a high school production of "Grease," the Broadway musical, was banned, and in Mount Diablo, California, *Ms. Magazine* was taken out of the school library.[17]

Leading the movement were the Moral Majority, the Christian Broadcasting Network, Heritage Foundation, Pro-Family Forum and other religious and conservative groups. "Their focus," said *The New York Times*, "is no longer a specific book or course of study but rather the very nature of public education itself." Their target was "secular humanism," which they saw as a philosophy that places man at the center of the universe and encourages free thought and scientific inquiry without deference to a supreme being and without absolute standards of ethics.[18]

Thus, the Reagan Administration and its allies in Congress, who were elected largely on their vow to "get the government off our backs," set out instead to give the government control over some of the most intimate aspects of American lives.

While removing almost all restrictions disliked by business, they sought new restrictions over individual lives. While showing concern about human rights under Communist rule, they did not mind violating the rights of free speech in the United States by implying that critics were Communists or immoral.

In the words of Burton Zwiebach, a professor of political theory at Queens College, "the conservatives' policies show that freedom is no more than a slogan." He said the whole program showed "the hollowness of the conservatives' commitment to freedom." Said the ACLU, "If the Moral Majority has its way, you'd better start praying. Their agenda is clear and frightening: they mean to capture the power of government and use it to establish a nightmare of religious and political orthodoxy."[19]

Gary Potter, president of Catholics for Christian Political Action, spelled out the moralists' aims more literally by saying: "When the Christian majority takes over this country, there will be no satanic churches, no more free distribution of pornography, no more abortion on demand and no more talk of rights for homosexuals. After the Christian majority takes control, pluralism will be seen as immoral and evil, and the state will not permit anybody the right to practice evil."[20]

8

Helping the Rich Get Richer

*This is what you want. This is what you've
been asking for. We're going to give it to you —
if you'll help us.*
                    Treasury Secretary Donald Regan[1]

One way to understand President Reagan's economic
philosophy is to look at his tax cut package. It all hangs out
there. Simply put, the package was designed to stimulate the
economy by reducing taxes, mostly for business and the well-
to-do, because they are more likely to invest the savings in productive enterprises. Under this theory, people in lower-income
brackets would benefit eventually from an increased number of
jobs created by expanded investments, and the government
would get more revenues because more people would be paying
taxes at lower rates.

Reaganites called this the "supply-side" theory because its
aim was to encourage new production and thus "get the
economy moving again," to use the President's oft-stated
words. Critics called it "trickle-down" economics, the idea that
the more profitable business becomes, the more likely some of
the milk and honey will trickle down to those at the bottom of
the scale.

A timely bible for supply siders happened to become a best-
seller just as the new Administration took office. *Wealth and
Poverty,* by George Gilder, program director of the International Center for Economic Policy Studies in New York, arrived in the nick of time, with a philosophical underpinning for
the "new beginning." Budget Director Stockman liked the
book so much that he had dozens of copies distributed to top
Administration officials. The book was a modern-day version
of Adam Smith's *The Wealth of Nations,* a ringing defense of

old-time capitalism and free enterprise with minimum government control.

With this tome in hand, Reagan decided to propose individual tax cuts of 10 per cent per year for three years, an idea that had been kicking around Congress since 1978 in a bill titled, "Kemp-Roth," named for its Republican sponsors, Rep. Jack Kemp and Senator William Roth. The cuts were to be equal in percentage terms for everyone starting July 1, 1981. For business, Reagan offered greatly relaxed depreciation rates with substantial savings designed to stimulate new investment in property and equipment. The business tax plan was similar to one also considered in Congress nicknamed "Conable-Jones" for its House sponsors, Republican Barber Conable and Democrat James Jones.

BORN IN BUSINESS WORLD

Both plans originated in trade organizations, which figured prominently in both advisory and financial capacities in the Republican Presidential campaign. They had been pushed hard on Capitol Hill by business-oriented Political Action Committees which have come to dominate campaign contributions for Congressional candidates in recent years.

Business interests had helped write such tax proposals into the Republican Party platform. When Ronald Reagan was nominated, he was already locked into Kemp-Roth and Conable-Jones, which he enthusiastically endorsed during the campaign. Like many candidates before him, he figured that favoring substantial tax cuts would boost his chances of victory.

Once in office, he naturally installed advocates of such taxes in key policy positions in his Administration, from Budget Director to Under Secretary of the Treasury for Tax and Economic Policy. The latter position, which had been upgraded from assistant secretary, was given to Norman Ture, who had originally developed much the same proposals while working for the National Association of Manufacturers. There was no evidence that any serious alternatives were considered.

Under normal circumstances, virtually any tax cut would be widely accepted. But many leading economists did not like what Reagan proposed. They considered the plans too risky because of the nation's high inflation rate and large federal deficits. They feared that taxpayers would not put their newly acquired funds into savings accounts and productive investments in sufficient amounts to turn the country around.

Some officials of the Reagan Administration later acknowledged problems. Both Treasury Undersecretary Ture and Murray Weidenbaum, chairman of the Council of Economic Advisers, agreed with critics that Kemp-Roth was inflationary. They recognized that the Administration was basing its forecasts on hope rather than evidence. When asked by House Democrats for evidence that Kemp-Roth would work, Treasury Secretary Donald Regan said that while there really was no evidence that the theory would work, there was evidence that the old theories had not worked. While campaigning for the Presidential nomination, George Bush had called Kemp-Roth "voodoo economics," a term that rose up to haunt him later.

WALL STREET WORRIES

Critics outside the government included many conservative advocates of "supply-side" economics. One of them was Henry Kaufman, executive partner of Salomon Brothers, a leading investment house on Wall Street. He called the Reagan tax plan "exceedingly expansionary" and said it would bring even higher interest rates and continued inflation. He said it would be better to balance the budget in fiscal 1982, adding that credit markets were already in a "precarious" condition and would be made worse by the tax cuts.

Liberal economists were even more critical. Walter Heller, former chairman of the Council of Economic Affairs under Democratic administrations, called supply side economics "Laetrile for the cancer of inflation." He said the Administration was "hooked on the supply-side fairy tale" into thinking that the proposed cuts would result in much increased work efforts, savings and investments when "nothing in the historical record supports" such an idea.

Heller's comments were especially pertinent, because he was the architect of a successful tax plan under President Kennedy frequently cited by the Reaganites as proof that their plan would work. Heller said conditions were far different then, however, with a balanced budget and an inflation rate of only 2 per cent.

When Kemp-Roth first gained currency in Congress in 1978, *Business Week* called it "irresponsible" and said it would "touch off an inflationary spiral (that) would wreck the country and impoverish everyone on a fixed income."[2] More recently, *The New York Times* said the plan was too much of a gamble. "If Kemp-Roth promises anything for the nation's chances of ending stagflation," said the paper, "it is harm. It is too small to generate the growth the Administration expects from it and too large and potentially inflationary to gamble on."[3]

A study by the Brookings Institute came to similar conclusions. Reporting on a conference held in 1979, the widely respected think tank often linked to the Democrats doubted that the proposed tax cuts would bring the economic growth expected. Although the cuts might have some effect, it said, they would not raise production enough to offset the cost to government "even with the most generous estimates of the total labor supply response."

The crux of the matter hinged on what recipients of the tax cuts would do with the money saved. A survey by *U.S. News & World Report* in March while the bill was being discussed indicated that people in middle- and lower-income brackets would spend the cash on themselves immediately while upper-income people would save and invest "much" of the money.[4] A Roper Poll in August reported that only 8 per cent of 2,000 adults interviewed said they would invest the proceeds, and 22 per cent said they would save them.[5]

One reason why so many people would spend the money instead of invest it was the relatively small amount involved for most taxpayers and the high cost of living. Although President Reagan was technically correct in saying that taxes would be cut "across the board," the effect of applying the same percentage to all income levels meant little or no dollar savings in lower and middle income brackets, with the great bulk of dollar savings going to the wealthiest taxpayers.

For most people, those with incomes of $20,000 or less, the tax cuts were illusory. Social Security tax increases and inflation-caused "bracket-creep" would wipe out projected income tax savings, leaving these taxpayers with less money, rather than more, after taxes.[6]

As these offsetting factors began to become known, criticism grew, especially on the Democratic side of Congress.

There were hints that the Administration had not been altogether forthright in talking of tax cuts without mentioning the net negative effect on many taxpayers. There also were increasing fears that the tax cuts, on top of huge military expenditures, might send the economy into a tailspin.

Sensitive to these criticisms and fears, the Reagan Administration took steps to blunt them. It decided to reduce the first of three yearly 10 per cent cuts to 5 per cent and start it on October 1, 1981, instead of July 1. That made the plan 5-10-10 rather than 10-10-10 over a 33-month period. To answer the charge of deception, Administration officials decided to send their heaviest hitter to address a joint session of Congress marking his triumphal return from the assassination attempt. Citing what he called "common misconceptions," President Reagan said the tax discussion should not have to do with how much of a tax cut but "how much of a tax *increase* should be imposed on the taxpayer in 1982." Referring to a "gigantic tax increase . . . (already built into the system)," he said, "We are proposing nothing more than a reduction of that increase. The people have a right to know that even with our plan, they will be paying more in taxes, but not as much more."

In his television appeal for Congress and the public to support the tax reduction package, he chose not to go into the large number of proposed new breaks for well-to-do Americans. They included virtually wiping out inheritance taxes in an effort to help inheritors of farms and small businesses keep from selling out in order to pay the taxes, a common complaint. Also in the plan was a substantial reduction in the capital gains tax used primarily by wealthy people to get away from higher individual income rates and a reduction in the top rate for individuals. As the measure proceeded through Congress, the Administration tacked on numerous other benefits, mostly for the wealthy, in order to win passage.

CUTS IN BUSINESS TAXES

The proposed cuts in business taxes did not receive as much attention as those for individuals, because they were not as controversial. Leading Democrats were not averse to providing further tax incentives to business to help stimulate the economy. However, the scope of the Reagan plan met increasing criticism since it would virtually wipe out the system of spreading capital costs over the lifetime of the items involved. As originally proposed, the plan would have allowed businesses to write off the cost of buildings in 10 years instead of 30 years or more, to write off most machinery and equipment in five years instead of many times that, and most motor vehicles in three years instead of the usual five years or more. This proposal became known as 10-5-3.

In response to critics, Reagan officials later decided to pare it down to 15-10-5-3 by having most business structures depreciated in 15 years instead of 10. Public utility structures would still be allowed 10 years for depreciation.

Business backers of the tax cut argued that American firms needed the cuts to keep up with inflation and to compete better with foreign companies. These interests had complained for years about taxes even while the corporate share of federal tax revenue dropped from about 30 per cent in 1955 to only 14 per cent in 1979.

Their campaign for more "capital formation" took on the aura of a religion, spearheaded by the American Council for Capital Formation, which had many business leaders among its members. "Our federal income tax system," said the Council, "is biased in favor of consumption and against the saving and productive investment so necessary to help reverse our declining productivity. Reflecting depression-oriented social views favoring income distribution from rich to poor, the individual income tax system is characterized by steeply progressive marginal rates. These high rates blunt incentives to work, save and invest."[7]

Did American voters give a mandate to reverse that alleged bias? They certainly did, said the Council. "On November 4," declared the Council, "American taxpayers recognized these deficiencies and voted for true tax reform appropriate for the 1980s — lower taxes, a fairer tax burden and taxes that do not unduly penalize productive work, saving and investment."

Actually, added the Council, true tax reform had gotten started with legislation in 1969 and 1976 which reduced rates on savings, cut maximum capital gains from 49 to 28 per cent, cut the corporate tax rate and liberalized the investment tax credit, which gives business firms extra deductions for new machinery. Passed over completely by the Council and its allies, however, was the question of why more breaks should be added to these earlier ones at a time when, according to the Commerce Department, business investment was at the highest point since World War II.[8]

RATIONALE QUESTIONED

Another question raised by critics related to the claim that American business was at a disadvantage in competing with foreign firms because of lower depreciation rates in this country. A study by the International Monetary Fund showed that depreciation rates were much costlier to business in Japan and West Germany, the two most productive countries in the world. The same study pointed out that Great Britain had the most generous rates and yet the hard-pressed island had the least to show for it.

According to Jay Angoff of the Tax Reform Research Group, the proposed rates would be so generous to some firms that they would bring negative tax rates, in which the government would owe companies rather than the other way around. Harvard Professor Dale Jorgensen said the business tax plan was "like applying a gold-plated band-aid to a gunshot wound. It is by far the most expensive form of treatment you could conceive of, and is totally ineffective in stopping the flow of blood."[9]

The London *Economist* called the idea "snake oil," saying that U.S. corporations were not over-taxed by international standards. The prestigious magazine went on to say that "investment booms arise mainly from an encouraging economic climate, not from accelerated depreciation schemes."[10] It suggested, instead, that the Reagan Administration reduce the federal deficit or lower interest rates.

One of the main purposes of lower depreciation rates was to bolster basic industries such as automobiles and steel. But tax reductions do no good when there is little or no profit to tax, as was the case with these industries for several years. Several economists also pointed out that the generous rates would be available to all businesses, including ones not considered productive, thus thwarting the purpose of the plan.

Business firms already had a host of tax incentives keyed to tax savings, including deferral of foreign income until earnings are brought home, the 10 per cent investment tax credit for job-producing expansions and special benefits for American exporting firms. In addition, firms could hire expert tax advisers to take advantage of every possible opportunity to avoid paying taxes. As a result, many large corporations pay no income taxes year after year, and many others pay at rates lower than a family of four would pay. According to former Rep. Charles Vanik, who kept annual tabs of corporate tax rates, 14 large firms with pre-tax earnings totaling more than $3.5 billion paid not a dime to the U.S. Treasury in 1978. These firms included U.S. Steel, Occidental Petroleum, Lockheed, Boeing and American Airlines. Companies paying less than 2 per cent of earnings included Chase Manhattan Corporation, Allied Chemical, Standard Oil of Ohio, Gulf Oil and Rockwell International. Over 25 years, the average portion of corporate earnings paid in taxes to the federal government dropped by half, from 38 to 19 per cent, according to Rep. Vanik, while the scheduled tax rate was 46 per cent.

CRITICS IN BUSINESS

As debate intensified over the total tax package, it became apparent that not all business representatives favored it and not all Reagan lieutenants were as sanguine as the President about it. At a hearing before the House Ways and Means Committee, business economist Jack Carlson said the individual cuts "would risk excessively stimulating consumer spending, driving up inflation and interest rates and depressing housing activity." A former Nixon official, Carlson was speaking as vice president of the National Association of Realtors. *Fortune* magazine concluded that the accelerated depreciation rates would distort business decisions on investments and create new business subsidies.

Consumer representatives were also opposed. Stephen Brobeck, executive director of the Consumer Federation of America, pointed out that neither personal nor corporate savings had declined in recent years. In testimony before the House Ways and Means Committee, he noted that although the percentage of disposable personal income put into savings was lower in the last five years than in the previous five, it still was higher than in the early 1960s. On the other hand, the proportion of corporate surplus to gross income was higher in the last five years than during all previous five-year periods back to the mid-1950s. Such figures, he said, "suggest that any additional corporate savings produced by further acceleration of depreciation allowances would not stimulate needed business investment."[11]

Brobeck contended that Reagan's depreciation proposals would do little to stem declining productivity, stagnant real wages and double-digit inflation because they failed to come to grips with rising energy prices, volatile interest rates and "myopic corporate planning which tends to maximize short-term profits and waste money on non-productive corporate mergers, real estate, currency, metals and collectibles."[12]

There also was considerable concern over contradictions between the inflationary effect of tax cuts and the opposite effect of strict monetary controls espoused by Reaganites. While some Administration officials were predicting a net effect that would be inflationary, Berryl Sprinkel, Treasury Undersecretary for Monetary Affairs, foresaw "a slowdown in economic activity" because of the tight money policy.[13]

LOOPHOLES KEPT OPEN

A big problem with the Reagan plan was the rosy assumptions made for production, living costs and other factors. The program was based on the premise that total national production (Gross National Product) would jump from a 1.1 per cent increase in 1981 to increases of 4 to 5 per cent in subsequent years, and consumer prices would drop steadily from an 11.1 per cent increase in 1981 to 5.5 per cent in 1984, while the unemployment rate dropped in smaller steps. Numerous economists contended that these figures were too optimistic.

Jay Angoff of the Tax Reform Research Group summed up the Reagan tax package as a "crazy idea whose time has come. It keeps the poor poor and the working and middle class working and middle class, while helping the rich get richer. It does nothing to help solve the real problem with the American tax code — the $300 billion worth of tax expenditures or loopholes used primarily by rich individuals and corporations." If these loopholes were eliminated, he added, and all income were taxed at the rate set out in the tax code, everyone's tax rates could be reduced substantially and the federal deficit wiped out.[14]

Why did not the Reagan Administration close up at least some of the loopholes rather than create more and favor the wealthy over other taxpayers? That question came up with increasing frequency after the economic program was presented. When Budget Director Stockman was asked by Hobart Rowen of *The Washington Post*, he said: "This Administration was elected to cut taxes, not to raise them."[15] Actually, he had tried to close some loopholes early in the game but was shot down by higher authorities.

MAJOR FEDERAL TAX BREAKS*
(in billions of dollars)

Type of Tax Break	Corporations/Individuals	
Exclusion of benefits and allowances to military personnel	0	$1.6
Deferral of income of domestic international sales corporations (DISC)	$1.6	0
Expensing of research and development	2.0	0
Expensing of oil and gas exploration and development costs	1.9	.9
Excess of percentage over cost depletion for oil and natural gas	.5	1.6
Exclusion of interest on state and local industrial development bonds	1.0	.2
Exclusion of interest on life insurance savings	0	4.0
Dividend and interest exclusion	0	1.3
Deductibility of interest on consumer credit	0	5.3
Deductibility of mortgage interest on owner-occupied homes	0	19.9
Deductibility of property tax on owner-occupied homes	0	8.9
Deferral of capital gains on home sales	0	1.1
Accelerated depreciation	3.6	.2
Capital gains other than timber, iron ore and coal	.9	16.2
Capital gains at death	0	5.1

Type of Tax Break	Corporations/Individuals	

Reduced rates on first $100,000 of corporate income............................7.4........0

Investment credit other than (ESOP's) employee stock ownership plans, also rehabilitation of structures and energy.................................16.4......3.1

Parent personal exemption for students aged 19 or over............................0......1.0

Deductibility of charitable contributions other than education and health........4......7.1

Maximum tax on personal service income ....0.....1.7

Credit for child and dependent care expenses.................................0.....1.0

Exclusion of employer contributions for medical insurance premiums and medical care..............................0.....14.2

Deductibility of medical expenses..............0.....3.6

Deductibility of charitable contributions (health)..............................0.....1.4

Social Security benefits for retired workers.................................0.....9.0

Social Security benefits for dependents and survivors.........................0.....1.3

Exclusion of worker compensation benefits.................................0.....2.7

Exclusion of unemployment insurance benefits.................................0.....5.3

Net exclusion of pension contributions and earnings:
in employer plans.........................0....23.6

in plans for self-employed and others...............................0.....2.1

Exclusion of other employer benefits: premiums on group term life insurance ....0.....1.9

Type of Tax Break   **Corporations/Individuals**

Additional exemption for the elderly . . . . 0 . . . . . . 2.3
Exclusion of veterans disability
  compensation . . . . 0 . . . . . . 1.3
Exclusion of interest on general purpose
  state and local debt . . . . 4.0 . . . . . . 1.9
Tax credit for corporations receiving in-
  come from business in U.S. posses-
  sions 1.0 0
Other tax breaks . . . . 8.1 . . . . . . 9.0

Total for fiscal 1981 . . . . 48.8 . . . . 179.8

Total for corporations and individuals $229

*Based on estimated taxes avoided for fiscal 1981, not in-
  cluding changes voted by Congress in 1981 which are
  summarized elsewhere in this chapter.
Source: Joint Committee on Taxation, March, 1981.

SUGGESTED SAVINGS

There are some tax subsidies that no administration would
dare tackle, such as the interest deduction for mortgages on
principal residences. But there are many others that could be
eliminated at a substantial saving to taxpayers without stir-
ring up any more opposition than the proposed Reagan Budget
cuts did. Ralph Nader's Congress Watch, a lobbying group in
Washington, came up with a possible saving of $52 billion in
what it called "wasteful subsidies to business." It included
$22 billion in tax loopholes; $21 billion in energy subsidies,
mostly for synthetic fuel development; $1 billion in agricultur-
al subsidies, mostly for milk price supports; $2 billion in envi-
ronmental subsidies such as water projects; and $6 billion in
transportation subsidies to airlines, trucking firms and shipping.

The tax loopholes Congress Watch wanted to close or reduce
included expenses of intangible petroleum drilling, depletion
allowances for all industries, subsidies for multinational corporations, expense account living, capital gains for businesses,

the stepped-up basis for capital gains at death, interest on
state and local industrial development bonds and investment
credits for business firms.

"Our catalogue of subsidies," said Congress Watch, "ex-
amines only seven areas of the federal budget. Direct and indirect government assistance to corporations costs Americans
hundreds of billions of dollars annually. It is past time to end
this wasteful, inflationary misuse of taxpayer dollars. Why
won't this Administration follow through on its alleged free
market principles and release U.S. industry from its cocoon of
dependence on public money?"

Such questions were certainly valid subjects for debate, but
they ignored some hard political factors. Neither the Administration nor Congress seemed ready to tackle the most
powerful economic interests in the nation in order to achieve
equity in income taxes. Wealthy individuals and corporations
had a lot of money invested in the Administration and Congress, and they were determined to get some solid returns for
their investments.

CASH FOR COMMITTEE MEMBERS

For example, according to a study by Congress Watch,
members of the tax-writing House Ways and Means Committee received $1.7 million in contributions from business
Political Action Committees during the 1979-1980 campaign
period. Leading contributors were oil, steel, auto, airline and
multinational businesses.

The investment paid off handsomely. The Committee went
even beyond what the Administration wanted in business tax
cuts and virtually repealed corporate taxes. As a result total
government revenues from corporate taxes will drop from 13
to only 7 per cent, based on figures supplied by the Treasury
Department. The Committee voted to drop the basic corporate
tax rate from 46 to 34 per cent over five years and decided to
outdo Reagan's depreciation write-offs by allowing the entire
cost of new equipment and machinery to be deducted in one
year instead of five.

Additional sweeteners were offered to industries which had
contributed large amounts to Committee members. For the oil
industry, which was overflowing so much with money that it
was buying other businesses, the Committee offered new tax

breaks totaling about $14 billion over six years. They included exemption from the windfall profits tax for independent producers of 500 barrels or less of oil a day and additional credits for those who collect royalties on oil production. For airline, auto, mining, paper, railroad and steel companies — so-called "distressed" industries — the Committee voted to hand out Treasury checks totaling $3.3 billion for exchangeable tax credits not used because of low or zero profits in previous years. Some referred to the credits as "corporate food stamps." For multinational corporations, the Committee decided to exclude up to $75,000 in individual earnings from abroad, even though most Americans living abroad already paid little or no tax because of existing income exclusions.

INDIVIDUAL TAX CUTS

For individuals, the Committee accepted virtually the same 5-10-10 personal income tax deductions as the Republicans offered, totaling 25 per cent over three years but members voted to make the third-year cut dependent on economic conditions. Democrats forced a slight tilt in favor of people with incomes between $10,000 and $50,000, plus increased exemptions for those at the bottom of the income scale and increased credits for child care expenses and married taxpayers.

People at the upper end of the scale won much more. The Democrats went along with almost all of the Reagan tax breaks for wealthy individuals, including a drop in the top rate from 70 to 50 per cent, eased requirements for contributions to individual retirement plans (such as IRA and Keogh), increased exemptions for estate taxes and increased exclusions for gifts.

In an $8 billion bow to another "distressed" industry, Democrats decided to create "all-savers certificates" with tax-free interest from lending institutions. Chief beneficiaries would be savings and loan associations, which had lost lots of deposits to money market funds. In order to take advantage of this tax break, however, a taxpayer would have to be in the 32-per-cent-bracket.

The Committee set the pattern of Congressional maneuvering. Still smarting from a humiliating defeat on the budget, Democrats in the House decided to stop at nothing in order to win on the tax issue. That meant wooing the most conservative members of the Party, largely those from the South and

Southwest, with big favors for the oil industry and other wealthy interests.

The Democrats thus started a bidding war. But the Republicans ended it by matching virtually every sweetener. The result was almost complete agreement on a series of tax breaks far beyond any in American history. It also caused further skewing of the tax system in favor of the rich and big business, with the additional loopholes. The struggle for genuine tax reform — to make the system fairer to all taxpayers — suffered its worst setback, as the nation embarked on an economic program so full of risks that few economists outside the Administration saw much chance of avoiding serious trouble.

COMMERCIALS FOR CONGRESS

Any likelihood that the Democrats could have stopped the bandwagon was dissipated by the tremendous pressures applied on Congress by the Republicans and their friends in the business and professional worlds. All during the tax debate, full-page ads placed in key newspapers by these forces sought to drum up public support for the Reagan proposals. In addition, massive letter-writing campaigns were instigated through appeals to employees and stockholders. Small business groups also turned on the heat.

Just before the final vote, Republican legislators launched an unprecedented media blitz including paid advertising to increase pressure further. An ad campaign costing $500,000 over radio and television urged individuals to send messages to Congress with pleas for the Reagan package, not the Democratic package, even though there was little difference between the two. The National Conservative Political Action Committee (NCPAC) began equally costly advertising attacks against 13 Democratic legislators who had not endorsed all of Reagan's plan. And the Committee for Economic Recovery started running radio and TV ads depicting House Speaker Thomas P. (Tip) O'Neill as a deceitful "Christmas speaker" who offered a big package that looked like a tax cut but was not.

President Reagan turned the screws further by giving a nationally televised speech and inviting Democrats to Camp David. With the help of White House aides working for Nofziger, Democratic Governor Fob James of Alabama set off on a thirty-day speaking tour of seven southern states with appeals for the Reagan tax proposals. As a result, Congress was deluged with calls and letters.

In the end, House Democrats were left in complete disarray, with 48 voting for the Reagan plan and others suffering from profound disillusionment and despair. Michael Kinsley, writer for the *New Republic* magazine, a traditional bulwark of Democratic thought, summed up the situation in an article entitled: "The Shame of the Democrats." In it, he lamented the "panicky surrender to lobbying pressure by politicians desperate for support from any quarter," adding that they "sabotaged their own best strategy. Reagan's millions of middle-class supporters don't yet realize that his economic plan, proudly billed as 'not a redistribution program,' in fact, redistributed money from people like themselves to a thin stratum of the economic elite."[16] Said Democratic Rep. Toby Moffett: "We had the chance to be the party of frugality and low deficits, and we've blown it.".

TILT TOWARD UPPER BRACKETS

Democrats were not the only losers. Although all taxpayers appeared to get some tax savings because of the 5-10-10 cuts over three years, most of the breaks went to people in the upper brackets. According to the Joint Committee on Taxation, only 5.6 per cent of the population would get 35 per cent of the savings, while 41 per cent of the people at the bottom end of the scale would get only 8.5 per cent. For an individual with income of $20,000, savings would be only $326 in 1982 and for a married couple with the same income, the savings would be $332. Actually, the breaks were tilted even more toward the well-to-do, because the Committee did not figure in all the special breaks beyond the basic 5-10-10 reductions. The 5 per cent cut went into effect October 1, 1981. The 10 per cent cuts were slated to take effect July 1, 1982 and July 1, 1983. Because of the timing, actual reductions were 1.25 per cent in calendar 1981, 10 per cent in 1982, 19 per cent in 1983 and 23 per cent in 1984.[17]

Some individuals also stood to gain from reductions in capital gains taxes and maximum rates, expanded exemptions for individual pension plans, increased credits for child care and reductions in the windfall profits tax for people receiving oil royalties. In addition, there were higher exemptions for married couples, estate and business owners and Americans working abroad. Business tax savings came mostly in shorter depreciation writeoffs and larger tax credits for research and development. While the bill created a number of new loopholes, it closed one, the commodity tax straddle, a device to shelter taxable income for commodity speculators.

SUMMARY OF MAJOR TAX CHANGES

Individual Income Taxes

Across-the-board cuts: 5% starting October 1, 1981; 10% starting July 1, 1982, and 10% starting July 1, 1983.

Indexing: Taxes reduced to match increase in living costs starting in 1985.

Top bracket: Reduced from 70% to 50% as of January 1, 1982.

Capital gains: Top rate reduced from 28% to 20%.

Tax-exempt savings certificates: Up to $1,000 in interest income for individuals and $2,000 for couples after October 1, 1981, excluded from taxes with purchase of "All Savers Certificates."

Marriage penalty relief: Up to $1,500 deduction for lower earning spouse of two-earner couples for 1982 and up to $3,000 for 1983.

Sale of home: Exclusion from income for taxpayers 55 or older raised from $100,000 to $125,000 effective July 20, 1981, and period for replacing residence without capital gains tax increased from 18 months to two years.

Child care: Credit maximum raised depending on income and number of dependents, beginning in 1982.

Retirement income plans: Beginning in 1982, maximum annual deductible contribution to an Individual Retirement Account (IRA) is increased from $1,500 to $2,000, even for people in group plans; deductible in Keogh plans (for self-employed people) increased from $7,500 to $15,000.

Americans abroad: Income excluded from tax set at $75,000 in 1982, then increased $5,000 per year until 1986.

Estate and gift taxes: Exemption lifted from $175,625 to $225,000 in 1982 and increased annually to $600,000 in 1987, plus reduction in top bracket rate from 70% to 65% in 1982, dropping to 5% each year to 50% in 1985. Also increased annual gift exclusion from $3,000 to $10,000 as of 1982.

Charitable contributions: Individuals who do not itemize deductions may deduct some donations starting in 1982.

Stock options: Rate lowered to capital gains level and paid only when stock is sold.

Business Taxes

Depreciation: Write-offs reduced generally to 15 years for most buildings, 10 years for public utility property, five years for machinery and equipment and three years for most motor vehicles. Entire cost may be deducted in the same year for items costing $5,000 in 1982 and 1983 and up to $10,000 in 1986.

Investment tax credits: For items written off in three years, 6% of cost may be treated as credit; other items, 10%; except buildings.

Leasing: Firms with little or no profit will be free to transfer investment credits and depreciation benefits to other firms through leasing arrangements.

Research and development: Companies can deduct up to 25% for these costs.

Real Estate: Deductions allowed for rehabilitating non-residential buildings in use at least 20 years increased from 10% to 15% or 25%, depending on circumstances.

Small business: Corporate rates reduced in lower brackets in small firms, and accounting requirements relaxed.

Windfall profits tax: Rate cut gradually from 30% to 15% by 1986, and royalty owners to receive $2,500 credit toward that tax for 1981, plus larger credits in subsequent years.

Source: *The Economic Recovery Tax Act of 1981;* Joint Committee on Taxation, August 5, 1981.

BUSTING THE BUDGET

Altogether, the legislation created tax breaks of $750 billion over five years. Four-fifths of the savings will go to individuals and one-fifth to business. The final package was so huge that even some supporters voiced misgivings about it. "I want the Senators to know," said Pete Domenici, Republican chairman of the Senate Budget Committee, "that in order to have a balanced budget in fiscal year 1984 and beyond, we are going to be forced to make major and painful budget reductions beyond those being made this year. We could easily face the necessity of reducing spending by over $80 billion during the next two years."

Democratic Rep. Don J. Pease predicted that figure would be the amount of deficit in 1984, the year Reagan planned to balance the budget. He said he had asked the Congressional Budget Office, the Brookings Institution and the Republican-oriented American Enterprise Institute to predict 1984 figures on the assumption that additional budget cuts were not made and economic factors such as inflation, interest and unemployment did not meet Reagan's optimistic hopes. All three sources, he said, predicted a deficit of about $80 billion. Pease himself said the tax bill would lead to continued high interest rates, stagnate economic growth and "business bankruptcies by the score."[18]

Such large tax cuts over so many years amounted to taking a big risk that everything Reagan predicted would fall into place perfectly. Pease and many others were saying that such hopes were not realistic, and the combination of tax and budget changes would be disastrous for the country. Reagan's own economists were forced to admit that the country did not live up to their expectations during their first six months in office. Some 40 states with tax rates tied to federal ones stood to lose as much as $27 million by 1986, according to Citizens for Tax Justice, a private research group.[19]

In a speech to investors, Richard Nixon's Secretary of Commerce Peter G. Peterson said that when the Reagan economic program was fed into computers, nine out of the 10 readouts said: "Does not compute."

9

Shooting Up the Working Poor

We are shooting real bullets.
Rep. Phil Gramm
(Democratic co-sponsor
of Reagan's budget bill)[1]

On the July day when President Reagan and his friends were celebrating passage of his tax bill containing bonanzas for business and the wealthy, and Congress was completing action on a budget that slashed social programs and boosted money for the Pentagon, an article was published in *The Los Angeles Times* from "Myissha Jones," a clerical worker in Southeast Los Angeles. Choosing to use a pseudonym to avoid drawing "the wrong kind of attention" to her family, she said:

"Ronald Reagan, it's safe to say, has never lived for as much as a weekend in my neighborhood, and I don't think he has even an inkling of how we are already suffering from the economic policies that, he says, will benefit us somewhere down the line. He doesn't understand how the people of the ghetto live; many of them do not fully understand his budget and tax cuts. However, they all understand the bottom line: The rich will get richer, and the poor will get poorer." She proceeded to describe "the effects of living a life of desperation," including having her son arrested and brother shot while she lived like a prisoner in her locked apartment for days for fear of being attacked by hoodlums.[2]

In one sense, Myissa Jones was a rarity. Not many denizens of depressed areas had the desire or ability to write a publishable letter. But she was far from alone in her situation. Indeed, millions of Americans were even less fortunate. At least, she had a job and private quarters that she could barricade if necessary. In fact, she seemed more concerned about crime than financial problems, although she obviously could

151

not afford to move elsewhere. For most people on the lower
rungs of society, the main worry is money.

It is both ironic and sad that a country that has attained
such scientific and economic success as the United States has
been unable to substantially reduce the proportion of citizens
in poverty and desperation. It has not been for lack of trying.
Lyndon Johnson's War on Poverty and efforts to build a Great
Society constituted the most recent efforts to strengthen
justice and redistribute some of the nation's wealth for the
good of all. Unfortunately, the Vietnam War got in the way,
and the failure to finance the war through higher taxes set a
pattern of federal deficits that has defied solution since.

Meanwhile, government spending to help those in need continued to increase, partly because of inflation but also because
of the tendency of government programs to continue growing
almost regardless of their effectiveness or lack of it. As taxes
rose to pay for the programs, a groundswell of resistance
began to make itself known in the tax revolt of a few years ago.
President Carter managed to cut back on some of the federal
burdens and nearly achieved a balanced budget. But like
presidents who preceded him, he failed to find a formula for
alleviating social problems and stimulating ecnomic growth at
the same time.

Inflation has become the biggest stumbling block. Since it
first became serious in the early 1970s, no administration has
found a way to stop the trend toward ever bigger price increases. People with limited incomes have been the hardest hit
because prices of essential items — food, fuel, housing and
health care — have risen faster than the average of all living
costs. These are the people most dependent on government
assistance for basic needs. Rising living costs have severely
added to the burden of life's problems not only for these
millions but for a government trying to help while carrying
nearly a trillion dollars of debt. By 1980, it was clear that the
nation needed to control government spending while preserving federal assistance for those who needed it to survive.

That was exactly what Ronald Reagan said he could do.
Demands for lower federal budgets had been a theme of his for
years. In 1980, he made it his top priority, along with cuts in
taxes and regulations. All during the campaign, he offered
assurances that he would reduce the budget without hurting

those who depended on government assistance. When elderly groups became worried about his earlier remarks about making Social Security voluntary, he told them to relax. When blacks and representatives of the poor became concerned about his hostility toward other programs in general, he promised them that they had nothing to fear.

ACTIONS BELIE PROMISES

But when the first outline of changes emerged from the office of Budget Director David Stockman, the fears and worries began to rise again. The size of the cuts alone — some $49 billion for fiscal 1982 (beginning October 1, 1981) — was far more than anyone expected and far more than any ever proposed before. In addition, there were to be $7 billion in new users fees for boat owners and others who use government services, generally without payment — totalling another $7 billion, for a total change of $56 billion. The user fees were not approved but were proposed again in September.

Stockman hastened to explain that cuts were not made indiscriminately or haphazardly although they were imposed virtually across the board. He said the main aims were to eliminate unintended benefits in the large entitlement programs, reduce benefits to middle- and upper-income groups, reduce subsidies, stretch out capital improvements and consolidate nearly 100 categorical grants with lower funding to states and municipalities. On the other hand, military spending was to be increased at a record rate — totaling more than $1.5 trillion over five years. The net result was a proposed budget of $695 billion, some $44 billion below Carter's for fiscal 1982. But the Reagan budget carried a deficit of $45 billion, well above Carter's projection of $27.5 billion. The campaign promise of a balanced budget was to be fulfilled only in the fourth year, fiscal 1985. But the assumptions made by Stockman's Office of Management and Budget raised a number of questions in Congress and in the financial community. Reagan officials had based their estimates on the hope that inflation and interest rates would drop substantially over the period.

The size of the proposed budget was particularly surprising, for it meant government spending would increase instead of decrease, as Reagan had promised in the campaign. His aides explained that the aim was now merely to "slow down the rate of growth." What pushed spending so high, of course, was the huge increases in the Pentagon budget, to an unprecedented $222 billion the first year, some $32 billion above Carter's projections for the same year.

CHANGE OF TUNE

Actually, relatively little of the total budget was available for cutting. By making the Pentagon exempt, along with some of the big social programs such as Social Security and Medicare in addition to some $95 billion in interest on the national debt, budget cutters were left with little more than $200 billion to play with. That figure also included sensitive social programs involving health, education and welfare, making the task even more difficult.

As for waste and fraud, two familiar demons of the Reagan campaign trail, they were rarely discussed after the Inauguration. Since they were not easily identifiable, there was no way to put a firm figure on them and throw them out. There was general agreement that the Pentagon was the biggest source of wasted funds, but Reagan's decision to increase its budget funds masked any savings.

Early polls showed broad public support for the general outlines of the plan to cut federal spending and taxes while strengthening the military. But when details of some budget cuts began to be known, fear gripped millions of Americans receiving some sort of government benefits. In an effort to reduce those fears, President Reagan hastened again to offer assurances. "Our spending cuts," he said in a speech to the nation, "will not be at the expense of the truly needy. We will, however, seek to eliminate benefits to those who are not truly qualified by reason of need."

HIT LIST STRIKES THE HEART

The storm really struck when Stockman's so-called "Hit List" emerged with detailed data in mid-February, due at first to the unauthorized dissemination of the draft document by the Democratic Study Group in Congress. The informal listing became an immediate best seller in Washington as every interest group sought to find out where it stood with the new Administration.

Most were deeply shocked by what they saw. Hardly a program or service was spared either complete elimination or
substantial reduction in funding. The cries of the wounded
were heard all over the Capital, prompting Administration officials to hastily put seven major programs into a so-called
"social safety net." They included basic Social Security
benefits, Medicare, Supplemental Security Income (welfare for
the blind, disabled and elderly poor), Head Start, school
lunches and breakfasts, veterans' benefits and summer jobs
for youths.

But a closer reading of the "Hit List" indicated that even
these programs were still endangered. For example, Stockman
planned to eliminate the $122 monthly minimum, student ben-
efits and some disability benefits under Social Security. He
also listed cuts in school meals (for children of families not on
welfare) and some veterans' benefits. Most Americans below
the poverty line were getting money from one or more of these
seven programs. So were many people far above the poverty
line. In 1981, the line was at $4,275 annual income for an in-
dividual, $5,660 for a couple and $8,400 for a family of four.

The "truly needy" received repeated assurances on continued assistance. But what did the term really mean? As explained by Administration officials, it referred to people who
could not survive without government aid. The term soon became a bad joke, however, with little laughing among the
millions still not sure how they would fare for the next four
years.

SAFETY NET COMES APART

On one occasion, HHS Secretary Richard Schweiker, watching a television interview of a disabled couple with seven
children living on government assistance, was asked by a reporter whether their benefits would be cut under the Reagan
proposals. He called the family a "classic case of those who are
most in need, the truly needy, and wouldn't have to worry
about being cut by the Reagan budget trims." But other Administration officials confirmed later that the family would
lose at least $6 a week in food stamps for each child in school as
well as other benefits because of reduced federal grants to
states for Medicaid, fuel assistance, and other social services.

To those unacquainted with government programs, the

"social safety net" sounded more protective than it really was. The main aim of the seven programs was to help veterans, the elderly and the disabled of all income levels. Three out of five Americans below the poverty line received either nothing or only a school lunch from these seven programs, according to a study by the Center for the Study of Welfare Policy at the University of Chicago. The Center estimated that most people in this category were working mothers who benefited more from other government programs on the cut list. These included Aid to Families with Dependent Children (AFDC), food stamps, fuel assistance and Medicaid, which provides free medical care for the poor. According to the Center, the typical working mother with two children would lose 15 per cent of her disposable income because of Reagan budget cuts mostly outside of the so-called "safety net," thus leaving her little better off than those depending entirely on government assistance.

A spokesman for Stockman acknowledged that low-paid workers eligible for welfare would be penalized. But he called the penalty "modest" and "not a major change in the work incentive," according to reporter David E. Rosenbaum of *The New York Times.*[3] "The policy decision," added the spokesman, "is that welfare is a safety net and not an income-supplement program."

This marked a radical departure from previous government policy that welfare payments to working parents provide an incentive for them to work and get away from government handouts. It also appeared to contradict Reagan's Workfare philosophy of encouraging people to work rather than depend on welfare. Thus the Administration hit hardest at the working poor, just the people it most wanted to help pull into the mainstream of society.

Between 20 and 25 million people with incomes below 150 per cent of the poverty line were to face reduced incomes because of cuts in only four programs: welfare, public service jobs, food stamps and school lunch programs, according to a study by the Congressional Budget Office (CBO) released in April. Many more would also be affected by cuts in other programs such as Medicaid, unemployment insurance, fuel assistance and health services.

The study drew a jab from Senator Edward Kennedy: "It is ironic and tragic," he said, "that an Administration which proclaims itself to be pro-family has given us an anti-family budget which will put even more pressure on the family structure of those already living at the economic margin. The budget could be the final factor that causes many more families to break apart. For them, the Administration's proposal is one of unequal justice and unfair sacrifice. It penalizes marginal families with children, those headed by women, and particularly those headed by nonwhite women."

PROMISE OF PROSPERITY

In response, Budget Director Stockman said the overall program of spending and tax cuts would benefit the economy by lowering inflation, cutting interest rates and expanding employment, all of which would "vastly outweigh" any income cuts. In his view, the projected income cuts that would hit nearly half of the people with incomes below 150 per cent of the poverty line would not be difficult for them to handle.

The President added: "I think our situation has been greatly distorted. I have to say that I think that some of the purveyors of these programs, the dispensers of these programs, are more worried about losing their position than they are about the people they represent and they're trying to create an image that we are picking on the poor because they don't want to lose their clientele."

The AFL-CIO called the budget cuts "madness." In testimony to the House Budget Committee, President Lane Kirkland of the union federation said "the evidence does not support" the Reagan theory that government spending and deficits cause inflation. He called it "pure fantasy" to believe that budget cuts would reduce tax burdens and improve living standards.

To the contrary, Kirkland said, such policies would add up to more inflation and more unemployment. He called the Reagan proposals "the most costly roll of the dice ever proposed for this nation by economic policy-makers." The Administration, he added, "is gambling with the well-being of those who can ill afford to gamble in order to provide a sure winner for the wealthy who are not asked to take any of the risks." The actions, he continued, "are inequitable, unfair and short-sighted. They are based on an untested theory, unrealistic projections and questionable logic."[4]

Columnist Carl Rowan called the budget cuts "total revolution" by people "not just trying to fight inflation (but) trying
to turn back all the clocks — to wipe out half a century of
social, legal, cultural and racial changes ... We are seeing an
effort in which the occupant of the Oval Office and his
ideological soul brothers seek to impose their ideology even
though the courts have spoken clearly and the people have had
their say through Congress."

Much of the criticism of the budget cuts centered around the
fact that middle- and upper-income people would not have to
sacrifice as much as others since many of them were in the
"social safety net" designed for the poor. For example, one-
third of the $150 billion spent yearly on Social Security
benefits went to people whose outside incomes exceeded their
government benefits. And 86 per cent of those receiving
Medicare payments had incomes above the poverty line, while
92 per cent of veterans and their families receiving benefits
also had income levels above the poverty level.[5]

Rather than cutting the non-needy out of these programs,
the new regime decided to help some of them even more. For
example, President Reagan confirmed his campaign pledge to
repeal the $5,500 limit on outside earnings for retired Social
Security recipients, thus dismissing an opportunity to save
billions for the U.S. Treasury.

SHIPPING PROBLEMS TO THE STATES

Reagan officials found it easier to shoot at those closer to the
economic edge. Among the preferred devices for doing so were
block grants. Picking up remnants of Ford and Nixon initiatives, budget planners decided to lump together about 90
federal services for shipment to states and communities in
seven block grants on the theory that local control would
reduce red tape and increase efficiency. Reagan aides also proposed cutting the funds by a typical 25 per cent to represent
administrative expenses saved at the federal level. This action
left local authorities in effect with reduced funds to handle
large programs with inflationary costs.

One big block grant was planned for programs mostly in the
Department of Health and Human Services. It included programs dealing with child abuse, runaway youths, energy
assistance to low-income people, community mental health
centers, research in primary health care, black lung clinics,

home health services, family planning, alcohol abuse services, drug abuse services, health education, venereal disease control, fluoridation, rat control, rehabilitation of the handicapped, the Community Services Administration (which ran Community Action Programs — CAPs — for the poor) and the Legal Services Corporation, which provided free legal assistance to the poor.

But Congress balked at throwing so many programs into block grants for fear that many would disappear because of budget cuts. Legislators voted to keep many as separate programs, including black lung clinics, migrant health services, venereal disease control, research in primary health care, family planning and rehabilitation of the handicapped. In addition, two new programs were set up for tuberculosis control and counselling adolescents on the case for chastity, the latter at the request of Senator Jeremiah Denton.

Separate block grants also were established for maternal and child health, including seven programs relating to such problems as lead paint, infant death syndrome and hemophilia; preventive health and health services, including home health services, rat control, fluoridation, health education and rape crisis centers; and community services, including CAPs, which were authorized for only one more year. The Community Services Administration was abolished and some of its programs shifted to HHS.

Another part of the budget plan was to combine some 40 educational programs into two block grants with reduced funds. Congress decided, however, to keep separate programs for grants to schools for economically disadvantaged children, handicapped children and adult education while allowing about 30 others to be put into an educational block grant to the states. Among the latter were Follow Through, the Teachers Corps and school library programs.

ATTACKING LEGAL AID FOR THE POOR

The Administration had wanted to let the Legal Services Corporation die by throwing it into the huge block grant. But as a result of objections from numerous groups, including the organized bar which once opposed the program, Congress decided to continue the service separately at a reduced amount with added restrictions.

But through an oversight by President Carter, President Reagan inherited the authority to appoint the entire board which runs the Corporation. This gave him the opportunity to impose further restrictions by naming people who agreed with his opposition to the program. What bothered him and other political conservatives most was the program's success in contesting practices of wealthy growers and large corporations whom they counted as political allies. The fact that divorces were the most common type of case also bothered Reaganites who sought favors from religious groups. The second most common type of case, landlord-tenant disputes, also angered conservatives. Reflecting the feeling of many, Rep. Phil Gramm of Texas said during the Congressional debate: "The program has fallen into the hands of troublemakers who foment discord in the community." *The Washington Post* noted in an editorial that while trying to kill legal services for the poor, President Reagan did nothing to end the subsidy of legal services to corporations and rich people through tax deductions.[6]

Other programs which the Administration told Congress it wanted to eliminate or substantially reduce included:

AID TO FAMILIES WITH DEPENDENT CHILDREN.

This basic welfare program was slated for a 25 per cent cut along with a Workfare requirement that recipients would either be dropped or have reduced benefits. States were permitted to include the value of food stamps and housing subsidies as income in determining AFDC benefits and could prohibit payments to any family with more than $1,000 equity in addition to a house and car. The previous maximum was $2,000. States were also authorized to set up forms of Workfare. Administration officials later issued rules indicating they would enforce the $1,000 limit although it rarely had been enforced before.

FOOD STAMPS.

Reagan wanted a cut of $4 billion over three years. Led by Jesse Helms, Congress went further, tightening eligibility requirements so that about a million people will lose stamps altogether, and another million will get fewer stamps.

HEALTH CARE PROGRAMS NOT IN BLOCK GRANTS.

Reagan wanted to put a "cap" on Medicaid funds and raise fees for Medicaid patients. Congress decided to cut funds to the states less drastically: by 3 per cent in the first year and more in following years. But this will also force states to either reduce services or raise funds to fill the gap because of cost increases. Medicare recipients also will have to pay more for doctor and hospital bills because of changes agreed to by Congress. Furthermore, Congress went along with Administration requests to drop 30 per cent of 187 Professional Standards Review Organizations (PSROs) which monitor hospital and medical practices in order to hold down costs.

JOB PROGRAMS.

Reagan got his request for elimination of all 330,000 public service jobs under CETA (Comprehensive Employment and Training Act), some of which may be taken over by state and local governments where jobs include ambulance dispatchers, firemen and other essential services. In addition, Congress agreed with Reagan's request to cut job training programs substantially and eliminate the automatic 13 weeks beyond the 26-week maximum in unemployment compensation. Congress went along with Reagan's plan to kill an extra 26 weeks beyond the maximum 52 weeks in compensation for people who lose their jobs because of lower-priced imports. Hiring and job training services were also cut at Reagan's request.

SOCIAL SECURITY.

The Administration won Congressional approval for elimination of the $122 monthly minimum, but a wave of public protests later caused both houses of Congress to restore the minimum in October for those already getting it. As a result of other budget action, monthly benefits for 1.2 million college student dependents of Social Security recipients were eliminated.

EDUCATION.

Government aid was reduced for almost all programs, including those previously noted in block grants, though Congress refused to cut as much as Reagan wanted. It decided to require a family means test for college loans only when family income exceeded $30,000, ordered students to pay a 5 per cent assessment fee, raised the interest rate on student loans from 4 to 5 per cent and put a cap on basic education (Pell) grants. Congress also agreed with Reagan in slashing impact aid to schools near government facilities. Head Start was retained intact with increased funds after having been inadvertently omitted from the House bill. Indian education programs were cut substantially.

In the college loan program, new eligibility rules take into account varying costs of school. For a college costing $11,000 a year, a family income of up to $66,000 would still qualify for a $1,000 loan, but for a college costing $4,000, an income over $30,000 might disqualify an applicant.

HOUSING.

Congress agreed with Reagan's request to cut almost 50 per cent from the number of additional low-income families Carter would have made eligible for subsidized housing. It also agreed to raise rental payments for 10 million low-income people from 25 to 30 per cent of their income and raise eligibility requirements for acceptance in public housing projects. Money for farm home mortgages was cut by more than $300 million, and federal aid to communities was slashed by nearly $500 million. Reagan also wanted to eliminate low-interest loans for rehabilitating deteriorated houses. Congress retained the program with reduced funds.

TRANSPORTATION.

Reagan wanted to eliminate all Amtrak passenger lines except Boston-to-Washington trains at a time when patronage was increasing. Congress limited the cut to about one-third. The loss of $271 million out of $930 million in subsidies, however, will mean higher fares and elimination of some of the least profitable routes. Congress was asked to cut mass transit subsidies by more than one-third. Legislators did not go that far, but the cuts of nearly $200 million will mean higher fares in some places and cutbacks on subway construction in other places. The Administration planned to sell the Conrail freight system, and Congress agreed if the line does not meet a profitability test by October, 1983, with fewer government subsidies. Whether Conrail is made more profitable or sold, the net result will mean higher freight charges and higher prices for consumer products moved by rail. Conrail commuter lines are to be transferred to Amtrak after a year. The largest item, the federal highway program, was cut only 12 per cent, thus leaving the same emphasis as before on the most inefficient type of transportation at a time when the nation needs to conserve fuel. An effort by the budget office to raise the tax on fuel for private planes was dropped before it reached Congress because of protests from owners.

CHILD NUTRITION.

Congress went along with cuts of $1.5 billion in child nutrition programs, affecting nearly all of the 27 million children receiving school lunches. Smaller subsidies to schools and higher prices for meals will cause some of the 10 million youngsters getting lunches to lose them. Another 2 million youngsters getting lunches for 20 cents will have to pay at least twice that, possibly five times that amount. Some of the remaining 15 million may see their schools drop out of the program or raise prices because of the higher costs of participating in the program, according to Jeff Becker of the Community Nutrition Institute.[7] Congress also eliminated incentives for serving school breakfasts, which have been generally considered more beneficial than lunches. As a result, many schools were expected to drop out of the program now serving 3.5 million children. Summer feeding programs now serving 700,000 youngsters were cut by one-third. The Women and Infant Children (WIC) program was also cut, with a freeze on the number of recipients at 2.2 million in 1982 and further reductions for the next two years.

VETERANS PROGRAMS.

Reagan officials wanted to make substantial cuts in medical facilities and counseling centers even though general veterans' benefits were supposed to be in the "safety net." Congress made only minor changes including reductions in aid to veterans enrolled in correspondence schools, elimination of loans for college and vocational courses and restrictions on dental and burial benefits.

ARTS AND COMMUNICATIONS

The Administration wanted to cut funds in half for the National Endowment for the Arts and National Endowment for the Humanities, but Congress decided that cuts of one-third were enough. Congress also scaled down proposed cuts in public broadcasting subsidies, but the end result was a 25 per cent cut that left the Corporation for Public Broadcasting (CPB) some $42 million short of its previously scheduled budget for fiscal 1982.

The organization was authorized to experiment with advertising as a potential means of revenue. Since the Nixon Administration, Republicans had been aiming to cut or kill public broadcasting on the grounds that it tended to favor liberal viewpoints. If the CPB is not successful in raising its own budget, it might have to drop some of its highly popular news and public affairs programs, which conservatives particularly dislike. Congress also voted to accept part of a Republican plan to lengthen the life of commercial television and radio licenses from three years to five and seven respectively.

COMMUNITY DEVELOPMENT.

Congress refused to kill the Urban Development Action Grant (UDAG) program, as requested by Reagan, but slashed its funding. Although designed to revive blighted areas of cities, the controversial program gave grants through the states to large corporations such as the Sheraton Division of International Telephone and Telegraph Company for hotels, Prudential Insurance Company for a new office building and the Hilton Corporation for a new hotel.[8]

Reagan also wanted to kill the Economic Development Administration, which provides money for public buildings and industrial parks in both urban and rural areas. Congress decided to keep the program but cut its funding to less than half. And Reagan wanted to kill the Appalachian Regional Commission which helped that depressed area. Congress kept it alive, too, but with only one-seventh of its previous funding. Congress agreed with Reagan in approving $4.2 billion for Community Development Block Grants.

SUPPLEMENTAL SECURITY INCOME.

This basic welfare program was cut by tightening eligibility requirements and repealing disbursements to state vocational rehabilitation agencies for blind or disabled people.

NATIONAL CONSUMER COOPERATIVE BANK.

Here was a relatively small, one-year-old program that fitted perfectly into the Reagan philosophy of helping generate new businesses through loans which would be paid back to the government. But cooperatives traditionally have been disliked by other businesses because of their special privileges on loans and taxes. Reflecting this constituency rather than the free-market philosophy, Reagan officials moved to wipe out the bank entirely. But Congress rescued it with reduced funds for one year to give the organization time to get onto a self-sustaining basis.

DIRE PREDICTIONS

These were the biggest sticking points in the budget battle. They also represented most of the major budget changes except for the mammoth increases in military spending. Altogether, the reductions came to $35 billion for fiscal 1982 beginning October 1, 1981, plus even larger cuts for the following two years for a three-year reduction of $131 billion. The cuts were not as large as President Reagan wanted, but he and other Republicans lost no time in claiming victory. Because of the Pentagon increases and tax cuts, the budget cuts were expected to leave a deficit of $42.5 billion in the 1982 budget of $696 billion.

Like the cuts in the 1982 budget, future cuts will hit even harder at social programs, even slicing into the gigantic military budget, which more than offset all savings in the rest of government. Because of the huge impact on their constituents, many of those voting for the final legislative package did so reluctantly. "Make no mistake about it," said Rep. Leon E. Panetta, a Democrat who supervised the mammoth conference of some 250 House-Senate panels, "it will hurt. It will impact on people. There are children that will no longer be able to afford nutrition benefits. There are those that will lose housing assistance and education assistance. There are communities that will lose highway assistance and mass transit assistance."[9] Nevertheless, Panetta was one of the Democrats urging passage of the final bill because of what he called "a mandate to reduce federal spending."

At one point in the debate over the effects of the budget

cuts, Democratic Rep. Phil Gramm, co-sponsor of the Administration's budget bill, was challenged about his willingness to go through with the cuts affecting so many people of limited means. In an effort to assure his colleague, Gramm said: "We are shooting real bullets." The remark sparked a bitter response from fellow Democrat Thomas Downey: "You're firing real bullets, and when you hit some of these programs, you're going to kill real people."

Senate Budget Committee Chairman Pete V. Domenici called the budget "a crucial step in restoring national economic sanity." House Budget Committee Chairman James R. Jones echoed many other Democrats when he said the cuts would have a "direct and damaging impact on the lives of millions of Americans." Rep. Carl Perkins objected to using social programs to cure inflation. "Cutting back on federal spending for the needy," he told colleagues, "is not the way we are going to cure inflation." He cited "expert testimony" at a committee hearing that all the cuts would lower the inflation rate by only two-tenths of one per cent.[10] Rep. Parren Mitchell predicted that "we are going to be scrambling around trying to make up for the enormous hurt we have imposed on people."[11]

Some Democrats were particularly disturbed by the destruction of so many New Deal and Great Society programs. Referring to "discredited and self-defeating trickle-down theories which led to the Great Depression of the 1930s," Rep. George Crockett said "we have now opted for a return to past injustices and a rejection of present and future promises. Even worse, we have withdrawn support of firmly established productive and vitally needed domestic programs in order to underwrite the most costly armaments program in the history of the world." He claimed that the budget "will not cut government spending . . . will not combat inflation or unemployment. It is not designed to benefit the many, but to enrich the few."[12] Crockett charged that the public had been kept in the dark about the real choices: between putting money into food stamps or military weapons. He blamed "a public relations blitz and pressure from conservative groups," causing both the public and Congress to be "mesmerized into seeing only what the Administration wants them to see." Yet he said he sensed a "growing public awareness that these new policies favor the wealthy and big business over the workers and the underprivileged." He said he feared "fallout of social unrest and mounting rebellion that must inevitably flow from this deliberate widening of the deplorable gap that separates these two societies."[13]

SAVING BUSINESS PROGRAMS

Crockett was referring to the preponderance of cuts in programs affecting lower-income people and the avoidance of equal cuts in many programs affecting business, particularly big business. The biggest bonanza, of course, was the $1.5 trillion defense budget, much of which will go to large corporations without competitive bids. But there were other substantial business-aid programs that escaped damage or were increased in the budget, even though they were contrary to the Administration's free-market philosophy.

One was the Export-Import Bank, which Budget Director David Stockman wanted to trim by 16 per cent. When word of the planned cut got out, some of the big firms that have benefited from the below-market loans applied pressure on Congress and other Administration officials. Even Reagan's Commerce Secretary, Malcolm Baldridge, joined the campaign to restore the cut. Congress eventually added $700 million to Stockman's proposal.

Another was the synfuels program, which Stockman also wanted to cut back substantially. Congress went along with the deep cuts because efforts to develop new types of fuels had proven too costly and too complex to provide much encouragement in the prospects. But as a result of pressure from large firms already committed to some projects, the White House overruled its budget office and decided to grant $400 million to one project involving the Union Oil Company, $2 billion in loan guarantees to the American Natural Resource Company of Detroit and $1.1 billion in loan guarantees to the Exxon Corporation.[14]

Most other subsidies to business and agricultural interests were not touched because of their political clout. One was the set of government programs for the tobacco industry, including the estimated $280 million in annual allotments for tobacco growing. An important cause for passing over this matter was Senator Jesse Helms, the formidable North Carolinian who heads the Senate Agriculture Committee. Even though his wife was a recipient of tobacco allotment money, the Senator continued to insist that government support programs did not constitute any subsidy and took a militant position against any suggested change. Nor did Helms see any conflict between the subsidies and the free enterprise system he championed so avidly.

In some cases, even budget cuts served industry purposes. Such a reverse twist occurred in the Energy Department, where funds for enforcement of oil pricing regulations were slashed, not by 10 or 20 per cent, but by 70 per cent. Before price controls were lifted — ahead of schedule — by President Reagan, the Office of Enforcement had uncovered an estimated $12 billion in oil overcharges during the 1973-to-1976 period and was trying to collect the money on behalf of the public. It had charged every major oil company with being a pricing violator. The budget cuts, however, were so great that former Department General Counsel Paul Bloom called them "amnesty for the oil industry under the guise of budget cutting."[15] Although Energy Department officials later responded to the uproar by partially restoring the funds, overcharges occurring between 1976 and 1980 were likely to be left undisclosed because of staff cuts.

WORKING POOR HIT HARDEST

Hardest hit will undoubtedly be people from below to just above the poverty line. Almost all of the 25 million people below the line get some federal benefits either directly or through local agencies. Few of the restrictions for these people may seem large to budget cutters sitting in Washington: Fewer food stamps for some people, no $122 monthly minimum check from Social Security for others, higher prices for school lunches or no more free lunch, 20 per cent higher rent payments for public housing.

But these seemingly small changes could be devastating to people already on the edge of society. For the so-called "working poor," such reductions could push them into the ranks of "the truly needy." Administration officials acknowledged that cuts in some aid programs would probably make additional people eligible for food stamps and welfare payments. That would mean more applicants at a time when these programs were being cut.

Reagan officials assumed that cuts in social programs would

cause the poor to work harder and get more jobs. But economist Lester Thurow said it was more likely that they would work less in order to regain eligibility for benefits they lost. "Suppose you are one of the working poor," he wrote, "and have a sick child. One choice is to work harder — perhaps by taking a second job — in order to pay the necessary medical bills. Another is to quit working to make yourself eligible for Medicaid. To pose the choices is to give the likely answer."[16]

CRUNCH AT LOCAL LEVEL

The crunch will hit hardest at the local level, particularly in the handling of block grants. All the grants will arrive with 25 per cent taken off the top, allegedly representing the cost of federal administration avoided by the transfer to the states. Inflation might boost the cut to 35 per cent, according to the Congressional Budget Office. To that must be added state administrative costs. That means an effective cut closer to 50 than 25 per cent. Budget cuts scheduled for the following two years will have an even greater impact.

Many people eligible for benefits from block grants would thus not get them or would get only a portion because of the cutbacks. These people may even find that some entire programs will be shelved by local officials in favor of other programs in the same block grant. States will have the authority to allocate funds to various communities and may do so on the basis of political pressures rather than where the greatest needs lie.

While the block grant scheme was being devised by the Reagan Administration, the "new federalism" idea was generally well received. But the changes made by Congress disappointed many state and local officials who will bear the burdens of any adverse results. At the National Conference of State Legislators in July, delegates were described by *New York Times* reporter B.D. Ayres Jr. as very worried about the effects. In a speech to the group, President Reagan urged them not to lose faith in his "dream," which was to ship even more programs to the states, eventually doing away with block grants and giving the states the taxing authority to finance them.[17]

Among the critics was Florida State Representative Richard S. Hodes, president of the Conference. "They told us," he said, "they were going to consolidate individual programs into block grants that we would control without federal strings, and we replied, 'Fine.' Then they told us they would cut the money in the block grants but that we'd save some money by running the programs without federal red tape. And again, we said, 'Fine.' We ended up with deeper cuts than we expected, fewer block grants and more red tape."[18]

Another critic was Peter Shapiro, Essex County Executive in Newark, New Jersey. Writing in *The New York Times*, he noted that state and local officials at first thought Reagan block grants were a Christmas tree filled with gifts. But, said Shapiro, the tree is "booby-trapped. In reality, the Reagan block grant proposal is not a program to let local creativity loose from the constraints of federal restrictions but rather is a clever political device to make local officials take the rap for the hardest part of federal budget cutting." He predicted that "the withering away of federal support for human needs will be devastating," especially in the Northeast and Midwest.[19]

His comments were echoed in a report of the Joint Economic Committee of Congress saying "the federal cutbacks will mean increased fiscal strain and fewer services for local citizens," especially in older cities like Boston, Detroit and Baltimore. The effects from loss of economic development funds, transit subsidies, wastewater treatment aid, public service employment and reduced support for health, education and social programs may be "severe," particularly in the Northeast and Midwest.[20]

OTHER VICTIMS

Among the indirect victims of the budget cuts was a vast array of voluntary citizen groups focusing on everything from civil rights to consumer affairs. Many had come to depend heavily on government funds for their existence, including loans, grants, contracts and money to pay the cost of testifying before governmental agencies. Among the largest recipients were civil rights groups. The National Urban League collected more than $100 million a year, mostly in job-training funds which were reduced. Others included Jesse Jackson's Operation PUSH, the National Council of Negro Women and the Martin Luther King Jr. Center for Social Change. Many other organizations operating in the "public interest" will also be affected.

Americans in all income brackets will have to adjust to reductions in Social Security benefits, Medicare, student aid, federal pay and pensions and various government programs such as water cleanup projects. Reductions in subsidies will also be felt in higher prices for various products and services, such as postal services and public transportation, particularly rapid transit and train service. Everyone will also be affected in some measure by the cut in funds for social research which totaled $1 billion in the previous administration. Chief losers will be universities and private firms that study such things as criminal behavior, economic development, preventive health and human relations.[21]

The budget cuts added up to an abrupt reversal of government policy, from compassion for the poor and helpless to a greater concern for property and the weapons of war. Reagan officials decided to jettison decades of programs designed to build up the country's investment in people, preferring to put the savings into a drive for more material goods.

The thrust of the change was almost too much for some people to accept. House Speaker Thomas P. (Tip) O'Neill do doubt spoke for many when he said: "This budget will close the door on America."

10

Looking for World War III

You can have a winner in a nuclear exchange.[1]
George Bush

With the Iranian hostage crisis resolved in the last minutes of the Carter Administration, the biggest cloud over the head of American foreign relations was lifted with fortunate timing for the incoming regime in Washington. Although the country was not at war with any nation at Inauguration time, there were still numerous and serious threats to peace around the globe. They included the Russian invasion of Afghanistan, the threat of the same in Poland, tensions with European allies, the Iraqi-Iranian war and Arab-Israeli turmoil in the Middle East, a host of miniwars in Africa, internal dissensions throughout Latin America, incipient friction with China over Taiwan and rising frustrations over Japanese imports.

Underlying these problems was a less visible one with even broader implications: the danger of nuclear war, not only between the superpowers but between one or more of the dozen smaller nations with nuclear capability. The Israeli raid on the Iraqi nuclear plant served as a stark reminder of this imminent danger.

Other threats to international stability included revolutions in numerous countries for human rights and increased trade, which bumped up against the interests of propertied classes and multinational corporations in preserving the status quo. Complicating these conditions further were the fundamental threats to life itself from increasing commercialization, pollution and depletion of natural resources. Efforts to control these threats depend to a great extent on communication and cooperation through international organizations, which face new tensions.

As Ronald Reagan took office, many people were wondering

whether he would be able to fulfill his campaign promises of restoring American power and prestige in the world. During his long pursuit for the Presidency, he had frequently exhibited a lack of knowledge and understanding of today's world with his unstudied comments that jarred experts in the fields involved.

A 1950 VIEW OF THE WORLD

At various times, he had advocated sending American military personnel to Afghanistan, Cyprus, Ecuador, Egypt, Lebanon, North Korea, Pakistan, Rhodesia and the Sinai. When tensions arose in Angola in 1976, he said it was "time to eyeball it with Russia." When the Soviets crossed into Afghanistan, he told a friend that the answer was to blockade Cuba, a suggestion he later retracted after talking with campaign aides.

Like many diehard military officers and political reactionaries, he felt that the reason the United States lost in Vietnam was because of unreasonable restraints (presumably against use of nuclear weapons) imposed by the White House. "There is a lesson for all of us in Vietnam," he told a VFW convention in August. "Let us tell those who fought in that war that we will never again ask young men to fight and possibly die in a war our government is afraid to let them win."[2]

In his view, the Carter Administration had unnecessarily demonstrated signs of weakness in allowing Iran to take over the American embassy and hold American hostages for so long. He felt that this country should support any government that stands its ground against communism, regardless of whether that government is an oppressive dictatorship or tolerates some democratic principles. A review of his radio talks, speeches and newspaper columns over the years by Ralph Nader's Citizen Research Group turned up enthusiastic endorsements of such despots as Park in South Korea, Marcos in the Philippines, Somoza in Nicaragua and Pincochet in Chile.[3]

The record of assassinations and other bizarre acts by the CIA did not disturb him either. As a member of the Presidential Commission appointed in 1976 to investigate the agency after the Watergate revelations, he acknowledged that "there had been some misdeeds." But, he added, "almost without ex-

ception, every one of them had been corrected internally by the
CIA before there had ever been an investigation."⁴ He referred
to the widespread criticism of the secret agency as "sniping"
and urged that it and other intelligence agencies be allowed to
"do their jobs" without interruption.⁵

In military matters, candidate Reagan frequently implied
that the country should use its entire arsenal of weapons if
necessary to "preserve peace." Like many conservatives, he
became convinced that the SALT II (Strategic Arms Limitation Talks) agreement had allowed the Soviets to pull far ahead
of the United States in military power. So he favored junking
the agreement and greatly increasing American fire power.

He was also convinced that the Soviets directed nearly every
outbreak of violence or dissension in the world. Like a football
player that he was in college, he tended to view all international affairs as essentially a contest between a freedom-loving
Uncle Sam and a conniving, grasping Russian bear. "Let's not
delude ourselves," he told *The Wall Street Journal* in June,
1980, "the Soviet Union underlies all the unrest that is going
on. If they weren't engaged in this game of dominoes, there
wouldn't be any hot spots in the world."⁶

To him, the struggle for human rights was not as fundamental as the struggle between this country and Russia for
dominance in the world. In 1976, he told a private school audience: "Humanitarian impulses and benevolences are com-
mendable, and they have their place, but . . . it is time that we,
the people of the United States, demanded a policy that puts
our nation's interests as the first priority."⁷ He apparently
meant that this country should support virtually any regime,
regardless how authoritarian, against those who wanted to
overthrow such a government. He was ready to believe that
people who oppose established authority are automatically
Communists or Communist sympathizers even though they
may merely be seeking democratic rights.

George Bush was cut from the same cloth. In an interview
with *The Los Angeles Times* during the campaign, he said,
"You can have a winner in a nuclear exchange."⁸ He seemed
oblivious to the fact that a nuclear war between the two superpowers would leave both a mass of irradiated ashes. Yet as a
former director of the CIA, he was in a position to know better
than almost anyone how futile such a war would be. He also

shared Reagan's view of human rights. On a visit to the Philippines after taking office, he told the ruthless Marcos that "we love your adherence to democratic principles," despite a rigged election giving Marcos an unlimited term as President.

Although the attitudes of Reagan and Bush deeply concerned many experts on foreign affairs, they were not much different than those of the average American, a factor which undoubtedly helped in the election. Numerous polls show that most people see the world nearly as simply as they do and are willing to take considerable risks in order to "stand up to the Russians," as Reaganites frequently said. A poll by *Time* magazine at Inauguration time reported that 80 per cent felt Reagan would make progress in re-establishing American prestige abroad and 86 per cent felt he would succeed in improving the nation's defenses, while 57 per cent even felt that he would achieve peace in the Middle East.[9]

BOOSTING THE PENTAGON

In Reagan's eyes, improving the nation's defenses meant much greater spending than ever before. President Carter had agreed with European allies to increase the military budget above the inflation rate while holding down the rest of the nation's budget to that rate. As President, Reagan went far beyond that by proposing $32 billion more for the Pentagon in 1982 and a total of $1.5 trillion over five years. That would mean a buildup three times the one for Vietnam and a jump in the defense share of the budget from 24 to 32 per cent, in contrast to proportions of 1 to 5 per cent for major U.S. allies.

Why spend so much more on the military while cutting into people-oriented programs such as food stamps and aid to children and the disabled? It was a matter of promises and priorities. Reagan and his aides felt that a substantial boost for the Pentagon was necessary to fulfill campaign pledges and to show the world that at least in terms of money, the United States was determined to bolster its defenses. They particularly wanted to send that message to Moscow.

For several years, right-wing defense experts had been pointing ominously to an allegedly growing budget gap between what the United States and Russia spent each year on arms. In his address to Congress on February 18, Reagan quoted CIA figures showing that the gap since 1970 was $300 billion. On this basis, an extra $184 billion for the Pentagon over four years did not appear out of line.

But there was considerable disagreement about what the Soviets actually were spending on military items. CIA estimates were refuted by several authorities, including Professor Franklyn D. Holzman of Tufts University. He concluded that military spending was about equal in the two countries. More important was whether the Russians had expanded their fire power. On that point, there was general agreement that they had. Since 1970, while U.S. strategic forces doubled their nuclear weapons, the Soviets tripled theirs and pulled ahead on missile submarines. According to John M. Collins of the Congressional Research Service, the Soviets also had pulled ahead on numbers of naval, ground and air forces but decreased their number of intercontinental ballistic missiles to a point about 25 per cent more than American ABMs. And Russia was said to have half of what the united States had in nuclear aircraft.[10]

GAPS IN WEAPON DATA

Missile "gaps" and bomber "gaps," however have had a spotty history in politics. Citing more famous — and equally illusory — ones of the 1950s and 1960s, author Mark Green accused the Administration of exaggerating the Soviet threat. "One can regard [the Soviet] government as despotic and imperialistic," he wrote in the *Village Voice*, "and still believe that the Russians are NOT coming. Yes, they have more missiles on submarines, but 55 per cent of ours are within target range at any time compared to 15 per cent of theirs. Yes, their military manpower exceeds ours by 75 per cent, but they have two hostile borders to defend and we have Canada and Mexico."[11]

Author James Fallows noted another problem in comparing numbers. In his book, *National Defense*, he cited the fact that the number of American fighter planes had fallen from 18,000 in the mid-1950s to 7,000, but added that the comparison fails to indicate the greater sophistication and cost of current aircraft. He said it also failed to indicate a deeper problem: that many pieces of military equipment, such as the M-16 rifle and F-16 plane, had become so complicated that they suffered from frequent breakdowns and could not be handled properly by the current crop of recruits. "Instead of fewer planes doing more," said Fallows, "fewer planes can each do less . . . The more complex fuel control breaks down eight times as often as the simpler one, and takes six times as long to fix . . ."[12]

Comparing numbers of weapons was discredited back in 1976 by an even better known authority, Henry Kissinger, Secretary of State in the Nixon and Ford Administrations. He said the idea of military superiority when each side can annihilate each other "has no operational significance."

Military planners for the Reagan Administration ignored these drawbacks. One of the first acts of the Navy was to approve production of 1,366 McDonnel Douglas F-18 Hornets, the most costly jet fighter ever devised, at about $32 million apiece. Pentagon officials also did not seem worried about the possibility that the Soviets would try to match the record American increases, further escalating the arms race. Nor did Congress appear concerned enough to do much questioning of cost estimates, weapon plans or policies, as *Washington Post* reporter Robert Kaiser pointed out two months after the Reagan requests were presented on Capitol Hill. "Few politicians in Washington," he wrote, "seem to be considering (the military request) just yet. Congress is rushing into the new defense program with unanimity and, thus far, with very little scrutiny."

As a result of the 1980 elections, pro-military legislators increased their dominance in Congress. At the Senate Armed Services Committee, Pentagon booster John Tower took over the chairmanship. His aides told reporters that their aim was not to take time for a serious look at the requests but to rush them through before legislators had to vote on the more politically sensitive cuts in social programs.[13] The net result, like many others in the past, was another effort to increase military spending even beyond the sights set by the White House.

What the Administration got was a free choice. Congressional leaders left it up to the Pentagon to fill in the details of which weapons systems to build and which ones to junk. Columnist Flora Lewis called it "putting the military cart before the national security horse." The underlying notion, she said, was that the United States should build up its visible capacity to use force, and then decide what power should be used as support. "The assumption," she said, "is that if the arsenal is big enough, the country will be ready for whatever might come along . . ."

REVIVING OLD IDEAS

In their haste to boost military spending, Reagan officials did not have time to consider many new options, so they decided to revive some old concepts that had been put on hold, including the ABM, MX missile and the B1 bomber. A big factor in the revival of these highly controversial weapons was lobbying pressure by the companies that stood to profit from them. Even before the Pentagon had decided what to do with the MX, for example, some firms anxious to get contracts hired Smith and Harroff, a Washington public relations firm and political consultancy, to win over public opinion. According to *Washington Post* reporter Maxine Cheshire, the firm was hired to do public opinion surveys in Nevada and Utah, where the MX network would be located, in preparation for an advertising campaign later.[14] The White House eventually decided to place MX missiles in existing silos in other states.

Other defense contractors used ads to generate grassroots support for record Pentagon increases. For example, the LTV Corporation took out full pages ads to trumpet its belief that "we must honor our defense commitment."

A big question apparently not faced by Reagan officials was whether American industry could handle such a large increase in defense business. An unpublicized study by the House Armed Services Committee in December, 1980, questioned the Pentagon's ability to get what it wanted in a "timely, efficient and economic manner." It said the defense industry had been "crippled" by decreasing productivity, antiquated equipment and shortages of skilled labor and certain materials. A further complication was the disappearance of numerous suppliers after Vietnam, leaving the Pentagon with only a few large firms — sometimes only one — to supply each item. In an analysis of the situation for *The National Journal*, writer Michael Gordon offered substantial evidence indicating that the defense industry could not possibly handle the extra business projected by the Reagan Administration.[15]

OVERLOOKING WASTE

Almost completely ignored was the matter of waste. No subject was pounded harder by candidate Reagan than government waste and corruption, for which the Pentagon had become a world-wide symbol. At least $15 billion is spilled through the cracks there each year, according to a recent study by a group of Congressional Republicans, all strong advocates of increased military spending. The General Accounting Office listed 15 areas of "cost reduction opportunities" totaling about $10 billion. Even the National Conservative Foundation found some $25 billion in Pentagon "fat," including golf courses, boating marinas, stables and "frivolous subsidies" of food prices for top military officers and use of enlisted personnel as servants for officers. Republican Senator Mark Hatfield, chairman of the Appropriations Committee, listed items for possible cuts totaling some $100 billion, including use of submarines for the MX missile rather than turning Nevada and Utah into a nuclear railroad switchyard.

Among those concerned was Senator Barry Goldwater, one of the staunchest supporters of a strong military force. He joined fellow Senator Howard Metzenbaum in declaring: "Runaway costs characterize our entire defense procurement program. These vast expenses have nothing to do with maintaining the strength of our military forces. They are, pure and simple, the result of a system that permits Department of Defense officials to operate as though the public purse has no limits. It is a system that can and must be changed."[16]

Yet the best that Reagan waste hunters could do was to find $1.7 billion to be saved in slowing weapons development and restricting travel and office expenses. The President seemed to think that putting Caspar Weinberger (also known as Cap the Knife for his reputation as a budget cutter in the Nixon Administration) in charge of the leakiest department would make haste with the waste. But the problem only got larger and more politically difficult.

Military expenditures tend to be inflationary in themselves because they produce goods for which there are no buyers in the marketplace. That means more dollars chasing the same amount of civilian goods, the classic prescription for higher prices. Merely talking about more military supplies can be inflationary. Within a month of Reagan's defense requests, supplies of some defense-related materials — aluminum, electric motors, and castings, to name a few — became tighter and prices began to escalate rapidly. Reagan fanned the fires further by announcing plans to increase stockpiles of strategic metals and boost military aid to other countries.

Much of the military problem was attributed to poor management. "The Pentagon can't spend what's been appropriated for them already," claimed Rep. Joseph P. Addabbo, chairman of the Defense Subcommittee of the House Appropriations Committee. He maintained in March that the Pentagon had some $120 billion under contract that had not yet been spent.[17] Rep. Les Aspin charged that unspent military funds had risen 80 per cent in four years while other government expenditures had increased only 39 per cent.

Further aggravating the situation was the fact that military work goes largely to highly skilled workers and therefore does not help much with unemployment. Reagan officials undoubtedly were hoping defense contractors would hire many of the workers laid off by auto and steel companies.

RECRUITING PROBLEMS

It was ironic that just when the military services were planning a record expansion, they found themselves losing technicians so fast that not enough remained to handle the weapons already available. In April, Jack Anderson reported that the calibre of soldiers had dropped to the point where 90 per cent of nuclear technicians who took a basic test in Europe failed. Failure rates were only lightly less for artillery crewmen, computer programmers, tank crews and anti-aircraft crews. One unit discovered that a third of its supervisory personnel was functionally illiterate. In joint exercises with NATO allies, American crews regularly finished last in the competition. In some places, highly expensive airplanes sat idle for lack of trained crews or proper parts. [18]

Much of the personnel problem was linked to voluntary recruiting, which tended to attract poor and uneducated people who had trouble getting or keeping a job in civilian life. Yet Reagan stuck by his oft-stated campaign pledge to oppose a draft, despite general agreement that it would raise the educational level and despite a July, 1981, report from the Army saying it needed 100,000 more soldiers than the "voluntary concept" could raise.

Reagan also ran into serious problems in recruiting top officials of the State Department. One of the problems was Jesse Helms. The ultra-conservative Senator quickly and quietly put a firm hold on some eight key appointments at the assistant secretary level. Helms, who the late columnist John Osborne said "personifies ugly conservative extremism," explained that he was merely trying to make sure that all of those named had views coinciding with those of the President.[19] In fact, he was trying to force his own views on State Department policy by holding up Senatorial confirmation until he got the appointees he wanted. While the White House observed the infighting silently, Helms succeeded in pressuring some appointees to pay him lip service. It was not until the end of April that he reluctantly allowed the confirmations to proceed, while expressing undiplomatic misgivings about some of the nominees.

Among other controversial nominations were those of Richard Allen as White House national security adviser, Jeane Kirkpatrick as United Nations Ambassador, William Clark as Deputy Secretary of State, Ernest Lefever as an assistant secretary and Alexander Haig as Secretary of State, as discussed in Chapter 4.

THE HAIG PROBLEM

None was more controversial than Haig. Yet none of the candidates for Secretary of State fitted the requirements of Reagan and his principal advisers better than he did. Haig shared their basic views that the Soviets were the principal source of world tension and that the United States should take a hard line to confront them around the world. As a career general who had headed NATO (North American Treaty Organization) forces in Europe, he fully agreed with the plans for building up American military power to help "close the window of vulnerability," a phrase that became repeated often by Reagan and his aides.

The mention of his name, however, stirred up bitter memories for many Republicans as well as Democrats, largely because of his role in the Nixon White House during the Watergate cover-up. They did not like the idea of having such a

man represent the United States around the globe. They were
particularly concerned about the tapes that revealed his advice
to Nixon on how to thwart investigators in the Watergate affair, his wiretapping of reporters and fellow White House officials while working as an aide to Henry Kissinger and his
pressure on Vice President Gerald Ford to pardon Nixon if the
President resigned. Some critics also were offended by Haig's
reputation as a "bootlicker" to higher officials who boosted
him up the ranks so rapidly.

Because of rumors that Haig had been even more deeply involved in the Watergate cover-up than publicly reported,
Democrats in the Senate sought to obtain hitherto unheard
tapes. But they were blocked by Republicans who had enough
votes for confirmation.

Senate approval, however, did not end the Haig matter. It
only opened up a new phase, which began on the day he took
office. Shortly after Reagan had taken the Presidential oath,
Haig presented the President with his own plan for taking full
charge of all foreign policy matters. He was apparently concerned that if he did not stake out his turf quickly and surely,
he might wind up in a power struggle with Richard Allen, the
President's national security adviser, and other White House
officials. Haig knew well the difficulties that previous
Secretaries of State had encountered, and he did not want to
fall into the same trap.

But instead of strengthening his role, the memorandum immediately put him into the catbird seat of controversy. Publicity about the incident forced President Reagan to put down the
proud general with a firm but gentle reminder that Reagan
would reserve the ultimate power to handle foreign affairs in
his Administration. The boldness and quickness of Haig's
thrust startled other Reagan officials and put them on notice
to keep a close watch on his future moves.

Within a few weeks, Reagan was pushed into another
dispute when Haig attempted to have himself named head of a
crisis team at the White House. Reagan made it clear that Vice
President Bush was the more logical person for the job as second in line to the Presidency. Still another bizarre episode
arose shortly after Reagan was shot. Appearing before television cameras in the White House, Haig announced in quivering
words, "I am in control here," even though there was no

reason or authority for him to assume command of the government at that point.

He also stirred the pique of Defense Secretary Weinberger
because of a foreign policy chart excluding Weinberger, and he
jarred Commerce Secretary Malcolm Baldridge by holding his
own meetings with the Japanese in efforts to get voluntary
reductions in automobile imports. At that point, Reagan apparently made him sheathe his sword, for the infighting seemed to decrease.

But not the headlines. They began to focus on his hard-line
statements and willingness to jump into many of the world's
hot spots with a theme from the 1950s: that the Soviets were
behind all the tensions in the world and were the greatest
threat to world peace. He told the House Foreign Affairs Committee that the Soviets had a "hit list" in this hemisphere with
designs "for the ultimate takeover of Central America." Bringing back the old "domino" theory, he said the first target was
seizure of Nicaragua, then El Salvador, Honduras and
Guatemala, in that order.

MIDDLE EAST

In further testimony, Haig said it might be necessary to
send American troops to help preserve peace in the Sinai and
to relax legislation barring American aid to Pakistan because
of its secret development of nuclear devices. All these moves
were called necessary to counter communism.

Haig saw "Soviet adventurism" in South Asia, Southwest
Africa, the Persian Gulf and the Middle East as well as Latin
America. The "most dangerous" trend, in his view, was "the
growth of Soviet military power, which is now capable of supporting an imperial foreign policy." Touring the Middle East
later, he kept up the line that it was the Soviets who were the
prime troublemakers there. Such a view was news to the Arabs
and Israelis. Later, the State Department said Haig had been
misunderstood.

More accurately, what was misunderstood was the whole
Middle East situation. The fixation on a Soviet threat appeared to blind Administration leaders to more fundamental
issues between Israel and the Arab nations there. One was
what to do with the Palestinian refugees seeking autonomy instead of control by Israel. Another was what to do about new

Jewish settlements on captured Arab land. Previous adminis-
trations had tried to get Israel to make some concessions on
these points but failed. The only bright spot was the Israeli-
Egypt pact involving return of the Sinai Peninsula to Cairo.
Impartial experts on the Middle East, including the European
Economic Community, generally agree that no solution to the
deep conflicts in the area is possible without a plan to solve the
Palestinian and West Bank disputes.

But Administration officials chose to give top priority to the
proposed sale of five AWAC radar observation planes for
Saudi Arabia. The purpose was two-fold:

● To show friendship to a key Arab state and thus offset to
some extent the much greater aid for Israel, which receives
more American aid each year than any other nation, and

● To give the United States a better way to watch
developments such as potential Soviet incursions in the
general area, through cooperative use of the data obtained by
the wide-ranging devices.

But Administration officials miscalculated the depth of opposition to the sale in Congress when it was proposed in the
Spring. It did not realize the power of the Israeli lobby, which
corraled more than a majority of both the House and Senate on
a petition to block the sale.

Instead of giving up, however, Administration officials
decided to hold back temporarily and try again. Meanwhile,
Israeli planes bombed the Iraqi nuclear plant, and the White
House decided to hold up a shipment of fighter planes as a sign
of Washington displeasure. Secretary of Defense Weinberger
called the bombing a "shocking offense against international
law." Israel was reminded also of the law prohibiting recipients of American military equipment from using it for other
than defensive purposes.

Then, the Israelis, in retaliation for an Arab rocket attack
that killed three citizens, launched a bombing raid on a Beirut
residential area that killed over 300 people. The White House
voiced strong criticism of the raid, as did leading Jewish
groups and many others. They felt Israeli Prime Minister
Menachem Begin had gone too far.

But pressure to release the planes resumed, and the White
House eventually released the planes without having determined whether there had been any violation of the law on

defensive use of American military equipment. Administration officials again capitulated to the power of the Israeli lobby.

Despite this second hard lesson, Reagan and his aides decided to try again to get Congress to approve the AWAC deal. Opponents again lined up legislators against it, and the Administration was forced to shift gears again. Meanwhile, the White House announced a formal military alliance with Israel apparently without gaining any concessions from Israel. It meant even less likelihood that the Administration would be able to achieve the "strategic alliances" it sought in the troubled area.

The policy errors were quickly and forcefully underscored by King Hussein of Jordan. The normally discreet friend of the United States called the Reagan moves "simplistic." He said the Arabs did not agree with the American view that the Soviets were the main problem in the Mideast. He warned that unless the Palestinian and West Bank problems were resolved with justice, peace would not be found. He deplored the failure of Israel or the United States to take seriously a peace proposal to that effect by Saudi Crown Prince Fahd.

EL SALVADOR

Reagan officials set similar traps for themselves in many other parts of the world. None were more bizarre or embarrassing than the lessons they learned in El Salvador. Their plan began to unfold within days of the Inauguration. Articles began appearing in the press, including one by columnist Cord Meyer, a former CIA official, saying that Soviet arms were being shipped to rebels there through Cuba and leftist Nicaragua. Within a short time, President Reagan and Secretary Haig announced that they had picked El Salvador as the place where they would draw the line against "international terrorism" directed by the Soviet Union and its "Cuban proxy." They called it "a textbook case of indirect armed aggression by Communist powers." They announced that a group of American advisers had already been sent there, along with increased military supplies, including helicopters, to help the ruling junta combat the rebels. And they threatened to strike "at the source" (Cuba) of rebel supplies unless shipments were stopped.

The announcement immediately aroused a barrage of wor-

ries in the news media and elsewhere that such action could
lead to another Vietnam, which began in the same way, with
shipments of a few "advisers" and materials. Administration
officials appeared stunned by the adverse response, largely
because they had never understood the depth of the public
backlash against Vietnam.

Their attempts to calm public fears sounded so much like the
explanations of Vietnam that the fears were only fanned further. In answer to a question about El Salvador at a press conference, President Reagan replied: "What we're doing is going
to the aid of a government that asked that aid of a neighboring
country — and a friendly country in our hemisphere — (to) try
to halt the infiltration into the Americas by terrorists and by
outside interference, and those who aren't just aiming at El
Salvador but, I think, are aiming at the whole of Central and
possibly later South America and, I'm sure, eventually North
America . . . . We're trying to stop this destabilizing force of
terrorism and guerrilla warfare and revolution from being ex-
ported in here, backed by the Soviet Union and Cuba and those
others we've named."[20] He saw no need to send troops, he said,
echoing another reassurance given the public in the early
stages of Vietnam involvement.

As evidence of a Soviet plot in El Salvador, the State
Department issued a White Paper written by an American
Embassy officer in Mexico. The eight-page summary of
documents allegedly captured from Communists in El
Salvador indicated that a Communist Salvadoran had once
traveled to numerous countries, including Russia, on a shop-
ping trip for arms and ammunition. American reporters immediately relayed the "news" as valid proof of the charges,
although the State Department itself offered no proof, and the
documents were highly questionable. Editorial comment was
almost unanimously supportive, helping to quench the fires of
public concern.

But reverberations from an earlier event in El Salvador
began to puncture the calm. In a country where some 14,000
citizens had been brutally murdered — and many mutilated —
during the previous 12 months, the killing of four more was
hardly news. But the four were Americans and included three
Catholic nuns and another woman. Their bodies were found
beside a rural road near their burned out van. Ironically, the at-

tention given to El Salvador by the State Department in-creased coverage of these and other mass murders there.

Previously, Administration officials had tried to dismiss the brutal repressions of the populace in El Salvador as work of rebel forces, adding that conditions could be worse with a Com-munist takeover. At one point, Haig suggested that the women "may have tried to run a roadblock," implying that they were revolutionaries. Jeane Kirkpatrick, the newly ap-pointed U.S. Ambassador to the United Nations, offered a similar theory.

But an investigative FBI crew that went there reported no evidence that the four women were political activists. Later findings indicated that the real killers had been national guard troops, not a surprising conclusion in view of the thousands of other slayings blamed on them. The result was a severe set-back to the Administration's plan to pursue its simplistic theories in a world more complicated than ever. But, rather than reversing its policies, it started to downplay events in El Salvador.

A worse blow for the Administration came in June, with a story in *The Wall Street Journal* quoting the author of the State Department White Paper as admitting numerous errors and exaggerations. The cat was finally out of the bag. As discussed in Chapter 3, the whole Reagan plan to draw a line in El Salvador became a shambles.

HELPING THE JUNTAS

However, Reagan officials did not give up. They prepared a long list of countries, including others in Latin America, where they were determined to assist assorted dictators and military juntas in subjugating dissident elements, which were all con-sidered Communist terrorists. One was Guatemala, where military and police death squads similar to those in El Salvador had wiped out political opponents by the thousands. The Carter Administration had suspended aid there on the grounds of human rights violations. But Reaganites decided to resume it.

According to Allan Nairn of the Council on Hemispheric Af-fairs, the policy reversal was preceded by a series of junkets to the country by various right-wing American individuals and organizations, including Young Americans for Freedom, the

Heritage Foundation, Moral Majority, Young Republicans'
National Federation, American Conserative Union, Conservative Caucus and Reagan's own Citizens for the Republic, a
campaign fund-raising group. Resumption of aid was apparently arranged by ex-CIA official Vernon Walters, a Haig
aide, and included an agreement by the State Department to
stop criticizing Guatemalan human rights violations.[21]

Honduras was another sensitive spot, where a right-wing
government was reportedly planning to launch a war against
the leftist regime of neighboring Nicaragua. The State Department agreed to supply helicopters to help the Hondurans.

In July, the Administration added still other oppressive
governments to its list of new friends. It announced that the
U.S. government would no longer object to loans from international development banks to Chile, Argentina, Paraguay and
Uruguay. Carter had decided to oppose such loans in order to
pressure the countries to improve their human rights policies.
Reagan officials said the nations had made sufficient improvements. They also asked Congress for permission to
transfer military equipment from South Korea to Uruguay, a
country accused of having one of the worst records on human
rights.

As the Reagan policy evolved, columnist I.F. Stone tried to
blow the whistle. "Someone should remind Secretary Haig,"
he wrote, "that the class struggle was not invented by Karl
Marx, and that revolution is not a recent gadget manufactured
for export in Moscow. Social turmoil in Central America has
roots three centuries old, first in Spanish and then in North
American exploitation. The new forces of opposition are
diverse .... They all draw help from their opposite numbers
and sympathizers elsewhere in the hemisphere and in Europe.

"Even a deal with Havana or Moscow would only shut off a
trickle. It would not stem the tide of change. It is fed as much
by the Gospels and by Jefferson as by Marx. Were this the pre-
thermonuclear age, this Administration's reversion to a
mangy and time-worn demonology would only be of regional
concern. But with 50,000 nuclear warheads ready to go, the
whole world is threatened when such fantasies begin to invade
the realm of policy."[22]

Reagan's approach to world problems was especially pleas-
ing to large corporations, which the Administration seemed

ready to befriend whenever asked. Business influence on foreign policy has always been strong, particularly in Latin America and the Middle East, but never so strong as under the Reagan-Haig crew.

CORPORATE CONSIDERATIONS.

Business interests showed their muscle with a vengeance in early March when they got the State Department to abruptly dismiss all members of the U.S. delegation to a United Nations Law of the Sea Conference. The effect was to scuttle chances of getting international agreement on controlling exploration of the oceans for the sake of future generations. Delegates from 158 nations were assembled in New York to approve a final draft of work begun seven years before when they learned that the American delegates had been suddenly replaced by appointees more attuned to U.S. commercial interests.

The reason, said State Department officials, was the possibility that treaty restrictions would hamper U.S. military maneuvers. But military forces were exempted from the treaty. Closer to the real reason, reported Nicholas Burnett in *The Washington Post*, was pressure from lobbyists for several American mining companies, which opposed any restrictions. The key firms — Kennecott Copper, Lockheed Aircraft, U.S. Steel Corporation and International Nickel — were similarly opposed to sharing seabed treasures with a common pool including Third World nations. Each company headed a consortium of firms poised to explore the ocean bed.[23]

Commercial interests also got in the way of the grain embargo which Carter had imposed against the Soviet Union as punishment for invading Afghanistan. During the campaign, Reagan repeatedly voiced opposition to the embargo in farm areas, where it was unpopular because of its inhibiting effect on food prices. But when Reagan took office, he began to fear that lifting the embargo might indicate a softening of the Administration's hard line regarding the Soviets. The political turmoil in Poland caused Secretary Haig to advise against lifting the embargo until it was clear that the Soviets would not invade Poland. Yet the President, finding pressure from farmers paramount, decided to lift the embargo in April while the danger of an invasion was still substantial. Administration

officials spent the next few days insisting that the decision indicated no change in attitude toward Moscow.

Lifting of the embargo raised a wry bread-and-butter issue
that spread further embarrassment over the Reagan hard-
liners. Jealous of wheat farmers, dairy farmers pointed to some
400 million pounds of surplus frozen butter, which the government was stuck with after buying it at subsidized prices. If the
Russians could buy American bread, why not butter, too, they
asked. But Haig said that to give them butter would "send the
wrong signal" to the Russians and would cost taxpayers about
$50 million. In order to save face, he then turned around and
sold it at an even larger loss to New Zealand for re-sale to
Russia. Thus, while the Administration was trying to appear
tough with the Russians, it managed to give them both bread
and butter at bargain prices — the latter at $1 a pound — while
many Americans were paying double that price.

TILT TOWARD SOUTH AFRICA

Economic considerations were also key factors in the Reagan
policy on South Africa. The widely perceived "tilt" of the Administration toward that racially segregated nation was due
more to American imports of gold, diamonds and other
minerals than to any other factor. In a television interview,
President Reagan called the nation "strategically essential to
the free world in its production of minerals we all must
have . . ."[24]

But racial factors were also involved in the new "tilt."
Carter had ruled out renewal of formal relations with the country's apartheid policies. But because of pressure mainly from
southern conservatives led by Senator Helms, Reagan officials
became more and more willing to risk alienating American
blacks and others seeking to "improve" relations with South
Africa while maintaining an official "neutrality."

The "tilt" gradually became more pronounced. In June, the
trade embargo was lifted partially to allow shipment of
medical supplies. By late August, the Administration removed
all doubt about its feelings after 4,000 South African troops in-
vaded Angola illegally in order to wipe out guerrillas that
threatened South Africa's control of neighboring Namibia.
The action quickly brought a resolution of condemnation by
the United Nations Security Council, 13 to 1, with the United

States casting the only negative vote. The vote came just one day after Assistant Secretary of State Chester Crocker vowed that the U.S. would not "choose between black and white" in dealing with South Africa. The action, which was condemned particularly by civil rights leaders, marked the first split with American allies which had sought for five years to arrange a plan for Namibian independence.

Further adding to the anger of blacks, particularly those in African countries, Reagan earlier asked Congress to repeal the Clark Amendment, a law banning U.S. aid to guerrillas fighting in Angola (and northern Namibia) for control of rich mineral deposits. The Amendment had been passed by Congress in 1976 after disclosure of American covert aid to anti-Marxist forces in Angola. Reagan officials insisted that they had no plans to renew such aid but merely wanted to be freed from unreasonable restrictions. The request was made despite public warnings from Nigeria, a large supplier of oil to the U.S., that such action would be considered hostile toward the black movement in Africa.

AID TO MULTI-NATIONAL FIRMS

Reagan officials were so beholden to multi-national corporations that they opposed a world-wide move to restrict the promotion of commercial infant formula. At the request of three American firms, which sell about $150 million of the product overseas, the White House decided to cast the sole negative vote against a code approved by 118 other nations in the United Nations World Health Assembly.

Before the vote in May, both the State Department and the Department of Health and Human Services had advised against opposing the U.S. move. So had two top officials of the Agency for International Development (AID), who declared that they would quit in protest if a negative vote were cast. The threat failed to budge the White House, and their resignations were accepted. Reagan officials disregarded the risk of offending many Third World nations which favored the restrictions because of evidence that promotion of baby formulas led to many deaths and illnesses from water contamination in primitive areas.

While promoting foreign trade for American business, Administration officials showed no interest in developing the economic strength of countries that needed U.S. goods but did not have the means of getting them. Nor were they concerned about humanitarian needs for food and medical supplies. Although the United States already devoted the smallest percentage of its revenue to foreign economic aid of any western nation, Reagan officials decided to reduce that portion still more. And they did so with the flourish and deception of a Madison Avenue advertising agency.

When the new head of the Agency for International Development (AID) found some $28 million in unfinished projects in 11 needy countries, he decided to cancel them and dramatize the savings by issuing an over-size check for that amount to President Reagan. In a White House ceremony attended by a beaming Reagan, AID Administrator M. Peter McPherson cited Haiti as an example, saying he had found $1.5 million in unspent funds there. "We all know," he told reporters, "that Haiti is a poor country. There is no doubt in anyone's mind that foreign aid is a vital part of its lifeline. However, I have decided to cut $1.5 million from the Haitian program because it is not being effectively spent . . ."

The gimmick won massive newspaper space and lots of television coverage. One paper that did not bite was *The Baltimore Sun*, which commented: "What troubles us . . . is the intensity that has to go into trying to make hay out of cutting off funds to poor people . . . In Bangladesh, where annual income is less than $100 per person, you can buy a bowl of rice for about 10 cents . . . If we wanted to, we could play around with how many bowls of rice $28 million would buy . . ."[25]

Administration officials also cut back on the long-standing Food for Peace program, which helps poor nations buy American food with low-interest loans. The wisdom of the reduction was immediately questioned by leading experts on nutrition and world hunger. At hearings of the House Agriculture Committee in July, they said the emphasis on export trade ignores a greater need of helping needy nations develop their own food-growing capacities. They estimated that one-fourth of the world's population suffers from malnutrition or hunger. The hearings received virtually no attention from the media, however, since they occurred while the budget reconciliation was under way.

Although ostensibly done to reduce federal spending, many

foreign aid cuts were made with the hope that private business would take up the slack. Such a policy was especially welcomed by multi-national companies, which already benefited from special tax breaks and from an organization known as OPIC (Overseas Investment Corporation), a federally funded program that provides insurance against export losses.

In their book, *Global Reach*, Richard Barnet and Ronald Muller pointed out that some multinational firms have become larger than many nations and have become a law unto themselves. With their pressure to keep wages down and squeeze out large concessions from governments grateful for their payrolls, these firms tend to become destructive forces that leave the people and land they exploit in far worse condition than before. Such operations also tend to increase political tensions by increasing demands for new wants and rights that neither the companies nor host countries are able or willing to grant. These factors, they contend, do more to increase turmoil in Third World nations than the opportunism of Moscow.[26]

EXPANDING ARMS SALES

Weapon sales to other countries were also made a high priority of the new Administration. In late May, 1982 the State Department announced that it had dropped a number of restrictions left over from the Carter Administration concerning human rights, nuclear proliferation and regional balances. Speaking to the Aerospace Industries Association in May, James L. Buckley, Undersecretary for Security Assistance, called the restrictions "theology," amounting to "an American withdrawal from world responsibilties." He urged Congress to authorize low-interest loans to countries that otherwise could not afford to buy American weapons.[27]

In naming China and Pakistan as the first two major beneficiaries of the new policy, however, the Administration ran into another wave of criticism. Pakistan, a country which had refused to allow inspection of its nuclear production facilities, was slated to receive $3 billion in military and economic assistance over five years. The purpose was to shore up a nation threatened by the Soviet invasion of Afghanistan and prevent it from siding with Moscow. But announcement of the proposal immediately drew bitter protests from India and from critics who cited General Zia's long record of violating human rights.

Even more opposition arose to Haig's announcement that the United States would sell "lethal weapons" to the People's Republic of China. Former Secretary of State Cyrus Vance called it "needlessly provocative" and said it "substantially diminished . . . any influence we have left over the Soviet Union." *Pravda* called the move "an escalation of reckless policy . . . highly dangerous to the cause of peace," adding ominously that the Soviet Union "will take such measures that will be dictated by the emerging situation."[28].

NUCLEAR PROLIFERATION

The fact that many other nations had gained the ability to produce nuclear weapons did not seem to bother Reagan. In January, 1980, he had observed: "I just don't think it's any of our business."[29] After taking office, he changed his tune, saying that strict controls should be applied to nations with nuclear capabilities. But he saw no problem in selling nuclear power plants to any nation that wanted them even though they could be converted into bomb production.

Critics were especially concerned about the effect of increased arms sales on nuclear proliferation. The degree of concern apparently surprised Reagan officials, who issued a policy statement designed to calm the fears only after the Israeli raid on the Iraqi nuclear plant in June. The statement declared that the United States was determined to prevent the spread of nuclear weapons but that it would continue to ship nuclear fuel and technology, along with conventional arms, in order to bolster the "legitimate security needs" of recipient nations and reduce their motivation to produce nuclear bombs. "In the final analysis," said the document, "the success of our efforts depends on our ability to improve regional global stability and reduce those motivations that can drive countries toward nuclear explosives." It added that the United States would "not inhibit or set back civil reprocessing and breeder reactor development in nations with advanced nuclear power programs where it does not constitute a proliferation risk." Yet such a capability can produce plutonium for bombs. The statement only increased fears further. Critics charged that it would tend to promote rather than restrict nuclear weapons and would further destroy whatever effectiveness the nuclear proliferation treaty had.

As if these provocations were not enough, the Reagan Administration renewed the possibility of war with nerve gas. It convinced Congress to pass a proposal to equip a new chemical plant in Pine Bluff, Arkansas, for nerve gas production, which previous administrations had banned. An effort by Senator Mark O. Hatfield to kill the proposal of Senator John W. Warner lost, 50 to 48. Hatfield said the Administration-backed plan had not received adequate hearings or debate and would amount to "launching this country on a system that could bring disaster to the earth."[30] The plan was included without debate in an overall budget bill passed by the House.

One of the most momentous decisions of the Reagan Administration was to proceed with production of neutron weapons and store them in the United States rather than Europe, where opposition to them has been intense ever since they had been proposed in 1977. Designed for European operations, the nuclear devices produce fatal levels of radiation far beyond blast effects, resulting in maximum human casualties and minimum property damage. The announcement in August marked the launching of the biggest nuclear buildup in history, including new submarine missiles, new warheads for land and air-launched missiles, plus more bombs.

INCREASING TENSIONS WITH ALLIES

Neutron weapons were considered an essential part of an "integrated battlefield" strategy previously rejected by President Carter. It called for the capacity to fight conventional, chemical and nuclear wars in many parts of the world at once. Defense Secretary Weinberger contended that neutron weapons would add a deterrent that would make a Soviet tank invasion of Europe less likely and would help in future arms talks by allowing the United States to lead from strength.

But the decision caused a wave of bombings directed at Americans in Germany and increased the possibility of serious problems with other European allies, especially in France and other countries where anti-nuclear, anti-military sentiments were increasing. The protests from Moscow were particularly ominous. Tass called the move "another extremely dangerous step" toward intensifying the arms race and "enhancing the threat of nuclear war." The Soviet news agency called the neutron warhead "the most inhuman type of weapon of mass annihilation."

The net effect of all these thrusts, said Senate Minority Leader Robert Byrd, was a dangerous increase in "the global tension index." He said a foreign policy "predicated on a singular, ideological preoccupation with the Soviet Union . . . is doomed to failure and potentially harmful to our national interests." Among what he called "festering sores" that "can only be exploited to the advantage of the Soviet Union" were the Administration's misunderstanding of the Middle East, failure to recognize the seriousness of nuclear proliferation, an indiscriminate arms sales policy, the over-estimation of Soviet involvement in El Salvador and the lifting of the grain embargo. Byrd particularly questioned the "incessant rhetorical baiting" of the Russians by implying that their international influence was weakening while there was a danger of an invasion into Poland.[31]

Similar rumblings were growing in Europe. Gaston Thorn, president of the Commission of the European Communities, told *The International Herald Tribune* in July that Europeans were getting worried and anxious about Reagan's policies, both economic and political.[32] Newly elected Francois Mitterand of France was particularly disturbed about the Reagan stand in Latin America and the propensity to bait the Russians. German leaders voiced fears that the tough anti-Soviet line could cause the Russians to take military action in Poland or elsewhere. All were also worried about the effect of high interest rates here on their countries.

But the biggest worry was that the Reagan Administration might touch off a nuclear exchange with Russia through some sort of miscalculation. At the core of the Reagan military buildup was the discredited theory that there can be a winner in a nuclear war. Administration officials apparently assumed no other course was available as they promoted the MX missile and other weapon systems dependent on nuclear warheads while continuing to play a waiting game with the Russians on further negotiations for limiting weapons. Although President Reagan retreated somewhat from his insistence that the Russians change their ways before he would agree to any talks, his appointment of war hawks to handle such talks and his delay in responding formally to Leonid Brezhnev's early call for talks indicated little hope of progress in the near future. As *The New York Times* observed, "public interest in those talks seems to have declined even as the danger increases."[33]

DANGERS OF A NUCLEAR WAR

A similar conclusion was reached at a conference on nuclear war prospects in Holland in mid-April. "There is a growing feeling," said retired American Admiral Gene R. LaRocque, director of the Center for Defense Information, "that we are moving inexorably toward a nuclear war in Europe." He added that "it seems unfair that nuclear war will be fought over, and in, the nations which have nothing to say about whether nuclear weapons are to be used." He was referring to Western European nations, which have grown increasingly reluctant to allow nuclear weapons to be stationed there. He and others at the Conference on Nuclear War in Europe were especially wary of the increased American emphasis on military solutions to world problems. Instead of making the Western World more secure, said LaRocque, nuclear weapons were causing more anxiety than ever.[34] On the day of the Conference, India and Pakistan both announced new atomic tests.

But the dangers felt so vividly by some people did not seem to worry the Reagan Administration. It continued to send arms and other aid to virtually every country that showed an anti-Red flag while proceeding to build up the nation's military might at a record pace. It continued to perpetuate the myth that the Soviets were more militarily powerful and all that was needed for U.S. security was more nuclear fire power. The probability that the Soviets will step up their own weaponry was either not considered or dismissed as irrelevant.

It was enough to make some of the most thoughtful and knowledgeable people despair. One was George F. Kennan, the former U.S. Ambassador to Moscow. In an article in *Russia* quarterly, he said: "We are being carried along at this very moment towards a new military conflict — a conflict which could not conceivably end, for any of the parties, in anything less than disaster." He pointed out that "modern history offers no example of the cultivation by rival powers of armed force on a massive scale which did not in the end lead to an outbreak of hostilities. And there is no reason to believe that our measure of control over this fateful process is any larger than that of the powers that have been caught up in it in the past.''

Kennan made an emotional plea for some powerful voice to ask all who possess nuclear weapons to "cease this madness ... for the love of God, for the love of your children and of the civilization to which you belong ... You have no right to hold in your hands ... destructive powers sufficient to put an end to civilized life on a great portion of our planet ... Thrust them from you. The risks you might thereby assume are not greater — could not be greater — than those which you are now incurring for us all.''[35]

No one in the Reagan Administration was listening.

Appendix A

How Your Representatives Voted

Did your legislator in Washington vote the way you would have on the big Reagan changes in 1981?

Theoretically, Members of Congress are elected to represent the people of their districts and states in all matters considered by the legislative branch of the government. In the real world of politics, however, many things dilute true representation.

One is the problem of determining just how the people of a certain district or state feel about various issues. Polls and questionnaires do not necessarily give an accurate picture, since many who participate in them may be forced to come to a decision with faulty or insufficient information. There also may not be time for canvassing the public before a legislative decision must be made. Another problem is the extra influence exerted on lawmakers by large contributors and personal friends whose interests may not coincide with that of the public. Further weakening true representation is the fact that votes are occasionally traded among legislators without regard to the views of the public. The popular will may be thwarted further by demands of a political party or leader for joint efforts on certain issues. Adding to these problems is the complexity of many issues, resulting in votes that sometimes may be misleading without detailed explanation.

All these complications were at work in 1981 when the Reagan program was presented to Congress. Making the legislative job even more difficult were the sheer size of the demands and the limited time available for study and debate. Because of these difficulties, it is unreasonable to put much weight on any single vote or failure to vote on a matter of importance to a constituent. Far more indicative of a legislator's performance is the pattern that emerges from votes on key issues.

One Sweet Guy

In an effort to show the patterns for members of the 97th Congress on Reagan proposals, eight votes were selected in both the Senate and the House. Each topic was chosen not only for its importance to the public but for its ability to clearly indicate a political viewpoint. In an effort to make comparison easier, votes are listed as either "A" (against the Administration's position) or "F" (for the Reagan position). But readers should check each item to see if those designations correspond with their own views before evaluating a legislator's record.

SENATE VOTES

In the Senate, the eight issues included:

(1) A proposal by Senators Bumpers and Kennedy for a three-year individual tax reduction tilted much more than the Administration or the Democratic bills in favor of lower- and middle-income taxpayers. It would have increased the standard deduction and reduced rates more in the lower brackets than the other bills did. It was defeated on July 23 with 76 "no" votes and "22" "yes" votes. A "no" vote was for the Administration position.

(2) A proposal by Senator Moynihan to restore approximately $1 billion in school funds cut by the Reagan-dominated Budget Committee for elementary and secondary education. It was defeated on March 31 with 65 "no" votes and 33 "yes" votes. A "no" vote was for the Administration position.

(3) An amendment by Senator Biden to restore approximately $400 million for fuel assistance to low-income people. It was beaten on April 2 with 61 negative votes and 37 "yes" votes. A "no" vote was for the Administration position.

(4) A motion by Senator Moynihan to reduce money for water projects by $200 million and increase money for mass transit and student loans by the same amount. It was defeated May 11 with 55 negative votes and 30 "yes" votes. A "no" vote was for the Administration position.

(5) A motion by Senator Hatfield to block a strongly worded condemnation of the Administration's proposed cuts in Social Security benefits. The motion was passed on May 20 with 49 "yes" votes and 48 "no" votes. The action opened the way for a milder rebuke that passed by a 96-0 vote. A "yes" vote on the Hatfield motion was for the Administration position.

(6) A motion by Senator Helms to prohibit use of Medicaid

funds for abortions except to save a mother's life. The proposal was passed on May 21 with 52 "yes" votes and 43 "no" votes. A "yes" vote was for the Administration position.

(7) A motion by Senator Symms to require all but the poorest families to pay up to 30 per cent of their income as partial payment for food stamps. The proposal was defeated June 10 with 66 "no" votes and 33 "yes" votes. A "yes" vote was for the Administration position.

(8) A move by Senator Moynihan to prevent a reduction in funds for child welfare and foster care services. It was defeated on June 23 with 52 "no" votes and 46 "yes" votes. A "no" vote was for the Administration position.

HOUSE VOTES

In the House, the eight issues included:

(1) A motion by Rep. Obey to replace the official Republican budget plan with one involving a smaller increase for the military, fewer cuts in social programs and a balanced budget without a tax cut for fiscal 1982. It was beaten on May 6 with 303 "no" votes and 119 "yes" votes. A "no" vote was for the Administration position.

(2) The Gramm-Latta resolution, the basic Administration budget bill calling for $31 billion in revenue cuts. The measure was passed on May 7 with 253 "yes" votes and 176 "no" votes. A positive vote was for the Administration position.

(3) A motion by Rep. Ashbrook to bar use of federal funds for abortions under government employee health insurance. The motion was passed on May 13 with 242 "yes" votes and 153 "no" votes. A "yes" vote was for the Administration position.

(4) A motion by Rep. Bonior to eliminate funds for construction of a plant to produce nerve gas. The move was defeated on June 4 with 220 "no" votes to 135 "yes" votes. A "no" vote was for the Administration position.

(5) A motion by Rep. Weiss to prevent use of federal funds for development of neutron weapons. The move was blocked on June 11 with 293 "no" votes and 88 "yes" votes. A "no" vote was for the Administration.

(6) A proposal by Rep. Wilson to prohibit lawyers for the Legal Services Corporation from bringing class action suits against federal, state or local governments for any reason. The motion was accepted on June 17 with 241 "yes" votes and 167

"no" votes. A "yes" vote was for the Administration position.

(7) A motion by Rep. Bolling designed to require separate votes on major sections of the budget bill rather than one up-or-down vote. The move was an effort by Democrats to preserve some social programs from more drastic cuts. It was defeated on June 25 with 217 "no" votes and 210 "yes" votes. A "no" vote was for the Administration position.

(8) A proposal by Rep. Udall to replace the Administration's tax bill with one more favorable to lower- and middle-income people and less favorable to business and investor interests. It was defeated on July 29 with 288 "no" votes and 144 "yes" votes. A "no" vote was for the Administration position.

Following are tables showing the vote of each legislator in the Senate and House on these matters. Legislators are listed alphabetically by state, with party designation and whether each vote was for ("F") or against ("A") the Reagan Administration position. House members are also identified by district. Numbers over vote columns refer to the issues discussed previously in this section. A question mark indicates absence or failure to vote for or against.

SENATE VOTES

Name and State	Party	1	2	3	4	5	6	7	8
ALABAMA									
Denton	R	F	F	F	F	F	F	F	F
Heflin	D	F	F	F	F	A	?	A	F
ALASKA									
Murkowski	R	F	F	F	F	F	F	A	F
Stevens	R	F	F	F	F	F	A	A	F
ARIZONA									
Goldwater	R	F	F	F	F	F	F	F	F
DeConcini	D	F	A	F	F	A	F	?	A
ARKANSAS									
Bumpers	D	A	A	A	?	A	A	A	A
Pryor	D	A	A	A	A	A	A	A	A
CALIFORNIA									
Hayakawa	R	F	F	F	F	F	A	F	F
Pryor	D	A	A	A	A	A	A	A	A
COLORADO									
Armstrong	R	F	F	F	?	F	F	F	F
Hart	D	A	A	A	F	A	A	A	A

Senate Votes Cont'd

Name and State	Party	1	2	3	4	5	6	7	8
CONNECTICUT									
Weicker	R	F	A	A	A	A	A	A	F
Dodd	D	A	A	A	A	A	A	A	A
DELAWARE									
Roth	R	F	F	A	?	A	F	F	F
Biden	D	A	A	A	A	A	F	F	A
FLORIDA									
Hawkins	R	F	F	F	?	?	F	A	F
Chiles	D	F	A	A	F	A	F	A	A
GEORGIA									
Mattingly	R	F	F	F	F	F	F	F	F
Nunn	D	F	F	F	A	A	A	F	A
HAWAII									
Inouye	D	A	A	A	?	A	A	A	A
Matsunaga	D	A	A	A	A	A	A	A	A
IDAHO									
McClure	R	F	F	F	F	F	F	F	F
Symms	R	F	F	F	F	F	F	F	F
ILLINOIS									
Percy	R	F	F	F	A	F	A	A	F
Dixon	D	F	F	F	A	A	F	A	A
INDIANA									
Lugar	R	F	F	F	A	F	F	F	F
Quayle	R	F	F	F	?	F	F	F	F
IOWA									
Grassley	R	F	F	F	F	F	F	F	F
Jepsen	R	F	F	F	?	F	F	F	F
KANSAS									
Dole	R	F	F	F	F	F	F	A	F
Kassebaum	R	F	F	F	F	F	A	A	F
KENTUCKY									
Ford	D	F	A	A	F	A	F	A	A
Huddleston	D	F	F	F	?	A	F	A	A
LOUISIANA									
Johnston	D	F	F	F	F	A	F	A	A
Long	D	F	F	F	F	A	F	F	A
MAINE									
Cohen	R	F	F	A	A	F	A	A	F
Mitchell	D	A	F	A	A	A	F	A	A
MARYLAND									
Mathias	R	F	F	?	A	?	?	A	A
Sarbanes	D	A	A	A	A	A	A	A	A

One Sweet Guy

Senate Votes Cont'd

Name and State	Party	1	2	3	4	5	6	7	8
MASSACHUSETTS									
Kennedy	D	A	A	A	?	A	A	A	A
Tsongas	D	A	?	A	A	A	A	A	?
MICHIGAN									
Levin	D	A	A	A	A	A	A	A	A
Riegle	D	A	A	A	A	A	A	A	A
MINNESOTA									
Boschwitz	R	F	F	F	F	F	F	A	F
Durenberger	R	F	F	A	A	F	F	A	A
MISSISSIPPI									
Cochran	R	F	F	F	?	F	A	A	F
Stennis	D	F	A	F	F	A	A	F	A
MISSOURI									
Danforth	R	F	F	F	F	F	F	A	F
Eagleton	D	A	A	A	A	A	F	A	A
MONTANA									
Baucus	D	A	A	F	F	A	A	A	A
Melcher	D	F	A	A	F	A	F	A	A
NEBRASKA									
Exon	D	F	F	F	F	A	F	A	F
Zorinsky	D	F	F	F	F	A	F	A	A
NEVADA									
Laxalt	R	F	F	F	F	F	F	F	F
Cannon	D	F	F	A	?	A	F	A	?
NEW HAMPSHIRE									
Humphrey	R	F	F	F	F	F	F	F	F
Rudman	R	F	F	F	?	F	A	A	F
NEW JERSEY									
Bradley	D	F	A	A	A	A	A	A	A
Williams	D	A	?	A	?	A	A	A	A
NEW MEXICO									
Domenici	R	F	F	F	F	F	F	A	F
Schmitt	R	F	F	F	F	F	A	A	F
NEW YORK									
D'Amato	R	F	F	F	F	F	F	A	F
Moynihan	D	F	A	A	A	A	A	A	A
NORTH CAROLINA									
East	R	F	F	F	F	F	F	F	F
Helms	R	F	F	F	F	F	F	F	F
NORTH DAKOTA									
Andrews	R	F	F	F	F	F	F	F	F
Burdick	D	F	A	A	F	A	A	A	A
OHIO									
Glenn	D	A	A	A	A	A	A	A	A
Metzenbaum	D	A	A	A	A	A	A	A	A

Senate Votes Cont'd

Name and State	Party	1	2	3	4	5	6	7	8
OKLAHOMA									
Nickles	R	F	F	F	F	F	F	F	F
Boren	D	F	F	F	F	A	F	F	A
OREGON									
Hatfield	R	F	F	F	F	F	A	A	A
Packwood	R	F	F	F	F	F	A	A	F
PENNSYLVANIA									
Heinz	R	F	F	A	A	F	F	A	A
Specter	R	F	F	A	A	F	A	A	F
RHODE ISLAND									
Chafee	R	F	F	A	A	F	A	A	F
Pell	D	F	A	A	A	A	A	A	A
SOUTH CAROLINA									
Thurmond	R	F	F	F	F	F	F	F	F
Hollings	D	F	A	F	F	A	A	A	A
SOUTH DAKOTA									
Abdnor	R	F	F	F	F	F	F	F	F
Pressler	R	F	F	F	F	?	F	A	A
TENNESSEE									
Baker	R	F	F	F	F	F	A	F	F
Sasser	D	F	A	A	F	A	F	A	A
TEXAS									
Tower	R	F	F	F	F	F	A	F	F
Bentsen	D	F	F	F	F	A	F	A	A
UTAH									
Garn	R	?	F	F	F	F	F	F	F
Hatch	R	F	F	F	F	F	F	F	F
VERMONT									
Stafford	R	F	F	A	F	F	A	A	F
Leahy	D	?	A	A	A	A	A	A	A
VIRGINIA									
Warner	R	F	F	F	F	F	A	F	F
Byrd	D	F	F	F	F	F	A	F	F
WASHINGTON									
Gorton	R	F	F	F	F	F	F	A	F
Jackson	D	A	A	A	F	A	A	A	A
WEST VIRGINIA									
Byrd	D	F	A	F	A	A	F	A	A
Randolph	D	A	A	A	A	A	F	A	A
WISCONSIN									
Kasten	R	F	F	F	F	F	F	F	F
Proxmire	D	A	F	F	A	A	F	F	F
WYOMING									
Simpson	R	F	F	F	F	F	A	A	F
Wallop	R	F	F	F	F	F	A	A	F

HOUSE VOTES

State/District Name	Party	1	2	3	4	5	6	7	8
ALABAMA									
1 Edwards	R	F	F	A	F	?	F	F	F
2 Dickenson	R	F	F	A	?	F	F	F	F
3 Nichols	D	?	F	F	F	F	F	F	A
4 Bevill	D	F	F	F	F	F	F	A	A
5 Flippo	D	F	F	A	?	F	F	A	A
6 Smith	R	F	F	F	F	F	F	F	A
7 Shelby	D	F	F	F	F	F	F	F	F
ALASKA									
* Young	D	F	F	F	F	F	F	F	F
ARIZONA									
1 Rhodes	R	F	F	F	F	F	F	F	F
2 Udall	D	A	A	A	A	F	A	A	A
3 Stump	D	F	F	F	?	F	F	F	F
4 Rudd	R	F	F	F	F	F	F	F	F
ARKANSAS									
1 Alexander	D	F	A	A	F	?	F	A	A
2 Bethune	R	F	F	F	A	F	F	F	F
3 Hammerschmidt	R	F	F	F	F	F	F	F	F
4 Anthony	D	F	F	A	F	F	F	A	F
CALIFORNIA									
1 Chappie	R	F	F	F	F	?	F	F	F
2 Clausen	R	F	F	F	F	F	F	F	F
3 Matsui	D	A	A	A	F	F	A	A	F
4 Fazio	D	A	A	A	F	?	A	A	A
5 Burton, J	D	A	A	?	A	A	A	A	A
6 Burton, P	D	A	A	A	A	A	A	A	A
7 Miller	D	A	A	A	A	A	A	A	A
8 Dellums	D	A	A	A	A	A	A	A	A
9 Stark	D	A	A	A	A	F	A	A	A
10 Edwards	D	A	A	A	A	A	A	A	A
11 Lantos	D	F	A	A	A	F	A	A	F
12 McCloskey	R	F	F	A	A	A	F	A	F
13 Mineta	D	A	A	A	A	F	A	A	F
14 Shumway	R	F	F	F	F	F	F	F	F
15 Coelho	D	F	A	A	F	F	F	A	F
16 Panetta	D	A	A	A	A	F	A	A	A
17 Pashayan	R	F	F	F	?	F	?	F	F
18 Thomas	R	F	F	F	F	F	?	F	F
19 Lagomarsino	R	F	F	F	F	F	F	F	F
20 Goldwater	R	F	F	F	?	F	?	F	F
21 Fiedler	R	F	F	A	F	F	F	F	F
22 Moorhead	R	?	F	F	F	F	F	F	F
23 Beilenson	D	A	A	A	?	A	A	A	A
24 Waxman	D	A	A	?	A	F	A	A	A
25 Roybal	D	A	A	A	A	A	A	A	A
26 Rousselot	R	F	F	F	F	F	F	F	F
27 Dornan	R	F	F	F	F	F	F	F	F
28 Dixon	D	A	A	A	A	A	A	A	A

House Votes Cont'd

State/District Name	Party	1	2	3	4	5	6	7	8
29 Hawkins	D	A	A	A	A	A	A	A	A
30 Danielson	D	A	A	A	A	F	A	?	A
31 Dymally	D	A	A	?	?	?	?	A	A
32 Anderson	D	F	A	A	F	F	F	A	A
33 Grisham	R	F	F	F	?	F	F	F	F
34 Lungren	R	F	F	F	F	F	F	F	F
35 Drier	R	F	F	F	F	F	F	F	F
36 Brown	D	A	A	A	A	?	A	A	A
37 Lewis	R	F	F	F	F	F	F	?	F
38 Patterson	D	A	A	A	A	A	A	A	A
39 Dannemeyer	R	F	F	F	F	F	F	F	F
40 Badham	R	?	F	F	F	F	F	F	F
41 Lowery	R	F	F	F	F	F	F	F	F
42 Hunter	R	F	F	F	F	F	F	F	F
42 Burgener	R	?	F	A	F	F	F	F	F
COLORADO									
1 Schroeder	D	A	A	A	?	A	A	A	F
2 Wirth	D	F	A	A	?	A	A	A	F
3 Kogovsek	D	A	A	A	A	A	A	A	A
4 Brown	R	F	F	A	F	F	F	F	F
5 Kramer	R	F	F	F	F	?	F	F	F
CONNECTICUT									
1 Cotter	D	1	1	1	1	1	1	1	1
2 Gejdenson	D	A	A	A	A	A	A	A	A
3 Denardis	R	F	F	F	A	F	F	F	A
4 McKinney	R	F	F	A	A	A	A	F	F
5 Ratchford	D	A	A	A	A	A	A	A	A
6 Moffett	D	A	A	A	A	A	A	A	A
DELAWARE									
* Evans	R	F	F	A	F	F	F	F	F
FLORIDA									
1 Hutto	D	F	F	F	F	F	F	F	F
2 Fuqua	D	F	F	F	?	F	F	A	F
3 Bennett	D	F	F	A	F	F	A	F	A
4 Chappell	D	F	F	F	?	F	F	F	F
5 McCollom	R	F	F	F	F	F	F	F	F
6 Young	R	F	F	F	F	F	F	F	F
7 Gibbons	D	F	F	F	F	F	F	A	F
8 Ireland	D	F	F	?	F	F	F	F	F
9 Nelson	D	F	F	F	F	F	F	A	F
10 Bafalis	R	F	F	F	F	?	F	F	F
11 Mica	D	F	F	F	F	F	F	A	A
12 Shaw	R	F	F	F	F	F	F	F	F
13 Lehman	D	F	A	A	A	A	?	A	A
14 Pepper	D	A	A	A	?	F	A	A	A
15 Fascell	D	F	A	A	A	F	A	A	A
GEORGIA									
1 Ginn	D	F	F	A	F	F	F	A	F
2 Hatcher	D	F	F	A	F	F	F	A	F

House Votes Cont'd

State/District Name	Party	1	2	3	4	5	6	7	8
3 Brinkley	D	F	F	A	F	F	F	A	F
4 Levitas	D	F	F	A	F	F	A	A	F
5 Fowler	D	A	A	A	F	F	A	A	F
6 Gingrich	R	F	F	F	F	F	F	F	F
7 McDonald	D	F	F	F	F	F	F	F	F
8 Evans	D	?	F	?	F	F	F	F	F
9 Jenkins	D	F	F	A	F	F	F	A	F
10 Barnard	D	F	F	F	F	F	F	F	F
HAWAII									
1 Heftel	D	F	A	A	A	F	F	A	F
2 Akaka	D	A	A	A	F	F	A	A	A
IDAHO									
1 Craig	R	F	F	F	?	F	F	F	F
2 Hansen	R	F	F	F	F	F	F	F	F
ILLINOIS									
1 Washington	D	A	A	A	?	A	A	A	A
2 Savage	D	A	A	A	A	A	A	A	?
3 Russo	D	F	A	F	A	F	A	A	F
4 Derwinski	R	F	F	F	F	?	F	F	F
5 Fary	D	A	A	F	?	F	A	A	F
6 Hyde	R	F	F	F	F	F	F	F	F
7 Collins	D	A	A	A	A	A	A	A	A
8 Rostenkowski	D	F	A	F	F	F	A	A	F
9 Yates	D	A	A	A	A	A	A	A	A
10 Porter	R	F	F	F	A	?	F	F	F
11 Annunzio	D	A	A	F	F	F	A	A	F
12 Crane, P	R	F	F	F	F	F	F	F	F
13 McClory	R	F	F	F	F	F	A	F	F
14 Erlenborn	R	F	F	?	F	?	?	F	F
15 Corcoran	R	F	F	F	F	F	A	F	F
16 Martin	R	F	F	A	?	F	F	F	F
17 O'Brien	R	F	F	F	F	F	F	F	F
18 Michel	R	F	F	F	F	F	F	F	F
19 Railsback	R	F	F	A	A	F	A	F	F
20 Findley	R	F	A	A	F	F	F	F	F
21 Madigan	R	F	F	F	F	?	F	F	F
22 Crane, D	R	F	F	F	F	F	F	F	F
23 Price	D	A	A	A	?	F	A	A	F
24 Simon	D	A	A	F	A	A	A	A	F
INDIANA									
1 Benjamin	D	A	A	F	F	F	F	A	A
2 Fithian	D	?	A	F	A	?	F	A	A
3 Hiler	R	F	F	F	F	F	F	F	F
4 Coats	R	F	F	F	F	F	F	F	F
5 Hillis	R	F	F	F	?	F	F	F	F
6 Evans	D	F	F	F	A	F	A	A	A
7 Myers	R	F	F	F	F	F	F	F	F
8 Deckard	R	F	F	?	A	F	A	F	F
9 Hamilton	D	F	A	F	F	F	A	A	A

House Votes Cont'd

State/District Name	Party	1	2	3	4	5	6	7	8
10 Sharp	D	F	A	F	A	F	A	A	A
11 Jacobs	D	F	F	F	A	A	A	A	A
IOWA									
1 Leach	R	F	F	F	A	A	A	F	F
2 Tauke	R	F	F	F	A	F	F	F	F
3 Evans	R	F	F	F	F	F	F	F	F
4 Smith	D	F	A	F	A	F	A	A	F
5 Harkin	D	A	A	A	A	A	A	A	A
6 Bedell	D	F	A	F	A	A	A	A	A
KANSAS									
1 Roberts	R	F	F	?	F	F	F	F	F
2 Jeffries	R	F	F	F	F	F	F	F	F
3 Winn	R	F	F	F	F	F	F	F	F
4 Glickman	D	F	A	A	A	A	A	A	F
5 Whitaker	R	F	F	F	F	F	F	F	F
KENTUCKY									
1 Hubbard	D	F	A	F	F	F	F	A	F
2 Natcher	D	F	F	F	F	F	F	A	A
3 Mazzoli	D	F	F	F	A	A	A	A	F
4 Snyder	R	F	F	F	F	F	F	F	F
5 Rogers	R	F	F	F	F	F	F	F	F
6 Hopkins	R	F	F	F	A	F	F	F	F
7 Perkins	D	A	A	F	F	F	A	A	A
MARYLAND									
1 Dyson	D	F	F	F	F	F	F	A	A
2 Long	F	A	F	A	F	A	A	A	A
3 Mikulski	D	A	A	A	?	A	A	A	A
4 Holt	R	F	F	F	F	F	F	F	F
5 Hoyer	D	2	2	2	2	2	2	2	A
6 Byron	D	F	F	F	F	F	F	F	F
7 Mitchell	D	A	A	A	A	A	A	A	A
8 Barnes	D	A	A	A	A	A	A	A	A
MASSACHUSETTS									
1 Conte	R	F	F	F	A	F	A	F	A
2 Boland	D	A	A	F	?	?	A	A	A
3 Early	D	A	A	F	?	A	A	A	A
4 Frank	D	A	A	A	A	A	A	A	A
5 Shannon	D	A	A	A	A	A	A	A	F
6 Mavroules	D	A	A	F	A	F	A	A	A
7 Markey	D	A	A	F	A	A	A	A	A
8 O'Neill**	D								
9 Moakley	D	A	A	F	A	A	A	A	A
10 Heckler	R	F	F	F	A	A	A	F	F
11 Donnelly	D	A	A	F	A	A	A	A	A
12 Studds	D	A	A	A	A	A	A	A	A
MICHIGAN									
1 Conyers	D	A	A	A	A	A	A	?	A
2 Pursell	R	F	F	A	?	?	A	F	F
3 Wolpe	D	F	A	A	A	A	A	A	A

House Votes Cont'd

State/District Name	Party	1	2	3	4	5	6	7	8
4 Siljander	R	F	F	F	F	F	F	F	F
5 Sawyer	R	F	F	F	F	F	F	F	F
6 Dunn	R	F	F	A	A	F	A	F	A
7 Kildee	D	A	A	F	A	A	A	A	A
8 Traxler	D	F	A	F	?	?	A	A	F
9 Vander Jagt	R	F	F	F	?	?	?	F	F
10 Albosta	D	F	F	F	?	F	F	A	F
11 Davis	R	F	F	F	F	F	F	F	F
12 Bonior	D	A	A	F	A	A	A	A	A
13 Crockett	D	?	A	?	A	A	?	A	A
14 Hertel	D	A	A	F	F	F	A	A	A
15 Ford	D	A	A	A	A	?	?	A	A
16 Dingell	D	A	A	A	F	F	A	A	F
17 Brodhead	D	A	A	A	A	A	A	A	A
18 Blanchard	D	F	A	A	A	F	A	A	A
19 Broomfield	R	F	F	F	F	F	F	F	F
MINNESOTA									
1 Erdahl	R	F	F	A	A	A	A	F	F
2 Hagedorn	R	F	F	F	F	F	F	F	F
3 Frenzel	R	F	F	A	A	F	F	F	F
4 Vento	D	A	A	F	A	A	A	A	A
5 Sabo	D	A	A	A	A	A	A	A	A
6 Weber	R	F	F	F	A	F	F	F	F
7 Stangeland	R	F	F	F	F	F	F	F	F
8 Oberstar	D	A	A	F	A	A	A	A	A
MISSISSIPPI									
1 Whitten	D	F	A	F	F	F	F	A	A
2 Bowen	D	F	F	F	F	F	A	A	F
3 Montgomery	D	F	F	F	F	F	F	F	F
4 Dowdy	D	3	3	3	3	3	3	3	F
5 Lott	R	F	F	F	F	A	F	F	F
MISSOURI									
1 Clay	D	A	A	A	A	?	A	A	A
2 Young	D	F	F	F	F	F	A	A	F
3 Gephardt	D	F	A	F	F	F	F	A	F
5 Bolling	D	A	A	?	A	?	A	A	A
6 Coleman	R	F	F	F	F	F	F	F	F
7 Taylor	R	F	F	F	F	F	F	F	F
8 Bailey	R	F	F	F	?	?	F	F	F
9 Volkmer	D	F	F	F	F	F	?	A	F
10 Emerson	R	F	F	F	F	F	F	F	F
MONTANA									
1 Williams	D	A	A	A	A	A	A	A	A
2 Marlenee	R	F	F	F	F	A	F	F	F
NEBRASKA									
1 Bereuter	R	F	F	F	F	F	F	F	F
2 Daub	R	F	F	F	F	F	F	F	F
3 Smith	R	F	F	F	F	F	F	F	F

House Votes Cont'd

State/District Name	Party	1	2	3	4	5	6	7	8
NEVADA									
* Santini	D	F	F	F	?	F	F	F	F
NEW HAMPSHIRE									
1 D'Amours	D	A	A	F	F	F	A	A	A
2 Gregg	R	F	F	F	A	F	F	F	F
NEW JERSEY									
1 Florio	D	A	A	A	A	F	?	A	A
2 Hughes	D	F	A	A	F	F	A	A	A
3 Howard	D	A	A	A	?	F	A	A	A
4 Smith	R	F	F	F	A	A	F	F	F
5 Fenwick	R	F	F	A	A	F	F	F	F
6 Forsythe	R	F	F	A	A	A	F	F	F
7 Roukema	R	F	F	A	A	F	F	F	F
8 Roe	D	A	A	?	?	?	A	A	A
9 Hollenbeck	R	F	F	A	A	?	A	F	A
10 Rodino	D	A	A	A	A	A	A	A	A
11 Minish	D	A	A	F	A	F	A	A	A
12 Rinaldo	D	F	F	F	F	F	F	F	F
13 Courter	R	F	F	F	F	F	F	F	F
14 Guarini	D	A	A	A	A	F	A	A	A
15 Dwyer	D	A	A	F	A	F	A	A	A
NEW MEXICO									
1 Lujan	R	F	F	F	?	F	F	F	F
2 Skeen	R	F	F	F	F	F	F	F	F
NEW YORK									
1 Carney	R	F	F	F	?	F	F	F	F
2 Downey	D	A	A	?	A	F	A	A	A
3 Carman	R	F	F	F	F	F	F	F	F
4 Lent	R	F	F	F	F	F	F	F	F
5 McGrath	R	F	F	F	F	F	F	F	F
6 Leboutillier	R	F	F	?	F	F	F	F	F
7 Addabbo	D	A	A	A	A	F	A	A	F
8 Rosenthal	D	A	A	?	A	?	A	A	A
9 Ferraro	D	A	A	A	?	F	A	A	A
10 Biaggi	D	A	A	F	?	F	A	A	F
11 Scheuer	D	A	A	A	A	F	A	A	A
12 Chisholm	D	A	A	A	A	A	A	A	A
13 Solarz	D	A	A	A	A	F	?	A	A
14 Richmond	D	A	A	A	A	A	A	A	A
15 Zeferetti	D	A	A	F	F	F	F	A	A
16 Schumer	D	A	A	A	A	A	A	A	A
17 Molinari	R	F	F	F	F	F	A	F	F
18 Green	R	F	F	A	A	F	A	F	F
19 Rangel	D	A	A	A	A	A	A	A	A
20 Weiss	D	A	A	A	A	A	A	A	A
21 Garcia	D	A	A	A	A	A	A	A	A
22 Bingham	D	A	A	A	A	A	A	A	A
23 Peyser	D	A	A	A	F	A	A	A	A

House Votes Cont'd

State/District Name	Party	1	2	3	4	5	6	7	8
24 Ottinger	D	A	A	?	A	A	A	A	A
25 Fish	R	F	F	F	?	F	A	F	F
26 Gilman	R	F	F	A	F	F	A	F	F
27 McHugh	D	A	A	F	?	A	A	A	A
28 Stratton	D	F	A	F	?	F	F	F	F
29 Solomon	R	F	F	F	F	F	F	F	F
30 Martin	R	F	F	F	F	F	F	F	F
31 Mitchell	R	F	F	?	F	F	F	F	F
32 Wortley	R	F	F	F	F	F	F	F	F
33 Lee	R	F	F	F	F	F	F	F	F
34 Horton	R	F	F	A	F	F	F	F	F
35 Conable	R	F	F	?	F	F	F	F	F
36 Lafalce	D	F	A	A	?	F	A	A	A
37 Nowak	D	F	A	F	A	A	A	A	F
38 Kemp	R	F	F	F	?	F	F	F	F
39 Lundine	D	F	A	A	A	?	?	A	A
NORTH CAROLINA									
1 Jones	D	F	A	A	F	F	F	A	F
2 Fountain	D	F	F	A	F	F	F	A	A
3 Whitley	D	F	A	A	F	?	F	A	A
4 Andrews	D	F	F	A	F	F	F	A	A
5 Neal	D	F	A	A	F	?	F	A	A
6 Johnston	R	F	F	F	F	?	F	F	F
7 Rose	D	F	A	A	F	F	F	A	A
8 Hefner	D	F	A	A	F	F	F	A	A
9 Martin	R	F	F	A	F	F	F	F	F
10 Broyhill	R	F	F	A	F	F	?	F	F
11 Hendon	R	F	F	F	F	F	F	F	F
NORTH DAKOTA									
* Dorgan	D	A	A	F	A	A	A	A	F
OHIO									
1 Gradison	R	F	F	F	F	F	F	A	F
2 Luken	D	F	F	F	A	F	F	A	F
3 Hall	D	F	F	A	A	F	A	A	F
4 Oxley	R	4	4	4	4	4	4	4	F
5 Latta	R	F	F	F	F	F	F	F	F
6 McEwen	R	F	F	F	F	F	F	F	F
7 Brown	R	F	F	?	?	F	?	F	F
8 Kindness	R	F	F	F	F	F	F	F	F
9 Weber	R	F	F	F	F	?	F	F	F
10 Miller	R	F	F	F	F	F	F	F	F
11 Stanton	R	F	F	F	F	F	F	F	F
12 Shamansky	D	F	A	A	A	F	A	A	A
13 Pease	D	A	A	?	A	A	A	A	A
14 Seiberling	D	A	A	A	A	A	A	A	A
15 Wylie	R	F	F	F	A	?	F	F	F
16 Regula	R	F	F	F	F	F	F	F	F
17 Ashbrook	R	F	F	F	?	?	F	F	F

House Votes Cont'd

State/District Name	Party	1	2	3	4	5	6	7	8
18 Applegate	D	F	A	F	F	F	F	A	F
19 Williams	R	F	F	F	F	F	A	F	F
20 Oakar	D	A	A	F	A	A	F	A	A
21 Stokes	D	A	A	A	A	A	A	A	A
22 Eckart	D	A	A	A	A	A	A	A	A
23 Mottl	D	F	F	F	F	?	F	F	A
OKLAHOMA									
1 Jones	D	F	A	F	F	?	F	A	F
2 Synar	D	F	A	A	F	F	A	A	F
3 Watkins	D	F	A	F	F	F	F	A	F
4 McCurdy	D	F	A	F	F	F	F	A	F
5 Edwards	R	F	F	F	F	F	F	F	F
6 English	F	F	F	F	F	F	F	A	F
OREGON									
1 AuCoin	D	F	A	A	A	A	?	A	F
2 Smith	R	F	F	F	F	F	F	F	F
3 Wyden	D	A	A	A	A	A	A	A	A
4 Weaver	D	A	A	A	A	A	A	A	A
PENNSYLVANIA									
1 Foglietta	D	A	A	A	?	A	A	A	A
2 Gray	D	A	A	A	A	A	A	A	A
3 Smith	D	5	5	5	5	5	5	5	A
4 Dougherty	R	F	F	F	F	F	F	F	F
5 Schulze	R	F	F	F	?	F	F	F	F
6 Yatron	D	A	F	F	F	F	F	A	F
7 Edgar	D	A	A	?	A	A	A	A	A
8 Coyne, J	R	F	F	A	F	F	F	F	F
9 Schuster	R	F	F	F	F	F	F	F	F
10 McDade	R	F	F	F	F	F	A	F	F
11 Nelligan	R	F	F	?	F	?	F	F	F
12 Murtha	D	F	A	F	F	F	F	A	A
13 Coughlin	R	F	F	A	A	F	F	F	F
14 Coyne, W	D	A	A	F	A	A	A	A	A
15 Ritter	R	F	F	F	F	F	F	F	F
16 Walker	R	F	F	F	?	F	F	F	F
17 Ertel	D	F	A	A	F	F	F	A	A
18 Walgren	D	F	A	A	A	A	A	A	F
19 Goodling	R	F	F	F	F	A	F	F	F
20 Gaydos	D	A	A	F	F	F	F	A	F
21 Bailey	D	A	A	F	F	F	F	A	F
22 Murphy	D	F	A	F	?	F	F	A	F
23 Clinger	R	F	F	A	F	F	A	F	F
24 Marks	R	F	F	A	F	F	A	F	F
25 Atkinson	D	F	F	F	F	F	A	F	F
RHODE ISLAND									
1 St Germain	D	F	A	?	?	?	A	A	F
2 Schneider	D	F	F	A	A	A	A	F	F

House Votes Cont'd

State/District Name	Party	1	2	3	4	5	6	7	8
SOUTH CAROLINA									
1 Hartnett	R	F	F	?	F	?	F	F	F
2 Spence	R	F	F	F	F	F	F	F	F
3 Derrick	D	F	F	A	F	F	F	A	F
4 Campbell	R	F	F	F	F	F	F	F	F
5 Holland	D	F	F	A	F	?	F	A	F
6 Napier	R	F	F	F	F	F	F	F	F
SOUTH DAKOTA									
1 Daschle	D	F	A	A	A	F	A	A	F
2 Roberts	R	F	F	F	F	?	F	F	F
TENNESSEE									
1 Quillen	R	F	F	?	F	?	F	F	F
2 Duncan	R	F	F	F	F	F	F	F	F
3 Bouquard	D	F	F	F	?	F	F	A	F
4 Gore	D	A	A	F	F	F	A	A	A
5 Boner	D	F	A	F	F	F	A	A	F
6 Beard	R	F	F	?	F	?	F	F	F
7 Jones	D	F	F	F	F	F	F	A	F
8 Ford	D	A	A	A	A	A	A	A	A
TEXAS									
1 Hall, S	D	F	F	F	F	F	F	F	F
2 Wilson	D	F	F	A	F	F	F	F	F
3 Collins	R	F	F	F	F	F	F	F	F
4 Hall, R	D	F	F	F	F	F	F	F	F
5 Mattox	D	F	A	?	A	A	A	A	F
6 Gramm	D	F	F	F	F	F	F	F	F
7 Archer	R	F	F	F	F	F	F	F	F
8 Fields	R	F	F	F	F	F	F	F	F
9 Brooks	D	F	A	A	F	F	F	A	F
10 Pickle	D	F	A	A	F	F	F	A	F
11 Leath	D	F	F	F	F	F	F	F	F
12 Wright	D	F	A	F	?	F	F	A	F
13 Hightower	D	F	F	F	A	F	F	F	F
14 Patman	D	F	A	?	F	F	F	F	F
15 de la Garza	D	F	A	F	F	F	F	A	A
16 White	D	F	F	F	?	F	F	F	A
17 Stenholm	D	F	F	F	F	F	F	F	F
18 Leland	D	A	A	A	A	A	A	A	A
19 Hance	D	F	F	A	?	?	F	F	F
20 Gonzalez	D	A	A	A	?	F	A	A	A
21 Loeffler	R	F	F	F	F	F	F	F	F
22 Paul	R	F	F	F	A	A	F	F	F
23 Kazen	D	F	A	F	F	F	F	A	F
24 Frost	D	F	A	A	A	F	A	A	F
UTAH									
1 Hansen	R	F	F	F	F	F	F	F	F
2 Marriott	R	F	F	F	F	F	F	F	F
VERMONT									
* Jeffords	R	A	F	A	A	F	A	F	A

House Votes Cont'd

State/District Name	Party	1	2	3	4	5	6	7	8
VIRGINIA									
1 Trible	R	F	F	F	F	?	F	F	F
2 Whitehurst	R	F	F	F	F	F	F	F	F
3 Bliley	R	F	F	F	F	F	F	F	F
4 Daniel, R	R	F	F	F	F	F	F	F	F
5 Daniel, D	D	F	F	F	F	F	F	F	F
6 Butler	R	F	F	A	F	F	F	F	F
7 Robinson	R	F	F	F	F	F	F	F	F
8 Parris	R	F	F	F	F	F	F	F	F
9 Wampler	R	F	F	F	F	F	F	F	F
10 Wolf	R	F	F	F	F	F	F	F	F
WASHINGTON									
1 Pritchard	R	F	F	A	A	F	F	F	F
2 Swift	D	F	A	A	A	F	A	A	A
3 Bonker	D	F	A	A	A	A	A	A	A
4 Morrison	R	F	F	F	F	F	F	F	F
5 Foley	D	F	A	A	F	F	A	A	F
6 Dicks	D	F	A	A	F	F	A	A	F
7 Lowry	D	A	A	A	A	A	A	A	A
WEST VIRGINIA									
1 Mollohan	D	A	A	A	?	F	A	A	F
2 Benedict	R	F	F	F	?	F	F	F	F
3 Staton	R	F	F	F	F	F	F	F	F
4 Rahall	D	A	A	?	A	A	A	A	F
WISCONSIN									
1 Aspin	D	A	A	F	A	?	A	A	A
2 Kastenmeier	D	A	A	A	A	A	A	A	A
3 Gunderson	R	F	F	F	A	F	F	F	F
4 Zablocki	D	A	A	F	F	?	F	A	A
5 Reuss	D	A	A	A	A	F	A	A	A
6 Petri	R	F	F	F	F	F	F	F	F
7 Obey	D	A	A	A	A	A	A	A	A
8 Roth	R	F	F	F	F	F	F	F	F
9 Sensenbrenner	R	F	F	F	?	F	F	F	F
WYOMING									
* Cheney	R	F	F	F	F	?	F	F	F

* At large
** Speaker (votes only to break ties)
(1) Rep. Cotter became ill in March and died in September.
(2) Rep. Hoyer was elected in June to replace Rep. Spellman, who became ill.
(3) Rep. Dowdy was elected in June to replace Rep. Hinson, who resigned.
(4) Rep. Oxley took office in July to replace Rep. Guyer, who died.
(5) Rep. Smith was elected in July to replace Rep. Lederer, who resigned after conviction in the Abscam affair.

Source: The Congressional Record for dates indicated.

1982 Requirements For Selected Benefit Programs

Following are revised requirements for benefits from selected federal entitlement programs for the 1982 fiscal year beginning October 1, 1981:

AID TO FAMILIES WITH DEPENDENT CHILDREN

Changes include new work program options for implementation by states, new provisions aiming assistance at families most in need and new administrative procedures designed to lower costs, according to the Department of Health and Human Services, which administers the basic welfare program. Approximately $6 billion is scheduled to be saved over the next five years because of stricter requirements.

The program provides cash assistance to families with dependent children who become financially deprived due to death, disability or absence of a parent. In about half the states, assistance is also provided to families in which a parent is unemployed. Some 4 million families totaling more than 11 million people received such assistance before the changes went into effect. States share the costs about equally with the federal government.

Changes include:

● New requirements for identifying the principal wage earner of two-parent families in which one parent is unemployed. Benefits may be paid only when the principal earner is out of work. Previously, benefits were paid if either parent was unemployed.

● A ceiling on gross family income was set at 150 per cent of the state's need standard for a family to qualify for aid.

● Changes were made in the amount of earned income which can be disregarded when calculating benefit levels. For the first time, the amounts disregarded are standardized for all states: $75 for expenses associated with full-time work, and a $160 minimum "disregard" per child for child care expenses. In addition, the $30 plus one-third of income which has also been disregarded will be applied as a "disregard" only for four consecutive months. This "30-and-one-third disregard" previously applied without any time limit.

● States may now count food stamps and housing subsidies as income. AFDC payments include food and housing components, so the non-AFDC aid for these purposes is duplicative.

● States may allow families to have resources worth up to $1,000 (equity value). The family's home and a car (worth up to $1,500 equity value, or less at state option) are not counted in these resources, and a state may also exclude basic maintenance items essential to day-to-day living such as clothing, furniture and other similarly essential items of limited value. Twenty-five states already limit personal resources to $1,000 in value or less, with resources to be excluded varying from state to state. The previous federal limit was $2,000.

● Income received as a lump sum, like insurance payments or inheritances, will be considered to be available for the family's support for as many months as this sum would meet the state's monthly standard of need. Previously, a family could spend the entire amount in one month and immediately requalify for assistance.

● Income of a step-parent will be considered available to the family he or she is living with. Income used by the step-parent to pay alimony or child-support will be disregarded.

● Earned Income Tax Credit will be assumed to be available to the family on a monthly basis.

● Persons participating in a labor strike are not eligible for AFDC assistance.

● Age limit — AFDC eligibility is limited to children under 18, plus at state option 18-year-olds who are expected to complete high school before reaching 19. Previous optional coverage through age 20 is eliminated.

● Pregnant women (who are not already recipients) may qualify for AFDC assistance in the third trimester of pregnancy. Previously, coverage of pregnant women varied from state to state. Needy pregnant women may be eligible for Medicaid assistance for pre-natal care.

● The income and resources of an alien resident's sponsor are deemed to be available to the alien during the first three years after entry.

● No payment will be made if the total benefit due to the recipient is less than $10. However those who qualify for total benefits less than $10 remain in the "categorically needy" status, qualifying them for Medicaid coverage.

● To ensure accurate payments, states are required to compute payment amounts retrospectively. In this way, benefits are based on actual need for assistance in a given month, not on estimates of need. Previously, states could base their computation of payments on prospective estimates. In addition, the law now requires for the first time that recipients submit monthly reports on their income and other circumstances.

● New provisions authorize the Internal Revenue Service to collect overdue child support payments from tax refunds. Unemployment benefits are now treated as income available to be used for child support. A declaration of bankruptcy no longer releases a parent from child support obligations (closing a loophole that has permitted parents to avoid child support obligations).

Source: Department of Health and Human Resources

FOOD PROGRAM FOR WOMEN, INFANTS AND CHILDREN (WIC)

This program supplies supplemental foods and nutrition education to pregnant and breast-feeding women and to children up to age 5 from families with an inadequate income and nutritional risk.

The program, which has served more than 2 million people, is operated in cooperation with the 50 states plus territories, the District of Columbia and 29 Indian agencies. The government provides cash grants to state health departments, which distribute funds to local agencies.

Children and pregnant or breastfeeding women may receive milk, cheese, cereal, juice, eggs and dry beans or peanut butter.

Non-breastfeeding, postpartum women may receive similar items.

Changes include lower limits on family income in order to participate in the program. Limits were lowered from 195 per cent of the poverty level to 185 per cent, plus a standard deduction. States may set their own income cutoff limits anywhere between the federal guidelines and their own limits for free or reduced-price health care. However, income limits may not be set lower than the poverty line. To qualify for participation, the annual income for a family of four may not exceed $15,630, which is 185 per cent of the poverty line.

Source: Department of Agriculture

FOOD STAMPS

New rules to save $1.3 billion in federal costs in this program for 1982 include:

● A gross monthly income eligibility limit for all food stamp households except those with elderly or disabled members. Under previous rules, eligibility was determined on the basis of a household's net monthly income, a figure derived by subtracting the $85 food stamp "standard deduction" and any other allowable child care, excess shelter, earned income, or medical deductions from the household's gross monthly income. Eligibility now is calculated on gross income before deductions. Under the new rules, households whose gross incomes exceed 130 per cent of the official poverty line will be declared ineligible. The new gross monthly income limit for a family of four is $916, or around $11,000 annually.

● New regulations that alter the definition of a food stamp "household" and ban benefits to boarders and strikers. Previous rules enable a household that met the income and assets limits to get food stamps, even if the low income was the result of a family member on strike. Now, a striker household that applies for stamps will be denied benefits unless it was eligible to receive food stamps before the strike began. Such households, however, will not be entitled to increased benefits under the new rules.

● A new rule that pro-rates a household's first month's

benefits. Earlier rules permitted a household joining the food
stamp program to get a full month's allotment, regardless of
the day of the month that it applies. Now, a household will
receive benefits from the day that it applies instead of for the
whole month.

● A new regulation that freezes the standard and child care-
excess shelter deductions at $85 and $115 until July, 1983, and
bases the July increase on consumer price index data for the 15
months ending March 31, 1983.

● A delay in the cost-of-living update of the Thrifty Food
Plan.

● A change that allows households with earned income to
deduct 18 per cent of their gross earnings, rather than the current 20 per cent, to offset work-related expenses under new
rules covering the "earnings disregard."

MEDICARE

Changes include:

● Elimination of occupational therapy as a basis for initial
entitlement of home health services.

● Elimination of carryover from previous year of incurred
expenses for meeting the Part B deductible.

● Part B deductible is increased to $75 beginning January
1, 1982.

● Elimination of open enrollment for Part B. The January-
March enrollment period was reinstated.

● Limits on reasonable charges for outpatient services must
be established for hospitals or clinics.

● Part A co-insurance is now based on the current
year'sdeductible, rather than the deductible in effect at the
time the beneficiary's spell of illness began.

● Five dollars was added to the base figure of $40 in the for-
mula used in the annual determination of the inpatient
hospital deductible for Part A. This means a very substantial
increase in the Part A deductible and co-insurance amounts
beginning January 1, 1982.

SOCIAL SECURITY

Changes include:

● Elimination of the minimum $122 monthly benefit for
people not already receiving it and certain others who had been

receiving it, such as those living abroad and those already receiving federal, state or local pensions. Future benefits will be based on actual earnings, with no monthly minimum, except for retired nuns, who will be eligble for the minimum for 10 more years.

● Restrictions on payment of lump-sum death benefits. Eliminated is the lump-sum death payment where there is neither an eligible spouse nor an eligible child. Only surviving spouses who were living with the worker or were eligible to receive monthly cash survivor benefits upon the worker's death will receive the payment. If no spouse, payment will be made to a child eligible to receive survivor's benefits.

● Temporary extension of earnings limitations. Exempt age under the earnings test is 72 in 1982, 70 in 1983.

● Termination of the mother's and father's benefit when youngest child attains age 16, instead of 18. It does not apply in the case of a parent caring for a disabled child.

● Elimination of benefits for students 18 or older in post-secondary school and 19 or older in elementary or secondary, effective August, 1982. However, those 18 or older who were entitled to a child's benefit in August, 1982, and began school before May, 1982, will continue receiving benefits. Benefits will not be adjusted for cost of living but will be reduced each year and phased out.

Source: The National Public Law Training Center

Casualties of Reaganism

Here are some federal programs targeted by the President's budget cutters last April that were killed by Congress or will expire in 1982. Where available, 1981 budget figures are provided.

AGRICULTURE DEPARTMENT
- Rural housing supervisory assistance grants ($1 million)
- Equipment assistance for food and nutrition service program

CSA
- Entire agency eliminated, some functions transferred to HHS, grants to states shifted to block grants to states (administrative costs $42 million)

COMMERCE DEPARTMENT
- Funds for Commerce representatives on the 10 federal regional councils ($1.07 million)
- Office of Productivity, Technology and Innovation ($5.2 million) — some functions transferred to other parts of the department
- Regional development commissions ($44 million)
- Coastal Energy Impact Programs ($40 million)
- Coastal Zone Management State Grants
- Department's portion of the National Ocean Satellite System

EDUCATION DEPARTMENT
- Outreach program to encourage people to go to college ($2.2 million)

ENERGY DEPARTMENT
- Fossil Commercialization Program

• Synthetic fuels feasibility studies and cooperative agreements
• Small hydropower subsidies
• Innovative Conservation Delivery Demonstration
• State energy emergency planning grants
• Economic Regulatory Administration oil and allocation controls
• Standby gasoline rationing program
• Rate reform assistance to public utility commissions
• Foreign country energy assessments

ENVIRONMENTAL PROTECTION AGENCY

• Local financial assistance for resource recovery
• Solid waste technical assistance panels
• Noise control program

EXECUTIVE OFFICE OF THE PRESIDENT

• Council on Wage and Price Stability ($9.4 million)

HEALTH & HUMAN SERVICES DEPT.

• Dental training subsidies ($2.35 million)
• National Center for Health Care Technology ($4 million)
• Support for health maintenance organizations ($8.8 million)
• Nursing grants ($9.9 million)
• Merchant seamen health entitlement program and federal funds for Public Health Service hospitals and clinics

HOUSING & URBAN DEVELOPMENT DEPARTMENT

• Planning assistance grants to states and regional planning groups for multipurpose land use planning ($19 million)
• Neighborhood self-help development ($9 million)

INTERIOR DEPARTMENT

• Youth Conservation Corps

LABOR DEPARTMENT

• CETA (Comprehensive Employment and Training Act) jobs programs that subsidize public and non-profit sector jobs ($4.078 billion)

- Demonstration projects to help welfare recipients find jobs in 14 cities

SMALL BUSINESS ADMINISTRATION
- Nonphysical disaster loans
- Small business development center programs

TRANSPORTATION DEPARTMENT
- Waterborne demonstration project (a hydrofoil between New Jersey and New York) ($4 million)
- Automotive research program ($12.5 million)

Appendix D
REFERENCES

Introduction

1. *Consumer Lobby Report*, Consumer Federation of America, September 28, 1981
2. *Governors' Bulletin*, National Governors' Association, September 25, 1981
3. *The Washington Post*, September 26, 1981

Chapter 1

1. Inaugural Address, January 20, 1981
2. *The Washington Post*, March 23, 1980
3. *The Washington Monthly*, July 8, 1981
4. Ronald Reagan and Richard C. Hublen, *Where's The Rest Of Me?*, Dell Publishing Co., New York, 1965, p. 313
5. *Ibid*, p. 337
6. Robert Lindsey, Reagan, *The Man, The President*, MacMillan, New York, 1980, p. 48
7. *Ibid*
8. *The Washington Post*, June 6, 1980
9. Reagan, *op. cit.*, p. 343
10. *Ibid.*, p. 344
11. *Ibid*, p. 352
12. Lindsey, *op. cit.*, p. 49
13. *Ibid.*, p. 109
14. *The Washington Post*, August 10, 1981

Chapter 2

1. President Reagan, speech at West Point, May 27, 1981
2. *U.S. News & World Report*, November 17, 1980
3. *Ibid*
4. *Enterprise*, National Association of Manufacturers, March, 1981
5. Village Voice, April 8-14, 1981
6. *Time*, February 2, 1981
7. *The National Journal*, November 8, 1980
8. *The Washington Post*, November 3, 1980
9. *Time, op. cit.*
10. Council on Environmental Quality, October 9, 1980
11. *New York Times Book Review*, June 7, 1981
12. *The Washington Post*, March 15, 1981
13. *The New York Times*, May 29, 1981
14. *Ibid*

15. David Broder *et al, The Pursuit Of The Presidency 1980*, Berkeley Books, New York, 1980, p. 265
16. *The 1980 Campaign Promises Of Ronald Reagan*, Democratic Congressional Campaign Committee, 1981
17. *Village Voice*, March 25-31, 1981
18. *Business War On The Law*, Public Citizen, 1981, p. 29
19. *The New Yorker*, May 18, 1981
20. *The Atlantic*, June, 1981
21. *U.S. News & World Report*, November 17, 1980
22. *The National Journal*, May 23, 1981
23. *Time*, September 14, 1981
24. *The Washington Post*, September 14, 1981
25. *Village Voice*, April 14-18, 1981
26. *The National Journal*, May 23, 1981
27. Richard I. Kirkland Jr., "Fat Days for the Chamber of Commerce," *Fortune*, September 21, 1981

Chapter 3

1. Robert W. Merry, "The Press as Power Broker," *The Quill*, January, 1980
2. *U.S. News & World Report*, October 27, 1980
3. *Parade*, January 11, 1981
4. *Ibid*
5. *The Washington Post*, October 10, 1980
6. Katherine Winton Evans, "Candidates and Their Gurus," *Washington Journalism Review*, September 1980
7. "Notes on a No-Win Campaign," *Columbia Journalism Review*, September/October, 1980
8. *Ibid*
9. *Columbia Journalism Review*, July/August, 1980
10. *Ibid*
11. *Washington Journalism Review*, May, 1981
12. *Ibid*
13. *Washington Journalism Review*, November/December, 1980
14. *Newsweek*, October 27, 1980
15. *Columbia Journalism Review*, July/August, 1981
16. "Talking to a Mule," *Columbia Journalism Review*, January/February, 1981
17. *Editor And Publisher*, November 1, 1980
18. *The Washington Post*, April 11, 1980
19. *The New York Times*, April 2, 1980
20. *The New York Times*, April 16, 1980
21. *Time* press release, undated
22. *U.S. News & World Report*, June 8, 1981
23. Personal notes, June 5, 1981

Chapter 4
1. *The Washington Post*, November 23, 1980
2. *Ibid*
3. *Ibid*
4. *Ibid*
5. *The New York Times*, March 18, 1981
6. *Mother Jones*, September/October, 1980
7. *The Los Angeles Times*, August 17, 1981
8. *The New York Times*, February 8, 1981

Chapter 5
1. *Selecting A President: A Citizen Guide To The 1980 Election*, Citizen Research Group, Farrar, Straus & Giroux, New York, 1980, p. 96
2. *AFL-CIO News*, April 12, 1980
3. American Clothing and Textile Workers Union release, March 27, 1981
4. *American Journal of Public Health*, August, 1981
5. The New York Times, July 13, 1981

Chapter 6
1. Plaque over entrance to Governor Reagan's office, *R.W.R., The Official Ronald Wilson Reagan Quote Book*, Chain-Pinkham Books, St. Louis, 1980, p. 61
2. *The Washington Post*, April 17, 1981
3. *The Washington Post*, February 22, 1980
4. *Ibid*
5. *The Washington Post* March 15, 1981
6. *The Washington Post*, September 18, 1981
7. *The Wall Street Journal*, May 20, 1981
8. *The Washington Post*, June 24, 1981; *The Wall Street Journal*, June 25, 1981
.9 *The Wall Street Journal*, August 28, 1981
10. Common Cause, June, 1981
11. *R.W.R., op. cit.*, p. 50
12. "Presidential Control of Agency Rulemaking: An Analysis of Executive Order 12291," Library of Congress, June 15, 1981
13. "The Regulators: Legalizing Corporate Murder," *The Nation*, June 20, 1981
14. *Ibid*
15. Justice Department press release, June 24, 1981
16. *The Washington Post*, August 27, 1981
17. Ralph Nader press release, September 5, 1981
18. *The Washington Post*, June 28, 1981
19. *The Washington Post*, June 20, 1981
20. *The Washington Post*, August 12, 1981
21. *The Washington Star*, May 5, 1981
22. *The Washington Post*, July 8, 1981

23. *The Washington Post*, July 5, 1981
24. *The New York Times*, August 18, 1981
25. *The Wall Street Journal*, May 28, 1981

Chapter 7
1. Americans for Democratic Action press release, October 16, 1980, quoting *The Los Angeles Times*, March 21, 1975
2. *The Washington Post*, February 20, 1981
3. Accuracy in Media promotion, undated
4. *The Washington Post*, April 11, 1981
5. *The Boston Globe*, March 21, 1981
6. *The Washington Post*, March 6, 1981
7. *The Wall Street Journal*, May 1, 1981
8. *The Washington Post*, April 3, 1981
9. *Covert Action Information Bulletin*, April, 1981
10. *The Washington Post*, March 10, 1981
11. Justice Department press release, May 8, 1981
12. *Village Voice*, March 25-31, 1981
13. *Ibid*
14. Jack W. Germond and Jules Witcover, *The Washington Star*, April 20, 1981
15. Americans for Democratic Action press release, October 16, 1980, quoting *The New York Times*, October 23, 1975
16. *The Washington Post*, July 12, 1981
17. *The New York Times*, May 17, 1981
18. *Ibid*
19. *U.S. News & World Report*, "Outlook '81."
20. *Playboy*, January, 1981

Chapter 8
1. Speech to the U.S. Chamber of Commerce, March 5, 1981
2. *Business Week*, August 7, 1978
3. *The New York Times*, April 27, 1981
4. *U.S. News & World Report*, March 23, 1981
5. *The Washington Post*, August 5, 1981
6. Joint Committee on Taxation, April 9, 1981
7. American Council for Capital Formation newsletter, March, 1981
8. *People & Taxes*, March, 1981
9. *Ibid*
10. *AFL-CIO News*, April 28, 1981
11. Testimony, March 24, 1981
12. *Ibid*
13. "A Simulation of the Economic Effects of President Reagan's Fiscal and Monetary Proposals, 1981-1984." Joint Economic Committee of Congress
14. *People & Taxes*, February, 1981
15. *The Washington Post*, March 19, 1981

16. *The New Republic,* June 20, 1981
17. "The Economic Recovery Tax Act of 1981," Peat, Marwick, Mitchell & Co., 1981
18. Don J. Pease, *The Washington Star*, July 22, 1981
19. The New York Times, August 21, 1981

Chapter 9

1. Paul Savoy, *The Nation*, June 20, 1981
2. *Los Angeles Times,* July 30, 1981
3. *The New York Times*, March 20, 1981
4. *AFL-CIO Federationist*, April, 1981
5. *The New York Times*, March 17, 1981
6. *The Washington Post*, March 10, 1981
7. Personal conversation, July 8, 1981
8. *The Washington Post*, July 27, 1981
9. *Congressional Record,* July 31, 1981, H5781
10. *Ibid*, H5795
11. *Ibid*, H5821
12. *Ibid*, H5833
13. *Ibid*
14. *The New York Times*, August 1, 1981
15. *The Washington Post*, March 6, 1981
16. "How to Wreck the Economy," *New York Review of Books*, May 14, 1981
17. *The New York Times*, July 31, 1981
18. *Ibid*
19. *Ibid*
20. "The Regional and Urban Impacts of the Administration's Budget and Tax Proposals," Joint Economic Committee, July 31, 1981
21. *The Wall Street Journal*, March 27, 1981

Chapter 10

1. Quoted by Richard Barnet, *The New Yorker*, April 27, 1981
2. Frank Vander Linden, *The Real Reagan*, Wm. Morrow & Co., New York, 1981, p. 234
3. *Selecting A President: A Citizen Guide To The 1980 Election*, Citizen Research Group, Farrar, Straus & Giroux, New York, 1980, p. 102
4. *Ibid*, p. 101, quoting *Christian Science Monitor*, June 3, 1976
5. *Ibid*, quoting *The Washington Post*, February 6, 1977
6. *Ibid*, p. 102
7. *Ibid*
8. Barnet, *op. cit.*
9 *Time*, February 2, 1981
10. Michael Gordon, *The National Journal*, April 11, 1981

1981, quoting *U.S.*, *Soviet Military Balance* by
John M. Collins, McGraw Hill, New York, 1980

11. *Village Voice*, March 25-31, 1981
12. *National Defense* Random House, New York,
    1981 (press release)
13. *Congressional Quarterly*, March 14, 1981
14. *The Washington Post*, April 19, 1981
15. *The National Journal*, April 11, 1981
16. Center for Defense Information press release,
    June 3, 1981
17. *The New York Times*, March 19, 1981
18. Jack Anderson, *The Washington Post*, April 8,
    1981
19. *The New Republic*, February 14, 1981
20. Presidential press conference, March 6, 1981
21. *Covert Action Information Bulletin*, April, 1981
22. *The Baltimore Sun*, March 27, 1981
23. *The Washington Post*, March 22, 1981
24. *The Wall Street Journal*, March 2, 1981
25. *The Baltimore Sun*, August 8, 1981
26. Richard Barnet and Ronald Miller, *Global
    Reach*, Simon & Schuster, New York, 1974
27. *The Washington Post*, May 22, 1981
28. *The New York Times*, June 23, 1981
29. *Selecting A President, op. cit.*, quoting *The New
    York Times*, February 1, 1980, p. 101
30. *The Los Angeles Times*, May 22, 1981
31. *The Washington Post*, July 12, 1981
32. *The Washington Post*, July 9, 1981
33. *The New York Times*, April 13, 1981
34. *The New York Times*, April 28, 1981
35. *Russia I*, Chalidze Publications, Issue No. 1,
    1981